This volume is sponsored by
The Center for Japanese Studies
University of California, Berkeley

The Mito Ideology

The Mito Ideology

Discourse, Reform, and
Insurrection
in Late Tokugawa Japan,
1790–1864

J. VICTOR KOSCHMANN

UNIVERSITY OF CALIFORNIA PRESS
Berkeley   Los Angeles   London

University of California Press
Berkeley and Los Angeles, California

University of California Press, Ltd.
London, England

© 1987 by
The Regents of the University of California

1 2 3 4 5 6 7 8 9

Most of chapter 5 has appeared as
"Action as a Text: Ideology in the Tengu Insurrection,"
in Tetsuo Najita and J. Victor Koschmann, eds.,
Conflict in Modern Japanese History: The Neglected Tradition.
Copyright © 1982 by Princeton University Press.
Reprinted by permission of Princeton University Press.

Library of Congress Cataloging-in-Publication Data

Koschmann, J. Victor.
The Mito ideology.

"This volume is sponsored by the Center for
Japanese Studies, University of California,
Berkeley"—
Bibliography: p.
Includes index.
1. Japan—History—1787–1868. 2. Mitogaku.
3. Mito-han (Japan)—History. I. Title.
DS881.K66 1987   952'.025   86-4351
ISBN 0-520-05768-6 (alk. paper)

To Nicole, Mei-joy, and Andrea

Contents

Acknowledgments	ix
Introduction	1
The Problem of Method	4
Tokugawa Ideology	7
Tokugawa Reformism	14
Historiographical Perspective	16
1. Rectification and Myth	29
The Plight of the Domain	29
The Mito Historiographical Tradition	34
Rectification of Names	43
Natural Order Through Artifice	48
2. The National Essence	56
History as Entropy	57
Eternal Return Through Imperial Ritual	64
The Need for Action	77
3. Reform as Representation	81
Demarcating the Land	85
Grounding the Aristocracy	101
Spreading the Way	114
The Domain as Microcosm	125
4. Recruitment of Commoners	130
The Tenpō Legacy	131
The Intrusion of National Politics	139
Education as Ideology	142
Assassination at Sakurada Gate	149
5. Ritual and Action in the Tengu Insurrection	152
Mobilization and Oppression	157
Pilgrimage to the Origin	162
New Political Space	170

Coda: Mito Ideology as Text 173

Appendix: *Gekibun* (Call to Action) 175

Bibliography 177

Index 183

Acknowledgments

Support for this book from institutions was generous. The Japan Foundation and the University of Chicago's Center for Far Eastern Studies granted financial support. The staff of the Ibaraki-ken Rekishikan in Mito provided bibliographical help, and the Tokyo Fulbright Office cooperated with Professor Matsuzawa Hiroaki of Hokkaidō University to give me a chance to discuss the book's main ideas with a distinguished group of Japanese scholars. Translation help for that occasion was provided by Takechi Manabu of the Center for Social Science Communication in Tokyo.

Aid from individuals was indispensable. Nancy Lee Koschmann read and diplomatically criticized more drafts than either of us cares to remember. Professor Matsumoto Sannosuke of the University of Tokyo responded frequently, with characteristic warmth and insight, to my faltering efforts to understand Mitogaku. Professor Gary D. Allinson listened patiently on several occasions and also read the manuscript with a critical eye. A particularly conscientious reader for the University of California Press saved me from many errors. The roles of typist and computer consultant were cheerfully performed through many revisions by Jill Warner. Nancy A. Blumenstock did an excellent job of editing. And Mr. Hirato Kuniharu graciously allowed a painting in his possession to be reproduced as the jacket illustration.

But, most of all, I am profoundly indebted to my friends and mentors at the University of Chicago: Professors Harry Harootunian and Tetsuo Najita. Without the benefit of their scholarship on Japanese intellectual history, the exciting environment for study that they created at Chicago, and the quality of their professional support, this book would have been inconceivable. Of course, I alone am responsible for any remaining deficiencies.

INTRODUCTION

In the decades before troops from the great western domains of Japan, such as Satsuma and Chōshū, succeeded in bringing down the Tokugawa shogunate (or bakufu) in 1868, the foundations of that government and of its ruling house were shaken repeatedly from within. The source of this seismic activity was the ordinarily conservative and scholarly Mito branch of the Tokugawas, which at the turn of the nineteenth century began to function as the "epicenter" of Japanese ideological activism.[1] Samurai scholars in Mito coined such reformist slogans as "Revere the emperor and expel the barbarian" (*sonnō jōi*) and elaborated a nationalistic vocabulary centering on the semimystical concept of "national essence" (*kokutai*). They also carried out, under their zealous lord Tokugawa Nariaki (1800–1860), a far-reaching program of reform in the early 1830s that provided a model for the bakufu's own Tenpō Reforms.

Then, on the eve of the Meiji revolution, the Mito reformists turned to violence and rebellion. In 1860 they assassinated bakufu great elder Ii Naosuke (1815–1860) outside the imperial palace in Edo; and in 1864 they led a multiclass army of rebels on a meandering pilgrimage to the Tokugawa tombs in Nikkō and then set them against bakufu troops in the "most far-reaching, potentially disastrous, sanguinary, and costly insurgency faced by Edo since 1638."[2] These events threw Mito itself into civil war several years before conflict erupted on a national scale, thus effectively sidelining from the later struggle those Mito radicals who had not already been killed or im-

---

1. The seismological metaphor is from Noguchi Takehiko, *Edo no rekishika: Rekishi to iu na no doku* (Tokyo: Chikuma Shobō, 1979), p. 277.
2. Conrad Totman, *The Collapse of the Tokugawa Bakufu, 1862–1868* (Honolulu: University Press of Hawaii, 1980), p. 120.

prisoned. Their own political precocity was therefore responsible for denying them a role in the final overthrow of the bakufu. Nevertheless, no attempt to understand the ideological processes that accompanied the political and military demise of the Tokugawa order can afford to ignore events in Mito.

The house of Mito, whose domain lay three days and two nights' journey north of Edo, was one of three collateral houses (*gosanke*) to the line of Tokugawa shoguns who ruled Japan from 1603 to 1868. Mito domain was smaller and poorer by half than those occupied by the other Tokugawa branches, Owari and Kii,[3] but it was closer to Edo and its lords (daimyo) were favored in the popular mind with the title—entirely unofficial—of "vice-shogun" (*tenka no fuku shōgun*). This epithet seems to have arisen from a special shogunal dispensation that allowed the Mito lord to reside permanently in Edo rather than move frequently between Edo and his castle town, as did the rest of the 270-odd daimyo.

The prestige of Mito came not only from the status of its lords, but also from certain real accomplishments, the foremost of which was the program of historiographical compilation that intended to produce the *Dai-Nihon shi* (A history of great Japan). Initiated in 1657 by the second Mito daimyo, Tokugawa Mitsukuni (1628–1700), the project extended over a period of 250 years and was completed with the publication of 397 chapters in 1906. This enormous expenditure of erudition and resources won lasting fame for Mitsukuni and also encouraged among generations of Mito retainers the development of high levels of national consciousness, emperor-centered loyalism, and expertise regarding the institutional foundations of the Japanese polity.

Perhaps as the result of a certain "vision" acquired in the course of their historical research and reflection, Mito scholars such as Fujita Yūkoku (1774–1826) were among the first to recognize the threat to Japan posed by the Western powers in the late eighteenth and early nineteenth centuries. They re-

---

3. When created in 1609, Mito domain was assessed at 250,000 *koku;* by 1622 it was expanded in size to 280,000 *koku*. In contrast, Owari was 620,000 *koku*, and Kii, 555,000 *koku*. As a result of the Kan'ei cadastral survey of 1641, Mito was finally able to claim 350,000 *koku*. (The *koku* was a measure of volume—approximately 5.1 bushels—used to express the yield of land in rice.)

Introduction

sponded energetically with exhortations, philosophical treatises, and political interventions that were designed not only to raise the crisis consciousness of their countrymen, but to repair defenses and reform institutions. Thus, for many later historians, the term "Mitogaku" (or "Mito scholarship") referred less to the monumental historical undertakings of Mitsukuni and his successors than to the much more timely and practically oriented works produced in the decades prior to the Meiji revolution.[4]

Although historians generally agree that Mitogaku played a role in the era immediately preceding the overthrow of the Tokugawa regime, they are by no means unanimous in their evaluation of that role. Their differences of opinion often focus on the degree of "influence" that Mito thought is believed to have exerted on the individual *shishi* (men of high purpose) who are credited with initiating the revolutionary process that brought down the bakufu. Thus, for example, they may cite Yoshida Shōin's sentiments toward a late Mito text, for example, *Shinron* (A new thesis) by Aizawa Seishisai (1781–1863), as the acid test of Mitogaku's anti-establishment role.[5]

It is indisputable that many of the individuals who led the anti-bakufu movement had gone through some sort of "Mito experience." Maki Izumi (1813–1864), Yoshida Shōin (1830–1859), Kusaka Genzui (1840–1864), and Umeda Unpin (1815–1859) all went to Mito at least once between the mid-1840s and early 1860s and left evidence of having read and pondered major works by Mito ideologues. Yoshida, particularly, stayed in Mito for a full month in late 1851 and early 1852, and spent time with Aizawa, Toyota Tenkō (1805–1864), and other Mito personalities.[6] He also seems to have traveled the Mito countryside, observing the degree to which the philosophy of *sonnō jōi* had penetrated rural society.[7]

What these radicals most likely imbibed in Mito, however,

---

4. A typical exponent of this view was the Taishō-period historian Kikuchi Kenjirō, cited in Bitō Masahide, "Mitogaku no tokushitsu," in Imai Usaburō, Seya Yoshihiko, and Bitō Masahide, eds., *Mitogaku*, Nihon shisō taikei 53 (Tokyo: Iwanami Shoten, 1973), p. 562.

5. For an example of such discussions, see ibid., p. 558.

6. Matsumoto Sannosuke, *Tennōsei kokka no seiji shisō* (Tokyo: Miraisha, 1969), pp. 65–72.

7. Yoshida Toshizumi, "Kōki Mitogaku to Kiheitai shotai," *Ibaraki-ken shi kanpō* 2 (Feb. 1975): 92–102.

was not anti-bakufu rhetoric, but rather a certain world view that sharpened awareness of the external and domestic threats to the "divine land," emphasized the essential political and spiritual role of the imperial line, and instilled an activist sense of righteous indignation toward any who would stand in the way of the needed reforms. Indeed, the major criticism leveled at Mito thought by post–World War II historians, who looked for a thoroughly revolutionary impulse, is that, for all their moralizing and sometimes violent activism, Mito zealots never proposed the overthrow of the bakufu or the bakuhan social order.

As retainers in the house of the "vice-shogun," Mito activists were understandably disinclined to criticize the bakufu itself in any fundamental or direct manner. Even the Tengu insurrectionists announced their desire only to "assist the shogun." Nevertheless, even the less violent and iconoclastic forms of Mito thought and action were corrosive of the system from within.

THE PROBLEM OF METHOD

Beyond its obvious historical significance, late Tokugawa Mito interested me as a case study in the relationship between thought and action. Leading Mito ideologues claimed to believe that learning (*gakumon*) and politics (*matsurigoto*) were one,[8] and there was surely ample reason to take their claims seriously. Mito loyalists like Fujita Tōko (1806–1855) seemed as deeply involved in political action as they were in scholarship. Beyond that, there seemed to be deep structural parallels and symbolic relationships between Mito writings and the forms of political practice that engaged their authors. Writings as well as practice apparently were aimed at a kind of rectification, not only of "names," as in the Confucian tradition, but of social relations, land registration, and education. Both also seemed equally fraught with tension between historical instrumentality and ritually based hopes for "eternal return."

A number of recent works on the theory and methodology of interpretation were helpful in developing an approach to this

---

8. See Fujita Yūkoku, *Teishi Fūji*, in Imai, Seya, and Bitō, eds., p. 27.

material. Paul Ricoeur's hermeneutic theory and, particularly, his extension of that theory to cover the interpretation of actions as "texts"[9] provided a perspective on the Mito writers' own claims that scholarship and constructive enterprise should not be split apart and encouraged an openness to the semiotic complexity of action. Michel Foucault's method of discourse analysis and his intricate study of the shifting connections between language and the phenomenal world in European discourse[10] led away from a traditional focus on the idiosyncrasies of leading actors toward an attempt to grasp the historical structure of possibilities that always lies outside contemporary consciousness and yet powerfully conditions human knowledge, language, and action. Nevertheless, in the course of the project, Foucault's historical structuralism has been moderated when there seemed to be a place for the analytical theories of intentionality that Quentin Skinner applied to the study of intellectual history. Skinner's insight that intentionality resides "in" the text rather than "behind" it is useful in the study of both acts and texts.[11] Finally, the works of Victor Turner provided a storehouse of concepts and insights regarding ritual process and the liminal moment.[12]

The approach that emerged from these and other theoretical writings suggested some possible interpretations of the late Tokugawa Mito experience. There remained, however, a need to account for the changes that seemed to occur both within Mito discourse and in its connection to a sequence of contextual events. Among those changes, it seemed particularly significant that the social constituency addressed by that discourse had broadened in the mid-nineteenth century. An initial emphasis on the ruling *bushi* (samurai class) had shifted to allow increased attention to commoner elites. In order to conceptualize that shift, I had to expand my approach to include not just the

9. *Interpretation Theory* (Fort Worth: Texas Christian University Press, 1976), and "The Model of the Text," *Social Research* 38, no. 3 (Autumn 1971).
10. *The Archaeology of Knowledge and the Discourse on Language* (New York: Harper and Row, 1976), and *The Order of Things* (New York: Random House, 1970).
11. "Meaning and Understanding in the History of Ideas," *History and Theory* 8 (1969), and "Motives, Intentions, and the Interpretation of Texts," *The New Literary History* 3 (1972).
12. *Dramas, Fields, and Metaphors* (Ithaca: Cornell University Press, 1974), and *The Ritual Process* (London: Penguin Press, 1969).

meaning of Mito discourse, but also the problem of its effects. How did it transform lives and minds in a dynamic historical process? In order to address such a problem, it was necessary to supplement a theory of discourse and interpretation with a theory of ideology.

Ideology is a protean term, but, for purposes of this study, I found Louis Althusser's formulation to be the most persuasive. Althusser locates ideology, as a practice, precisely at the conjunction of thought structure and intentional action. From that position, "all ideology hails or interpellates concrete individuals as concrete subjects," thus equipping them to respond to the conditions of their existence.[13] One of the clearest and most accessible reformulations of Althusser's concept is by Göran Therborn, who applies it not only to the legitimation of stable power relationships, but also to the dialectical process by which human subjectivity is transformed, leading to change. For Therborn, therefore, a methodological commitment to viewing thought systems and other forms of consciousness *as ideology*

> means to look at them from a particular perspective: not as bodies of thought or structures of discourse per se, but as manifestations of a particular being-in-the-world of conscious actors, of human subjects. In other words, to conceive of a text or an utterance as ideology is to focus on the way it operates in the formation and transformation of human subjectivity.[14]

By this view, the difference between discourse and ideology is largely a matter of perspective or approach. It allows one to read a particular text *as discourse*, with primary attention to its internal constraints and structure, or *as ideology*, with a focus on the active articulation between discourse and human subjectivity. I will use both terms, depending on whether I want to emphasize one or the other aspect of a complex of texts and acts.

Therborn's concept of ideology also implies a dialectical field of tension between subordination and freedom. He illustrates that tension by pointing to the two opposing meanings of the

---

13. See Althusser, *Lenin and Philosophy and Other Essays* (London: Monthly Review Press, 1971), p. 173. For an explanatory discussion of Althusser's conception, see Rosalind Coward and John Ellis, *Language and Materialism* (London: Routledge and Kegan Paul, 1977), chap. 5.

14. *The Ideology of Power and the Power of Ideology* (London: New Left Books, 1980), p. 2.

word "subject" in English and French (the "subjects" of the prince and the "subjects" of history), which he terms subjection and qualification: "Ideologies not only subject people to a given order. They also qualify them for conscious social action, including actions of gradual or revolutionary change. Ideologies do not function merely as 'social cement.'"[15] There are, in other words, both an ordering, or constraining, aspect to ideology (subjection) and an emergent, transformative aspect (qualification).

In this study of Mito domain in the late Tokugawa period, therefore, I have attempted not only to view thought and action interpretively, as equivalent forms of textuality, but also to consider how thought, as ideology, enabled people to act under the historical circumstances that confronted them and, furthermore, to act in ways that sometimes undermined rather than supported the existing order.

TOKUGAWA IDEOLOGY

Any study of discourse and ideology in Mito in the late Tokugawa period must come to terms with at least some of the other forms of discourse that prevailed throughout the Tokugawa period (1603–1868) as a whole, and particularly with the ideological function of discourse in relation to early-modern Japanese society. Recent works by Herman Ooms and others have drastically revised the view, still commonly held in both Japan and the West, that the neo-Confucianism of Chu Hsi (1130–1200) clearly dominated Japanese ideological space in the seventeenth century. Neo-Confucianism was indeed important, but Buddhism and, especially, Shinto were often even more so.

According to Ooms, there were at least four major moments in the early construction of ideological hegemony under the Tokugawas: first, the Shinto-oriented self-deification of the victorious warriors Oda Nobunaga (1534–1582), Toyotomi Hideyoshi (1536–1598), and Tokugawa Ieyasu (1546–1616); second, the spinning of a multifaceted discourse on society by a range of ideologues, including the Zen preacher Suzuki Shōsan (1579–1655) and the Zen-apostate neo-Confucians Fujiwara

---

15. Ibid., p. vii. Emphasis added.

Seika (1561–1619) and Asayama Irin'an (1589–1664); third, the diversion of national religious ritual away from the imperial court toward a new center focused on the bakufu, and particularly on the tombs of Ieyasu who, through the machinations of the Tendai priest Tenkai (1536–1643), had been transformed into the avatar of a Shinto-Buddhist "god of all gods";[16] and fourth, Yamazaki Ansai's synthesis of neo-Confucianism and Shinto, which produced the sublime doctrine of Suika Shinto.

Yamazaki's synthesis of seventeenth-century ideology is of the greatest importance for an understanding of late Tokugawa Mito thought. That is particularly so because, by the end of the eighteenth century, Yamazaki's epigones in the Kimon school of neo-Confucianism had secured a strong position in the Bakufu College and through the Kansei Reforms had reestablished a kind of ideological orthodoxy.[17] Many Kimon ideas found their way into memorials written by Aizawa Seishisai and other Mito reformists in the early to mid-nineteenth century.

Yamazaki Ansai (1618–1682) began his adult life as a Buddhist monk but turned to the neo-Confucianism of Chu Hsi in his early twenties. After working for a while on a bakufu-sponsored historical project, he became interested in producing a neo-Confucian history of Japan. Although he abandoned the project after several years of research, he retained a strong interest in early Japan, which he diverted to the study of mythology and Shinto doctrine. So assiduously did he pursue this interest that in 1669 he was initiated into the esoteric tradition of Ise Shinto,[18] and in 1671 he received instruction in Yoshida Shinto.[19] From this time on, he devoted himself to discovery of the "Way" in Japan's Shinto tradition.

In a manner directly relevant to my concern with ideology,

16. Ooms, *Tokugawa Ideology* (Princeton, N.J.: Princeton University Press, 1985), p. 177.

17. Ooms, *Charismatic Bureaucrat* (Chicago: University of Chicago Press, 1975), chap. 6; Robert L. Backus, "The Kansei Prohibition of Heterodoxy and its Effects on Education," *Harvard Journal of Asiatic Studies* 39, no. 1 (1979): 55–106, and "The Motivation of Confucian Orthodoxy in Tokugawa Japan," *Harvard Journal of Asiatic Studies* 39, no. 2 (1979): 275–338.

18. Ooms, *Tokugawa Ideology*, p. 222. Also called the Watarai school of Shinto, Ise Shinto centers on the Outer Shrine at Ise.

19. Yoshida Shinto (or Yuiitsu Shinto) was begun by Yoshida Kanetomo (1435–1511) and considers Shinto to be the origin of Confucianism, Taoism, and Buddhism as well.

Ooms describes Yamazaki's synthesis in terms of a four-level hermeneutic developed in the West by patristic theologians and recently adapted to the study of ideology by literary critic Frederic Jameson. The levels of interpretation, as explained by Jameson, are the literal, allegorical, moral, and anagogical.[20] Ooms applies these levels to Yamazaki's ideological system as follows.

First, Yamazaki took the material on the "age of the gods" in the Japanese mytho-histories, particularly the *Nihon shoki* (Chronicles of Japan), to be literally true. This distinguished him from other major Confucian historians of the seventeenth century; even the Mito daimyo Tokugawa Mitsukuni was hesitant to include the mythical age in the *Dai-Nihon shi*.[21] Second, Yamazaki found in the text of pure Shinto not only history, but eternal truths as well. He believed that hidden within the mythic narrative were semiological traces, exemplars, numerological correlations, and etymologies that would unerringly lead the serious student to the universal Way. Third, once understood in this allegorical fashion, the texts were able to exert normative moral force; they now "addressed, grabbed, interpellated the individual and insisted on his ethical practice."[22] Fourth, the texts provided collective meaning to history by elevating Japan above all other nations as the divine land: the Land of the Gods.

Yamazaki's achievement, therefore, was the culmination of a century of ideological process:

> He worked out a comprehensive and systematic articulation of all core tenets of the Chinese with the Japanese tradition (the allegorical level of interpretation); he stressed more intensely than others the imperative of ethical practice (the moral level of interpretation) and laid the groundwork for a full development of the "nationalistic" dimension (the anagogical level of interpretation).[23]

The result was a closed system that veiled the coarse exercise of power and presented social inequality as an inalienable aspect of cosmic order.

20. Ooms, *Tokugawa Ideology*, p. 283; Jameson, *The Political Unconscious* (Ithaca: Cornell University Press, 1981), p. 31
21. Ooms, *Tokugawa Ideology*, pp. 223–24
22. Ibid., p. 284.
23. Ibid., p. 285.

Underlying this social agreement with respect to hierarchy was an ontology that equated mental and cosmic states. Virtues that were *innate to* man, such as reverence and loyalty, were also *inherent to* the makeup of the universe and would therefore manifest themselves spontaneously in social order.[24] The central virtue was reverence (*kei*); beyond that, loyalty. Rebellion was unthinkable. Therefore, according to Ooms, "the only political action that remained open for his followers, besides absolute loyalty to the lord and his ministers was remonstrance and, as its precondition, the maintenance of a certain economic independence from those in power."[25]

Yamazaki's seventeenth-century system retained its vitality throughout the eighteenth century, despite challenges. It was also reinvigorated in nineteenth-century Mito, where its moral and specifically ideological dimension—its capacity to transform human subjectivity—propelled commoners as well as warrior reformists beyond reverence into emergent forms of rebellious action.

Eighteenth-century discourse, part of which developed under the impact of another early Tokugawa school called *kogaku* (ancient studies), was also selectively incorporated by the Mito ideologues. In contrast to Yamazaki's Confucianized Shinto, which equated the human mind with the cosmos and sought to dissolve all other aspects of life—social, political, economic—into that "natural" whole, the early *kogaku* school focused attention on change and variety in the physical and social universes. In the early eighteenth century, the *kogaku* scholar Ogyū Sorai (1666–1724) redirected the normative force of the Way from a man-cosmos continuum toward the social world of constructive action and institutions. For Ogyū, the fact of human diversity meant that the Way could never be discovered solely through self-cultivation focused on reverence. Only social institutions, constructed in historical context by enlightened, benevolent rulers, could provide the basis for a moral order.

Ogyū's theoretical insertion of instrumental reason into the calling of the ruler was by no means unambiguous.[26] But it was

24. Ibid., pp. 218–19.
25. Ibid., p. 248.
26. Samuel Hideo Yamashita, "Nature and Artifice in the Writings of Ogyū Sorai (1666–1728)," in Peter Nosco, ed., *Confucianism and Tokugawa Culture* (Princeton, N.J.: Princeton University Press, 1984), pp. 138–65.

Introduction 11

partly as a result of the uncertainty sown by Ogyū and his predecessors that the eighteenth century brought a "moral crisis."[27] Precisely because it had been premised on similitude, the predominant seventeenth-century version of truth had failed to incorporate adequately what was different; because it was based on moral precepts, it had stood aloof from the "immoral"; and, as sanction for an orderly, naturalistic hierarchy, it had tried to ignore elements that did not fit: drifters, entertainers, masterless samurai, peasants uprooted from the soil, and, most seriously of all, the venal merchant culture of the cities.

However, many thinkers in the eighteenth century chose to focus on such anomalies in their full particularity, seeking only secondarily to reconcile them with a concept of truth and order. As they encountered irregularity and conflict where received paradigms taught that there should be only an orderly pattern of similarities, they often turned to a form of historicism that explained events as the effects of irrational passions, purposeful human instrumentality, and inexorable forces, all of which collided in patterns unique in time and place. They also attracted new social constituencies precisely in the sectors of society that had been excluded by neo-Confucian orthodoxy.

In their attempts to accommodate the experience of the merchant class, for example, Ogyū's successors dramatically altered the Confucian system. Kaiho Seiryō (1755–1817) immersed himself in the commercial life of Osaka in search of the internal secret of its vitality. What he found was a notion of precise calculation that made profit possible and thus facilitated exchange. When formulated in terms of a general rule, this discovery implied that everything, including the realm itself, could be considered a commodity with exchange value.[28] In Kaiho's philosophy, the neo-Confucian concept of principle was displaced from its position of ontological primacy by a homonym, meaning "profit" or "advantage." The effect was to affirm the life of the merchant as consistent with universal principle.

As he investigated the sources of merchant efficiency and productivity, Kaiho described in some detail the house rules of

---

27. See Tetsuo Najita, "Method and Analysis in the Conceptual Portrayal of Tokugawa Intellectual History" in Najita and Irwin Scheiner, eds., *Japanese Thought in the Tokugawa Period* (Chicago: University of Chicago Press, 1978), p. 19.
28. Ibid., p. 26.

the Masuya family, which in his view were admirably effective as motivating mechanisms. What emerged from his effort was a compelling portrait of life in a merchant house, with hardly a trace of the opprobrium reserved for that milieu by the samurai aristocracy. He went so far as to espouse an egalitarian view of society on the basis that all human beings share a common "life spirit."[29]

Kaiho was often equaled in his irreverence toward the samurai class by nativists, who sought to rediscover a Japanese tradition unsullied by Chinese accretions. Nativist scholar Motoori Norinaga (1730–1801) rejected the abstract language of Confucianism in favor of a poetic realism that promised to reanimate the Way of the Gods: "The Way of the Gods does not contain a single argument that annoyingly evaluates things in terms of good and evil, right and wrong, like the Confucian and Buddhist Ways. It is opulent, big-hearted, and refined. The essence of Japanese poetry suits it well."[30]

Motoori's naturalistic sensibility bestowed new dignity on the private life, unencumbered by the stern discipline and idle posturing of public affairs. To his mind the best policy for the common man was to obey unconditionally, because "the laws of each era are based on the will of the Gods."[31] In effect, of course, Motoori's complete reliance on divine will detracted from the prestige of rulers and samurai administrators, who claimed full credit for peace in the realm.

Hirata Atsutane (1776–1843) brought the nativist perspective out of the cities into the countryside. He also turned from Motoori's emphasis on aesthetics to a new concern for practical affairs and cosmology. Indeed, what seems to have emerged from the work of Hirata and later nativists was a concept of the community as a microcosm where procreation, work, and worship at the shrines of tutelary deities had divine significance as reenactments of the primal processes of world creation. The re-

29. Ibid., p. 31.
30. Maruyama, *Studies in the Intellectual History of Tokugawa Japan* (Tokyo: University of Tokyo Press, 1974), p. 170. On Motoori, see H. D. Harootunian, "The Consciousness of Archaic Form in the New Realism of Kokugaku," in Najita and Scheiner, eds., pp. 63–104.
31. Maruyama, *Studies*, p. 174.

Introduction

sult was a form of symbolic autonomy for local entities that was reflected in new concepts of legitimacy and ways of relating to higher authority.

Peasant movements gained new confidence in the phrasing of their demands for relief. They also adopted protest tactics that far exceeded in violence and assertiveness the petitioning customarily employed in the seventeenth-century "natural economy." Late in the Tokugawa period, village groups also joined millenarian *yonaoshi* (world renewal) movements and contributed to an upsurge of new religions, such as Tenrikyō, Konkōkyō, Kurozumikyō, and Fujikō. As manifestations of revolutionary energy, these groups shared an orientation to egalitarian forms of organization and a claim to represent particular social constituencies outside the purview of publicly established authority.[32]

There was, in other words, an explosion of discourse in the eighteenth century, which brought vividly to consciousness the incorrigible diversity pervading society. The development of a distinctive ideological formation in Mito in the early nineteenth century was part of that process, but it was also, to a great extent, a reaction against the relativism and disorder such diversity implied. Steeped in concepts of moral and political orthodoxy as a result of their labors on the *Dai-Nihon shi*, samurai reformists in Mito announced the need to reconstitute the unity between Heaven and Man. Because the Way of Heaven was no longer clearly evident in the phenomenal world, it was now up to men themselves to bring it back to life—to objectify it in texts, institutions, and demonstrative acts of heroism so that the moral imperative of the Way would again be clear to all. Once the Way was made manifest, uniformity would overcome diversity, and the hearts of the people would again be in complete accord.

---

32. See H. D. Harootunian, "Ideology as Conflict," in Tetsuo Najita and J. Victor Koschmann, eds., *Conflict in Modern Japanese History* (Princeton, N.J.: Princeton University Press, 1982), pp. 24–60. On peasant rebellion and *yonaoshi*, see Irwin Scheiner, "The Mindful Peasant," *Journal of Asian Studies* 32 (1972–73), and "Benevolent Lords and Honorable Peasants," in Najita and Scheiner, eds., pp. 39–62; also, contributions by Hashimoto Mitsuru, Stephen Vlastos, and George Wilson, in Najita and Koschmann, eds., pp. 145–94.

TOKUGAWA REFORMISM

Members of the samurai class took note of incongruities in the bakuhan system even within the first half-century of Tokugawa rule. One of the first of their major proposals for reform was the *Daigaku wakumon* (Questions on *The Great Learning*), finished in 1687 by Kumazawa Banzan (1619–1691).[33] Kumazawa calls for a variety of changes, including the manipulation of currency, the return of the samurai class to the land, relaxation of the *sankin kōtai* system of alternate-year residence by daimyo in Edo, official promotion by merit, and remedies for extravagance and chronic indebtedness in the samurai class. He justifies these reforms pragmatically, presenting them as necessary if the shogunate is to avoid the serious crisis that he believed would appear in the form of a Manchu invasion.

At the same time, however, the pragmatism of the proposals seems to contradict Kumazawa's own neo-Confucian convictions, which, like Yamazaki Ansai's, focused on moral self-cultivation as the basis for social order. Indeed, Kumazawa's writings suggest that he was torn between a belief in the Confucian ideal of a sage ruler, whose very presence on the throne can "spontaneously" bring society in resonance with a cosmic order, and a belief in an instrumental approach to government that emphasizes the need for interventions based primarily on practicality, if not expediency.[34] In a manner that prefigured the mentality of Mito reformists in the nineteenth century, therefore, Kumazawa felt that practical reforms were necessary to create the conditions under which a natural order could be fully operative.

Kumazawa's proposals predated the influence of Ogyū Sorai, but they anticipated not only some of the specific reforms Ogyū would later promote, but the dualism of his philosophical system. Although Ogyū played a central role in the development of historical relativism in Japanese Confucianism, he never abandoned his conviction that the authority of Chinese civilization under the ancient sages was "changeless and timeless."[35]

33. Kumazawa Banzan, "*Dai Gaku Wakumon*," *Transactions of the Asiatic Society of Japan*, ser. 2, vol. 16 (1938).
34. Ian James McMullen, "Kumazawa Banzan and *Jitsugaku*," in Wm. Theodore de Bary and Irene Bloom, eds., *Principle and Practicality* (New York: Columbia University Press, 1979), pp. 341–42, 355–67.
35. Yamashita, in Nosco, ed., p. 162.

Therefore, in his reform proposals, *Taiheisaku* (A proposal for a great peace) and *Seidan* (A discourse on government), "there is a conspicuous tension between the ever-changing historical reality and the institutions created by the sages and the early kings."[36]

Ogyū's proposals differed from Kumazawa's in ways that point to a stronger emphasis on practicality and historical adaptation. For example, contrary to Kumazawa's views, Ogyū accepted the necessity for a money economy and the freedom to buy and sell land. At the same time, they agreed on other points, most notably on the need to return the samurai class to the land (*dochaku*) and on the desirability of relaxing the *sankin kōtai* system.[37] They also agreed with each other, and with Confucius himself, on the fundamental premise that change should be "restorationist," and therefore its models should be found in the past.

Of course, reforms were not merely proposed in the Tokugawa period but were also periodically carried out, albeit not always in ways that either Kumazawa or Ogyū would approve of. Bakufu leaders attempted to reform society and polity on three main occasions: in the 1720s (the Kyōhō Reforms), in the 1780s and 1790s (the Kansei Reforms), and in the 1840s (the Tenpō Reforms). In the Kyōhō period, shogun Tokugawa Yoshimune (1684–1751) promised to restore the world to its condition at the time of Tokugawa Ieyasu; in the Kansei period, bakufu chief senior councillor Matsudaira Sadanobu (1758–1829) called for a return to the Kyōhō Reforms; and in the Tenpō period, chief senior councillor Mizuno Tadakuni (1794–1851) tried to restore the "spirit of the Kyōhō and Kansei reform eras."[38]

None of these bakufu reformers ever actually attempted the wholesale return of the samurai class to rural life, as advocated by Kumazawa and Ogyū, but they were all strongly motivated by the insolvency, indebtedness, and failing vigor of the ruling class. Moreover, all focused their remedial efforts on economic and financial retrenchment, with secondary emphases on the expanding bureaucracy, rural unrest, excessive or conspicuous consumption, and moral degeneracy. Some of the specific mea-

36. Ibid., p. 159.
37. Ibid., p. 163; J. R. McEwan, *The Political Writings of Ogyū Sorai* (Cambridge: Cambridge University Press, 1969), pp. 27, 57, 99.
38. See Conrad Totman, "Tenpō Reforms," *The Encyclopedia of Japan* 8 (Tokyo: Kōdansha International, Inc., 1983), p. 2.

sures adopted earlier by bakufu reformers were also tried by reformers in Mito in the early 1830s. These included the purge of officials, reform of tax assessment practices, sumptuary regulations, extraction of forced loans or contributions from merchants, promotion of military training, and enforcement of ideological or religious orthodoxies. However, I argue that, on balance, the Mito reformers were less concerned with economic improvement than with social and ideological rectification in the moral sense.

HISTORIOGRAPHICAL PERSPECTIVE

I have attempted above to place Mito discourse against the background of a Confucianized Shinto ideology that was elaborated in more or less finished form by Yamazaki Ansai in the seventeenth century and then challenged from various perspectives throughout the eighteenth. I suggest that the Mito ideologues drew heavily on the discourses of both centuries in their effort to reconstruct, through programs of reform, the institutional foundations for a natural order similar to that envisioned by Yamazaki. Indeed, they not only hoped to reactualize such an order, but to install it permanently as a bulwark against powerful forces for change.

In chapter 1, I will explore aspects of a paradoxical relationship in Mito discourse between confidence in an archetypal natural order, on the one hand, and a poignant sense of the corrosive power of language and history, on the other. In chapter 2, I will show how the paradox between history and an archetype of natural order—the latter now represented in the symbol of *kokutai*—is revealed in Aizawa's epic work, *Shinron*. In chapter 3, I will extend my interpretation to encompass action as a text, in an attempt to grasp the meaning of the Tenpō Reforms in Mito. In chapter 4, I will focus on the effect of the reforms and, especially, of the newly radicalized district schools on the subjectivity of local elites.

In chapter 5, I will describe the Tengu insurrection that drew Mito into a civil war in the mid-1860s, pointing out the ambivalent relationship between the largely rural, non-samurai Tengu force and the local population, which was often oppressed and plundered by that force.

Introduction

The view of Mito ideology I present in these chapters diverges somewhat from the traditional interpretations of Mitogaku with regard both to the internal constraints or structure of that discourse and its effectiveness in transforming human subjectivity. Some of the most persuasive and important existing interpretations of Mito thought have emerged from comprehensive attempts to elaborate a master narrative that can explain the Meiji Restoration of 1868 and specific features of the state and society that arose out of that event.[39] A leading example is Maruyama Masao, who treats major aspects of early-modern Japanese thought in terms of a contrast between nature and invention—between the view typical of the neo-Confucian school that society is an aspect of natural order, on the one hand, and the view of Ogyū Sorai and his successors that social and political institutions are made or invented (*sakui*) by men, on the other.

Maruyama believes social invention to be an essential element of modernity. Therefore, its divergence from theories of natural order "is not simply a technical problem inside the framework of feudal society, but . . . implies the world-historical problem of the conflict between the medieval view of social and state institutions and the modern bourgeois view." Accordingly, his project is to trace what he believes to be the development in the course of the Tokugawa period *from nature to invention*.

Maruyama postulates that the appearance in early-modern Japan of an idea of social invention was more or less inevitable:

> When social relations lose their natural balance and become less predictable, the authority of the society's norms or laws collapses. . . . In such a critical situation a body of thought is bound to emerge that stresses the idea of an autonomous personality [*shutaiteki jinkaku*] whose task it is to strengthen the foundations that uphold the social norms and to bring the political disorder under control. (p. 206)

The body of thought to which he refers, of course, is that of Ogyū Sorai, and the prototypical autonomous personalities are Ogyū's "Early Kings," who invented norms and endowed them with validity. Hence, in theory:

---

39. "Nature and Invention in Tokugawa Political Thought," in Maruyama, *Studies*, pp. 189–319. Maruyama does not necessarily still adhere to all parts of the argument presented here (ibid., introduction). (Subsequent page references to *Studies* are inserted in the text.)

By extending the analogy of the logic of "invention by the Early Kings" to all ages, the ascendancy of persons over ideas was firmly established for the first time. This made it possible for political rulers to engage in inventive activities, *directed towards the future*, in order to overcome the crisis confronting them. (p. 218)

In fact, the transition from nature to invention was far from smooth and, ultimately, incomplete. Ogyū's own system was not entirely free of the logic of natural order, because in content it still relied on "the natural elements that constituted primitive feudalism: an agricultural livelihood, a natural economy, a family-based master-servant relationship, and so on" (p. 222).

Moreover, there was a "revival of the ideology of natural order" in the late eighteenth century, which, in conjunction with the immaturity of industrial production, caused the logic of invention to stagnate (pp. 302–3). Not until after the Meiji Restoration of 1868, in the popular rights movement, did the theory of invention truly come into its own:

It was the emergence of the Movement for Freedom and Popular Rights that established the supremacy of the theory of invention in the post-Restoration period. *Here the doctrine of invention was at last able to develop its implications to their conclusion in a clear-cut theory of man-made institutions.* (p. 312)

The Meiji developments signified a major breakthrough, but one that had been prepared in advance by Tokugawa thought:

Just as the enormous energy of a river as it breaks out of a dam is the product of the slow accumulation of hydraulic power during the containment, the irresistible spread of the theory of invention after the Meiji Restoration could not have occurred without these hidden developments beneath the surface of the feudal system. (p. 314)

However, Maruyama concludes his essay on a less triumphant note. The Meiji period soon brought its own revival of theories of natural order, and they succeeded again in overshadowing the invention-oriented conception of popular rights: "Apparently on the verge of recapturing his freedom as an autonomous personality with respect to the social order, having eliminated the restrictions of the estate system in the Meiji Restoration, man was to be swallowed up again by the new Leviathan, the Meiji state" (p. 319).

There is a markedly Hegelian cast to Maruyama's vision of the "inexorable infiltration" of the theory of invention through something akin to the "cunning of reason" (p. 284). He seeks to provide for Tokugawa thought a teleological resolution of its contradiction between nature and invention by casting the former as traditional and the latter as progressive. When he approaches a text, therefore, he tends to focus on the *degree* of invention revealed in it, thereby either obscuring the extent of coexistence between invention and natural order where they appear together or portraying such modes as transitional and therefore somehow incomplete. Among the works he treats in the latter manner are those of Ogyū who, as noted above, failed to "free himself" completely from the conviction of natural order. Treatment of the former kind is dealt out to Mito thought, which enters into Maruyama's narrative as part of the late Tokugawa reaction against the theory of invention. According to Maruyama, Aizawa Seishisai's theoretical premise is a "belief in the natural order in its purest form" (p. 305).

Although this book documents at length the importance in Mito thought and action of archetypes of natural order, it is difficult to ignore Mito's equally apparent (and contradictory) sensitivity to historical change and emphasis on the need for constructive "invention" as the means of representing a natural order. In contrast to Maruyama, and from a different perspective, therefore, I have proposed that it is precisely the *contradictory combination* between a degenerative concept of history and the possibility of a natural order that defines the law of existence of Mito discourse. Indeed, I would argue that this dualism in Mitogaku can be brought fully into view only when chronology is suspended, at least temporarily, and both *thought and action* are viewed synchronically with attention to their structural articulation and modes of interdependency. As Ricoeur suggests, structural analysis is useful—perhaps even essential—as one dimension of a comprehensive strategy of interpretation.[40]

40. See Ricoeur, *Interpretation Theory*, pp. 82–88, and "The Model of the Text," p. 559.

I also depart from some leading portrayals of Mitogaku with respect to the ideological function and effectiveness of that school of thought. Here the standard view is best expressed by Tōyama Shigeki, although Maruyama's treatment is generally consistent with it.[41] Tōyama argues, in the first place, that Mitogaku was one variety of the *sonnō jōi* thought of late Tokugawa Japan that provided the "ideological foundation of the Meiji Restoration."[42] Because such thought was based on Confucian "arguments concerning names and statuses" (*meibunron*), it tended toward the normative application of ideal categories while lacking the inner compulsion to work within or change reality. It tended, therefore, to "degenerate into an academic form of conceptual amusement."[43]

Second, Tōyama argues that debates in the names-and-statuses mode served most often to "rationalize the existing power structure." They led to a "feudal ideology" whose proponents, like Nariaki himself, sought only to strengthen the existing system.[44] Therefore, *sonnō jōi* thought, of the sort typical of Mitogaku, had to be transcended if a movement to overthrow the bakufu was ever to emerge. According to Tōyama, that was accomplished not in Mito, but in the great western domains of Satsuma and Chōshū. Thus, "From the time of the opening of the ports in the Ansei period, Mitogaku gradually lost its place in the mainstream of the Restoration movement."[45]

Third, in order to become revolutionary, *sonnō jōi* thought had not only to throw off its preoccupation with "names and statuses," but to forge a link with the non-samurai classes and address the problems that affected them. Tōyama explains:

> In sum, two very different qualities coexisted in *jōi* thought. The first expressed the feudalistic world concept of the privileged *bushi* class, whose members sought to avoid the collapse of the feudal system as a result of opening the country to foreign intercourse [*kai-*

---

41. See Maruyama, *Studies*, pp. 304–6, 353–67.
42. Tōyama Shigeki, "Mitogaku no seikaku," in Nakamura Kōya, ed., *Seikatsu to shisō* (Tokyo: Shōgakkan, 1944), p. 176, and Tōyama, *Meiji ishin*, p. 58. I have used the summary of Tōyama's main points provided by Yoshida Toshizumi, "Kōki Mitogaku to Kiheitai shotai," *Ibaraki-ken rekishi kanpō* 2 (Feb. 1975).
43. Tōyama, *Meiji ishin*, p. 59.
44. Ibid., p. 62.
45. Tōyama, "Mitogaku no seikaku," in Nakamura Kōya, ed., pp. 195–96.

koku]. The second expressed the national awareness [*kokuminteki dokuritsu ishiki*] of ordinary people, catalyzed by their attempt to avoid the added burdens on their livelihood imposed as a result of opening the country. That is, *jōi* ideology was not the direct expression of a popular sense of national unity and independence, but instead was distorted by rigid feudal attitudes. . . . It was when the *sonnō jōi* movements took up the problem of people's livelihood [*kokumin seikatsu*] and appealed to the general populace that it can be said to have begun to develop from merely a movement of *bushi* to a movement of the whole people; and from a feudal to an antifeudal movement.[46]

Specifically, regarding the conversion from a movement oriented to *sonnō jōi* to one aimed at overthrowing the bakufu (*tōbaku*), "the transition was accomplished through the consolidation by lower *bushi* forces of a hegemony that more widely incorporated members of the rich peasant and merchant strata." For Tōyama, the critical moment in this transition was when Chōshū, "finding it necessary to prepare for retaliatory attacks [by foreign ships], proceeded in that unlikely circumstance to take the emergency measure of arming ordinary people."[47] The result was the Kiheitai (special militia) and other Western-style forces (*shotai*) that included commoners.[48]

Tōyama recognizes that the Kiheitai was "certainly not a modern national army premised on popular liberation [from feudalism]." It was selective and always under the control of military aristocrats. In other words, such groups represented the "induction into feudal military forces of [commoners] who thus became 'quasi-samurai.'" Tōyama's statement of their significance is labored but precise:

> The strength of such units resulted not only from the awareness [on the part of their leaders] that, if human resources were to replace the corrupt *bushi* bureaucracy, they had to be drawn from such strata as foot-soldiers, rural samurai, rich peasants, and rich merchants. That strength also stemmed from the capacity of the

---

46. Ibid., pp. 200–1.
47. Tōyama, *Meiji ishin*, pp. 136–37.
48. On the Kiheitai/shotai, see Albert M. Craig, *Chōshū in the Meiji Restoration* (Cambridge: Harvard University Press, 1961), pp. 170–85; Thomas Huber, *The Revolutionary Origins of Modern Japan* (Stanford: Stanford University Press, 1981), pp. 120–25.

low-ranking *bushi* reformists who led the movement (in the confrontation with the people [*minshū*], mediated by the rich peasant and merchant strata) to employ toward their own purposes the anti-feudal energy of those people. As that occurred, the reformists were made aware that their own class interest dictated the distortion and suppression of that energy, and were impelled to develop policies, of the sort typical of absolutist leaders, that are designed both to appeal to the people and also to deceive them.[49]

The keen sensitivity to the function of ideology that is revealed in this and other passages marks a high point in Tōyama's consistently stimulating analysis. Contrary to the preoccupation of leading Western historians with the numbers and backgrounds of peasants relative to samurai in the *shotai*, and their concern about whether or not such groups were "true" peasant militia or, on the contrary, were dominated entirely by samurai, Tōyama's emphasis here is on the practice of ideology and the process by which ideological hegemony was extended among samurai and other groups. Rather than disputing the degree of "revolutionary energy from below," Tōyama recognizes that a process of subjection is likely to accompany the formation of active subjects.[50]

However, Tōyama's careful treatment of the Kiheitai units also reflects a sweeping interpretation of the Meiji Restoration, which he sees as the "twenty-four year [1853–1877] process of the formation of absolutism."[51] Thus, his synthesis presents an overarching interpretation of modern Japanese history.

49. Tōyama, *Meiji ishin*, p. 138.
50. Craig, e.g., argues that the *shotai* "were clearly not pure peasant militia" because "the samurai component was sizeable" (*Chōshū in the Meiji Restoration*, p. 272). He also observes that the majority of the commoner members of the *shotai* "joined to obtain the coveted symbols of the feudal class" (p. 274); that they "fought only when . . . they were catalyzed by the firm control of extremist samurai leaders"; and that the "willingness of the Chōshū bureaucrats to arm the peasants and to train them in the use of modern weapons suggests that they were totally unaware of any revolutionary potential among the Chōshū peasantry." Therefore, he finds it difficult to sustain the Marxist "thesis of a revolutionary peasant movement" (pp. 276–77). However, because of his desire to discredit the notion of any "revolutionary energy" among peasants, he does not explore with any subtlety the dynamics of the process by which, as Tōyama argues, lower samurai consolidated a form of ideological hegemony that allowed commoners to be mobilized as active subjects.
W. G. Beasley, in *The Meiji Restoration* (Stanford: Stanford University Press, 1972), also focuses on the question of whether or not commoners acted as "independent entities" (p. 72).
51. Tōyama, *Meiji ishin*, p. 327.

Without necessarily contesting Tōyama's interpretation, it is essential to confront his account with the evidence offered below, which suggests that Mito ideology, too, was "in action" at least from the Tenpō period on and was effective in qualifying and recruiting, first, *bushi* aristocrats and, then, commoners for lives of restorationist activism.[52] Mito ideology both subjected (Tōyama says "distorted" and "suppressed") the energies of ordinary people and qualified ("appealed to," "used") them to engage in political action. Once understood *as ideology*, that is, Mitogaku no longer appears to fit so nicely into the historical niche prepared for it by Maruyama and Tōyama. Indeed, when events in Mito are juxtaposed correctly against those in Chōshū and elsewhere, the Meiji Restoration begins to look less like the culmination of an identifiable stream of causally linked elements than what Tetsuo Najita has called a "composite of diverse and simultaneous transformations taking place throughout society."[53] As such a view suggests, there appears to have been a great deal of redundancy among events in Chōshū, Tosa, Mito, and elsewhere, and to assign particular causal significance to one over another can easily be misleading.

With respect to a third type of study of late Tokugawa Japan, my interpretation of events in Mito emerges as less a revision than a counterpart. Thomas C. Smith has argued that the penetration of rural society by market forces led to a proliferation of tenancy and the growth of a class of rich, local landlords (*gōnō*). This new village elite identified itself increasingly with the samurai and rich merchant classes and, Smith suggests, eventually produced some individuals who joined loyalist samurai in the struggles leading to the Restoration.

Smith's analysis emphasizes the role of economic development in the reorganization of class relations in rural Japan. Rapid urban growth and the rise of commerce in the context of an increasingly broad-based market system in the mid-Tokugawa period presented rural folk with new incentives:

> Enormous quantities of grain, fish, timber, and fibers were required to feed, clothe, and shelter the growing population of the

---

52. Yoshida Toshizumi has also criticized Tōyama on this point ("Kōki Mitogaku to Kiheitai shotai," pp. 89–102).
53. Tetsuo Najita, "Introduction," in Najita and Koschmann, eds., p. 20.

towns. Most of it came by way of local markets and merchants from Japanese farming and fishing villages, since foreign trade contributed almost nothing. What a task and what opportunities were set for villages which in the eighteenth century had produced little or nothing for sale! And what social adjustments were required to meet the challenge successfully![54]

The market provided new opportunities for nonagricultural by-employment, causing a labor shortage in some rural areas. The immediate result was a decline in the numbers of indentured servants and the other more or less bonded laborers who had formed the basis of traditional, household-based agriculture (*tezukuri*). Traditional farmers turned initially to shorter term workers and hired for wages, but, as wages rose, new forms of agricultural organization had to be developed.

Meanwhile, technological advances and their dissemination led to increased productivity and expanding surpluses for some farmers. But, rather than stimulating the formation of larger farming units and thus economies of scale, the result was a gradual reduction in the size of such units until the nuclear family revealed itself as the most efficient. The specific nature of early-modern Japanese technological developments, which included commercial fertilizers, increased plant varieties, the extension of irrigation, and new methods of planting, transplanting, weeding, and harvesting, was to increase "not only per-acre yields but per-acre labor requirements as well." Such advances also made farming "more intricate":

> Far from simplifying and making more uniform the multitude of tasks that confronted the labor force (as mechanical innovations presumably would have done), innovations actually increased the demands made on every farm worker. They demanded of him more specialized knowledge and skill, more attention to detail, the exercise of more initiative and judgement. . . . To speak metaphorically, rather than impelling farming forward to a manufacturing stage of production, these operations served to strengthen its handicraft character.[55]

---

54. Thomas C. Smith, *The Agrarian Origins of Modern Japan* (Stanford: Stanford University Press, 1959), p. 68.
55. Ibid., pp. 101, 105.

Introduction

The result, therefore, of commercialization plus technological advances was widespread tenancy, which allowed increasing concentration of land *ownership* while the actual *management* of farming devolved to ever-smaller units, settling finally on the nuclear family. Village populations were increasingly polarized between a few rich landlords and many landless tenants; moreover, the relationship between these two levels became increasingly distant and contractual, penetrated by what Marx and Engels called the "cash nexus." This created new possibilities for conflict, not only between rich and poor, but between traditional elite and nouveau riche.

Moreover, and most interesting for my purposes, this "new class" of large landlords (who were also often "capitalists" of one kind or another) set itself culturally above the common run of peasant and aspired to a more aristocratic status and lifestyle: "Unable to resist temptation, many wealthy peasants took concubines, frequented inns and hot springs, collected books and art objects, built fine houses, studied poetry, painting, and even the military arts." They purchased surnames and the right to bear arms and, furthermore, "began to cultivate the fine arts and invade the fields of scholarship and speculative thought, all previously the special province of warriors and the city rich."[56] Once their abilities had extended to the military and cultural arts, they were available for political mobilization in the impending crisis:

> [N]either swords and surnames nor learning and military training obliterated the distinctions between wealthy peasants and warriors. But they lessened the psychological distance between the two classes, and this may have prepared the way for a political alliance of elements of each during the crisis the country faced in the last decades of Tokugawa rule.[57]

Smith concludes, "It is not surprising, therefore, to find evidence of peasants taking part in the Restoration movement."[58]

The exceptional merit of Smith's study is to delineate clearly the impersonal, market forces that helped produce a new vil-

---

56. Ibid., pp. 128, 177.
57. Ibid., p. 179.
58. Ibid., p. 204.

lage elite in the late Tokugawa period. However, demonstrating the existence of a particular class as an objective, social entity does not suffice to show the emergence of a new political actor. As argued by Althusser, Therborn, and others, it is the specific function of ideology to produce subjects who are qualified to respond actively to the conditions of their existence. Without ideology, a new class might exist, but its members would remain politically inert.

Thus, my book may be seen as complementary to Smith's in that it seeks to view the production of historical subjectivity in the late Tokugawa period from the perspective of ideology rather than socioeconomic development. Given the objective existence in Mito domain of a new rural elite—an existence often noted by Yūkoku, his son Tōko, and others—I have tried to show how in Mito that elite was subjected to a form of hegemony through the reforms and the district schools, and thereby qualified to speak and act politically.

Mito ideology in the late Tokugawa period took full account of the reformist possibilities suggested by eighteenth-century relativism, constructivism, and economism, but it struggled internally to control and recontain those very tendencies. The Mito reformists shared Yamazaki Ansai's fundamentalist belief in the creation myths, the primacy of reverence, and the supernatural preeminence of the Land of the Gods over all other life on earth. They were convinced it was possible to reactivate a natural order in which spontaneous expressions of loyalty and filial piety would reinforce correct distinctions between rulers and ruled, and the imperial benevolence would radiate outward through ritual compliance.

But they also noted that loyalty and filial piety were no longer spontaneous, that "names and status distinctions" were out of alignment, and that ritual alone would never suffice to bring order. Therefore, they contrived to reactualize the conditions for spontaneity. They "rectified" names and statuses by constructing new ones where necessary, and they flexibly adapted mythical archetypes to contemporary institutional and cultural constraints. Thus, they sought to work within history in order to escape its degenerative forces. They also strove to use linguistic and other mediations to achieve a state of nature in which such contrivances would be superfluous. That is, they attempted to "write" the Way of Heaven, not only in texts, but in the configurations of ritual, routines of institutional structure, and conventions of daily life, so that it would become manifest in the spontaneous inclinations of the people.

Mito discourse—despite, or perhaps because of, its many paradoxes and contradictions—transformed the subjectivity of *bushi* scholars in the Tenpō period and put them in action. As it did so, it pushed them beyond Yamazaki's quietistic reverence to involve them in iconoclastic constructivism and instrumentality. But it did not stop there. By the 1850s, Mito ideology had begun to subject both *bushi* and commoners to a moral and political discipline that set them against entrenched political forces in Mito-han and the nation as a whole. And it eventually qualified them for an ethical commitment that went beyond both reverence and practicality to the sublime pursuit of sacred pilgrimage and martyrdom.

In Mito in the late Tokugawa period, therefore, the seventeenth-century ideology was not transformed, replaced, or overthrown. It was, rather, repossessed with such fervor that it became corrosive of the very political hierarchy that it had once helped legitimize.

1
RECTIFICATION AND MYTH

In the late eighteenth and early nineteenth centuries, samurai intellectuals in Mito began in earnest to focus their scholarly efforts on real social and economic problems. In 1797 Fujita Yūkoku prefaced one of his many memorials to the Mito daimyo with the lament: "Each year domainal finances are further depleted, and samurai mettle abates; each day the strength of the people wanes, and the foundation for government crumbles."[1] The sentiments expressed in Yūkoku's missive reflect the tendency toward political involvement that began to infuse the Mito historiographical institute (Shōkōkan) around the turn of the century. Moreover, the form of the document is itself symbolic. The learned yet practically oriented memorial to higher authority came to typify a union of scholarship and political action in Mito that reached its apex in the first half of the nineteenth century under the reformist daimyo Tokugawa Nariaki.

THE PLIGHT OF THE DOMAIN

The problems described by Yūkoku and his colleagues were by no means new. Mito had begun to experience serious financial distress as early as the Genroku era (1688–1703),[2] and in 1700 administrators made their first demand for donations from wealthy farmers and merchants. Nevertheless, samurai incomes stagnated, and discontent was pervasive. Reforms attempted during the Hōei period (1704–1710) led in 1709 to the largest peasant rebellion ever experienced in the domain. By 1774 the stipends of samurai retainers were withheld for the first time as

---

1. *Teishi fūji*, in Imai, Seya, and Bitō, eds., p. 26.
2. Seya Yoshihiko and Toyosaki Takashi, *Ibaraki-ken no rekishi* (Tokyo: Yamakawa Shuppansha, 1973), pp. 123–24.

"loans" (*okariage*), and in 1791 the domain administration announced that it would subtract fully half of their emoluments. The announcement dramatized the plight of the domain:

> You are all aware of the financial difficulties in which we find ourselves. Every year our accounts are more in the red, and our debt to the bakufu increases. Consequently, it has become difficult to continue to meet the needs of the domain. We have appealed once more to the bakufu and have succeeded in borrowing the considerable sum of 30,000 *ryō* [gold coins]. In return, however, we have been ordered to economize, even though in view of our intensifying poverty there is little that can be done. Therefore, next year, half of the annual stipends of retainers who receive 6 *koku* (or 6 *ryō* in cash) and above and one-third of the stipends of those who receive less than that will be withheld.[3]

The vast majority of retainers above foot-soldier level received more than 6 *koku* (a *koku* measured about 5.1 bushels of rice), so in effect the order meant a 50 percent reduction across the board. The precedent established here was repeated often in later years.

It was not uncommon in the Tokugawa period for daimyo as well as lower-ranking samurai to seek relief from insolvency by taking loans from merchants, and it appears that Mito had been involved in dealings with Kyoto merchants since the reign of the first daimyo.[4] Other loans were floated among Mito merchants, and, as samurai indebtedness increased, the traders sometimes became arrogant, openly demanding repayment, and at times refusing further services. In his monumental essay, *Shinron*, Aizawa Seishisai sums up the dilemma of the samurai aristocracy in a manner that echoes the perceptions of Ogyū in the early eighteenth century:

> The samurai are concentrated in the towns so they must obtain on the market everything they need for the entire year. They take their rice stipend—the value of which declines further each year—and exchange it for currency, which is constantly being devalued. Then, with that debased currency they seek to purchase commodi-

---

3. Ibid., pp. 126–27. (The *ryō* was a gold coin equal in the late Tokugawa period to 60 *momme*, the standard weight of each of which was 3.75 grams of silver.)

4. Ibid., p. 128.

ties at increasingly inflated prices. They are from the outset unable to meet their expenses, but the servants and help they employ are all accustomed to luxurious living so they cannot be maintained cheaply. The samurai are forced to turn to annual contract labor, but that also soon becomes too expensive. . . . Moreover, household needs, wife's allowances, entertainment expenses, and so on increase daily. Soon, it is no longer possible to make ends meet. As a result, the samurai become accustomed to receiving loans from the rich. Even among daimyo and other fief holders, there are virtually none who do not borrow. Crafty plutocrats wield unlimited power in the realm of finance, treating kings like children they can bounce on their knee. As a result, wealth has largely passed into the hands of the townspeople.[5]

Agriculture in Mito had never been prosperous. Low productivity was the rule, and natural disasters were frequent. Great famines scourged the land during the Kyōhō (1716–1736), Tenmei (1781–1788), and Tenpō (1830–1843) eras, and droughts, floods, drenching rains, and unseasonal freezes frequently took their toll of crops. Taxes in Mito were relatively high. The result was bare subsistence, if not starvation, for most peasants of the domain. Emigration to other domains was frequent, and at certain periods infanticide was widely practiced. As a result, the population of Mito decreased steadily in the late Tokugawa period.[6]

In the wake of such difficulties, Mito intellectuals were quick to find evidence of social disintegration. Aizawa complains that the fabric of community was rent by moral dissipation. Gamblers and gangs of drifters, he says, seemed to ignore legal restrictions, making themselves the uninvited guests of rural villages. There they "gather from dusk 'till dawn, corrupting the villagers with food, drink and games of chance." They are impossible to stop because "it is in the nature of the common people to love profit."[7]

Moreover, in recent years a variety of religious hucksters had flouted the Mito administration's traditional enmity toward Buddhism by hawking magical incantations. No sooner was one

---

5. *Shinron Tekiihen* (Tokyo: Iwanami Bunko, 1931), pp. 89–91.
6. Seya and Toyosaki, *Ibaraki-ken no rekishi*, p. 140.
7. Aizawa, *Shinron*, p. 131.

such group prohibited than a new one would spring up in its place.

> The Fuju-fuse sect of Nichiren Buddhism ... and other groups devoted to the Lotus Sutra were severely dealt with long ago. Recently however, countless individuals have again succeeded in gathering hordes of followers by establishing shrines to malicious deities or purporting to follow certain Buddhist canons. It is said that a group calling itself the Fujikō has attracted upwards of seventy thousand followers.[8]

There is little to be done, Aizawa says, because "the common people naturally fear the spirits."[9]

Aizawa emphasizes that, as the popular mind (*minshin*) became fragmented and corrupt, the danger of subversion would become increasingly serious. Here, of course, his concern for Mito merges with apprehensions about the fate of the nation as a whole. Foreign enemies could capitalize on Japan's weaknesses by seducing the people with Christian doctrine: "Once the minds of the people have been won over, we will have lost the country before the fighting even begins."[10] Aizawa feared and distrusted the very population whose hearts and minds he sought to win.

In sum, the problems that fueled the intellectual and political efforts of Mito samurai in the bakumatsu period included the economic predicament of the samurai class, the divisiveness and instability portended by signs of moral disintegration, the rise of new religious groups, and the fertile ground for foreign subversion these factors provided. The major question for consideration here, however, is not so much the specific nature of the problems themselves. As noted above, the major issues were by no means peculiar to the early years of the nineteenth century or to Mito domain. Of greater interest is the manner in which Mito writers defined or "encoded" the phenomena they perceived and the mode of action in which they responded.

---

8. Ibid. Mito-han favored Shinto, and in the 1660s got rid of over 50% of its Buddhist temples. A similar policy was initiated during the Tenpō reforms. See Mito-shi Shi Hensan Iinkai, ed., *Mito-shi shi* II/1 : 836–76 (cited hereafter as *Mss*). The Fuju-fuse sect is a branch of Nichiren Buddhism noted for its militant purity. It was outlawed along with Christianity in 1614 and persecuted throughout the Tokugawa period. On Fuju-fuse in the context of early Tokugawa ideology, see Ooms, *Tokugawa Ideology*, pp. 186–93.
9. Aizawa, *Shinron*, p. 131.
10. Ibid., p. 53.

Rectification and Myth

The problems outlined above were, in fact, construed as evidence of the failure of the samurai as a managerial class.[11] Fujita Tōko admonishes in his *Kōdōkanki jutsugi* (Commentary on the Manifesto of Mito Academy) that:

> After a long period of peace the hearts of the people have become frivolous. Farmers have engrossed themselves in side-jobs, while merchants and artisans are consumed by lust for profit. Nevertheless, in view of the abundance of grain, fabrics, and all kinds of implements that fill the land, we are hardly justified in criticizing all farmers, artisans, and merchants for laxity in the performance of their callings. When doctrine and learning are not disseminated, military preparations are slack, officeholders are left unaware of circumstances at lower levels of society, the benevolence of the sovereign fails to reach the common people, and the fate of the realm is in question, who are to blame? Are we not faced with these problems because those who are charged with governance have failed to carry out their responsibilities? Yet not only ordinary samurai but their elders as well remain completely unaware of their own inadequacy.[12]

But how was that failure explained, and what did it mean? How might we define, in other words, the ideological framework within which inchoate experience was transformed into specific problems requiring solution? As so often in the Confucian tradition, so now in Mito, the apparent failure of the rulers to recognize their culpability was seen as evidence that the true nature of the Way had been obscured. Tōko, for example, lamented that "it has been a long time since the Way became unclear,"[13] and then revealed the foundations of the late Tokugawa Mito project by remarking that "only when the Way (*dōgi*) is clarified can we put ourselves in order and rule over others."[14]

The Mito activists perceived that the normative state of spontaneity and natural virtue that they generally called the Way had been obscured by the ravages of time and heresy; therefore, they were preoccupied with the need to provide such mediations as would allow the Way to regain its full visibility and

---

11. Tōyama Shigeki, *Meiji ishin*, p. 63.
12. Fujita Tōko, *Kōdōkanki jutsugi*, in Imai Usaburō, Seya Yoshihiko, and Bitō Masahide, eds., pp. 319–20.
13. Ibid., p. 321.
14. Ibid., p. 327.

effectiveness in human affairs. This preoccupation caused them to focus initially on language and status distinctions as the pillars of moral and political construction. It later led them to mythical reconstruction and other, more radical, forms of action, both instrumental and performative.

THE MITO HISTORIOGRAPHICAL TRADITION

It is important to recall that the particular way in which problems were defined in Mito in the late Tokugawa period was the precipitate not only of a millennia-old Confucian restorationist legacy, but also of an historiographical ethos that stretched 200 years into Mito's own past. The clarification of norms through the writing of history was a living tradition in Mito and must be considered as inseparable from the political thought and action that occurred there in the nineteenth century.

The idea of a history of Japan, to be compiled by the Mito house, originated with the second Mito daimyo, Tokugawa Mitsukuni. The project was intended as a moral exemplar on the pattern of Chinese histories, and particularly the *Shih chi* (Records of the historian) by Ssu-ma Ch'ien (145–186 B.C.). The didactic purpose behind the project is dramatized in the following anecdote recounted in 1715 by Mitsukuni's adopted son and successor, Tokugawa Tsunaeda (1656–1718):

> At the age of eighteen, my father read the biography of Po I. He rose to his feet with the admiration he felt at Po I's high devotion to duty. Fondling the book, he said with a sigh: "If this book did not exist, one could not find out about the history of early China. If one had no histories to rely on, one could not cause future ages to know what should be emulated." Hereupon, he . . . conceived the determination to compile a history.[15]

Work apparently was begun on the history, which was to become known as the *Dai-Nihon shi* (A history of great Japan), in 1657. By 1672, an institute called the Shōkōkan had been estab-

---

15. Herschel Webb, "What is the *Dai Nihon Shi?*," *Journal of Asian Studies* 19, no. 2 (Feb. 1960):136. Po I was a self-denying son who fled to the wilderness rather than accept an inheritance against his late father's will. See his biography in the *Shih chi* (Records of the historian).

lished, and the project was proceeding under Mitsukuni's supervision. Talented scholars were recruited; they included men trained in most of the powerful philosophical schools of the time. It appears that the dominant viewpoint was that of the Hayashi Razan (1583–1657) school of *shushigaku,* or Chu Hsi neo-Confucianism. But the early relationship between the Mito historians and the Hayashis also seems to have been strongly competitive, inasmuch as the Hayashi school was working on its own Japanese history, the bakufu-sponsored *Honchō tsugan* (Comprehensive mirror of Japan).[16]

Because of the bakufu's rule that the Mito daimyo should reside in Edo, the Shōkōkan was located there as well, first in the annex to the Mito headquarters and later in the headquarters itself. This location facilitated recruitment, and the staff at the institute increased from about twenty in 1672 to between forty and fifty by the end of the century. In this early period, most came from outside the Mito band of retainers.[17]

The format of the history as it was planned by Mitsukuni conformed to the model for Chinese histories bequeathed by Ssu-ma Ch'ien. It was to be composed of the "Annals," consisting of a chronology; the "Essays," on special topics; the "Tables," which indicated relationships among elements in schematic form; and the "Biographies," which dealt with important but nonregnant personages. In its final form, the *Dai-Nihon shi* departed from this pattern in minor ways, as by including the Biographies immediately after the Annals rather than at the end, but overall the form was faithfully followed. Clearly, Mitsukuni intended the *Dai-Nihon shi* to be history in the Chinese mold. However, perhaps his most important departure from Chinese practice, one that indicates the early polemical thrust of the work in a specifically Japanese context, was the focus on the imperial line. Each chapter of the Annals contained only information relating to the reign of a single legitimate emperor, with no attention to military rulers or other de facto powerholders. This revealed Mitsukuni's emperor-centered philosophy of his-

---

16. Seya Yoshihiko, "Mitogaku no haikei," in Imai, Seya, and Bitō, eds., p. 513; also see Hashikawa Bunsō, *Fujita Tōko,* Nihon no meicho 29 (Tokyo: Chūō Kōronsha, 1974), pp. 28–32.

17. Seya, "Mitogaku no haikei," p. 515.

tory, which portrayed the imperial line "as the embodiment, mystic or symbolic, of Japanese society and nationhood."[18]

Their desire to include only legitimate emperors confronted the Mito historians with the need to determine legitimacy in several difficult cases. Three of their decisions on these cases were more or less iconoclastic in the early Tokugawa scholarly world and became known as the *san dai-tokuhitsu*, aptly translated by Herschel Webb as "Three Great Innovations." These were the decision that the ancient "Empress Jingū" was not an empress in her own right at all but rather a regent for her son, the Emperor Ōjin (201–310); the conclusion that in 672 the Emperor Tenmu (622–686) had usurped the throne of his nephew, Prince Ōtomo (648–672), who was himself a legitimate emperor; and the determination that, during the era of the great imperial schism in the early fourteenth century, the southern court at Yoshino, rather than the northern one at Kyoto, had been the orthodox line.[19] When included with the rest of the 73 chapters of the Annals and 170 chapters of the Biographies, which covered such people as consorts, regents, shoguns, and so on, these three conclusions highlighted the enormous accomplishments of the institute under Mitsukuni's supervision. His death in 1700 came after the Annals were finished and only shortly before the completion of the Biographies. Both of these sections were presented to the bakufu in 1720, and with that the "early" period of historiographical activity came to a close. Work at the institute virtually ceased for more than seventy years, and it was not until Tachihara Suiken (1774–1823) became director in 1786 that another spurt of productivity announced the inauguration of what modern historians would call "late Mitogaku."

In commenting on the philosophy of history embraced by the Mito institute in the early period, a specialist in Japanese intellectual history, Bitō Masahide, points to its emphasis on the moral evaluation of historical figures and confidence in a universal moral ideal capable of providing the basis for uniform judgments. These, of course, are qualities the early Mito philosophy held in common with the neo-Confucian tradition

---

18. Webb, "What is the *Dai Nihon Shi?*," p. 139.
19. Ibid., p. 141.

of Chu Hsi. Bitō contrasts these tendencies, moreover, against the philosophy espoused by the late Mito writers, who turned from the moral judgment of individuals to a concern with the history of particular institutions in Japan. In Bitō's view, these new preferences reflected the eighteenth-century influence of the schools of Ogyū Sorai and the nativists.[20]

The literary historian Noguchi Takehiko also points out the importance of the Chu Hsi tradition, which the *Dai-Nihon shi* historians held in common with the Hayashi school, but he focuses on the internal tensions that were evident in the Mito position, even in the early period. Emphasizing its preoccupation with the imperial court (*kōchōshugi*) and the nascent "nationalism" this implied, Noguchi argues that the Mito school courted the danger of undermining the legitimacy of the Tokugawa shogunate. In order to avoid such an indiscretion, the Mito historians had to preserve a delicate balance between imperial loyalism and Chu Hsi–type moral universalism. To some extent, these streams of thought were compatible: "universality" in the Japanese context could be interpreted as residing in the imperial line itself, which, because of its purity, continuity, and homogeneity, provided an unchanging source of rectitude. Nevertheless, this compromise required the abandonment of Chinese notions of legitimate dynastic change (*ekisei kakumei*) because the Japanese imperial line was continuous.

Moreover, as a guide to historical methodology, this view tended to divert attention away from the task of assessing good and evil (*kanzen chōaku*) as they were manifested in historical events, and toward an effort to demonstrate continuity and therefore legitimacy. The result was to obscure the articulation between moral ideal, as formally represented in the imperial line, and real historical events, such as military takeovers. In early Mito historiography, therefore, Noguchi finds that the underlying principle of history "loses its foundation in the actual historical process, and remains empty and floating as an abstract universal." When this abstract historical principle was applied, it inevitably gave rise to problems related to the "rectification of names and status distinctions":

---

20. "Mitogaku no tokushitsu," pp. 562–64.

Rebellions and traitorous acts occur in the real historical process, and the fortunes of the imperial household decline. But extending throughout such events there is always an element of pure continuity, giving the process homogeneity and forming the nucleus of historical time. That is the unbroken imperial line itself. And when that ideal of uniform historical time is, so to speak, frozen in its spatial dimension, the result is none other than an orderly arrangement of names and statuses (*meibunteki chitsujo*).[21]

When understood in this manner, the early Mito philosophy of history seems to come close to anticipating the problematic of Fujita Yūkoku's essay on the rectification of names, discussed in the following section. However, it is difficult to demonstrate a direct line of development between Mitsukuni's historiography and the late Mito explosion of thought and action. It is only when the abstract historical ideals of the earlier tradition are reconnected to historical reality—when an early philosophy of history is transformed into an active, engaged "historical consciousness"—that the paradoxes of the earlier discourse give way to the contradictions of the latter.[22] Playing an important role in that transition were the "moral crisis" of the eighteenth century and the changes that took place in both the personnel and the activity of the Mito historiographical institute.

Once the Annals and Biographies were complete, work on the history stagnated. The project had from the outset been planned to include two more sections, the Essays and the Tables. Apparently, some work was initiated in the early period on the Essays, which should have been the next stage, but the job did not go smoothly and finally ended entirely. That seems to have been the result of several factors, among them the death of Mitsukuni, the lack of enthusiasm on the part of some of his successors, and the financial difficulties perennially experienced by Mito-han. There also seems to be a specifically intellectual explanation.

The Essays were to be histories of institutions, not of emperors or other individuals, and were intended to focus specifically on the actual shape of religious and governmental structures as they had evolved under Japan's particular historical

21. Noguchi, *Edo no rekishika*, p. 129.
22. Ibid., pp. 143–44.

conditions. As eventually published, they carried such titles as "Gods of Heaven and Earth," which dealt with Shinto rituals and establishments, "Clans and Families," "Offices," "Food and Money," and "Military Affairs," which included an account of shogunal governments.[23] When understood holistically, these institutional topics demanded quite a different set of historical tools from those employed in work on the Annals and Biographies. It was only after the work of Ogyū Sorai and the nativists was widely disseminated and elaborated in the eighteenth century that the methodological and philosophical bases for institutional studies were firmly in place. Not until the mid-eighteenth century, therefore, did the intellectual climate favor an all-out effort to complete the Essays.[24]

At the same time, the turn in the direction of work on the Essays also meant a renewed willingness to treat mythical materials as historical fact. Of course, as the intellectual historian Maruyama Masao so cogently argues, Ogyū Sorai's rejection of Sung neo-Confucianism in favor of a fundamentalist insistence on direct readings of the Chinese classics was extended by eighteenth-century nativists like Motoori Norinaga to a renewed interest in Japanese mythohistories, particularly the *Kojiki* (Record of ancient matters).[25] Even though the nativists learned from Ogyū's methods, however, they reacted violently against what they took to be his Sinocentrism, replacing it with an exclusive focus on purely Japanese origins. Although the willingness of the late Tokugawa Mito historians to treat the "age of the Gods" as history was undoubtedly influenced by the eighteenth-century nativist return to myths, the Mito scholars did not share the nativist's hostility to Confucianism. Rather, they remained within a Confucianized Shinto framework that shared a great deal with the Kimon school, and their renewed belief in mythical accounts of the age of the gods can be viewed as a revival of the synthesis forged by Yamazaki Ansai in the early eighteenth century.[26]

Tachihara Suiken assumed directorship of the Shōkōkan

23. Webb, "What is the *Dai Nihon Shi?*," p. 142.
24. Bitō, "Mitogaku no tokushitsu," pp. 563–65.
25. *Studies in the Intellectual History of Tokugawa Japan*, pp. 135–85, 264–73.
26. Nakamura Akira touches on the relationship between Kimon and Mito thought in "Mitogaku no kokka-ron," *Ibaraki-ken shi kenkyū* 34 (March 1976): 1–18.

in 1786 on the appointment of the sixth shogun, Harumori (1751–1805), and finally injected the enthusiasm and dedication necessary to make new advances on the project. But Tachihara also was hesitant to make a heavy commitment of resources to the Essays and instead focused the institute's attention on annotation of the Annals and Biographies. This decision drew opposition from many members of his staff, who were anxious to get to work on institutions. A leading spokesman for the dissidents was Komiyama Fūken (1763–1840), who in 1789 argued in the tradition of Ogyū that it was essential to study "systems of government, laws, and documents."[27] It was Fujita Yūkoku, however, who confronted existing policy most directly and, as a result, eventually replaced Tachihara as director. Yūkoku's coup signaled the emergence of a strong sense of involvement in contemporary history among members of the institute; it also exemplified the late Mitogaku "union of scholarship and politics."

The dispute between the two factions that broke out in the 1780s and 1790s focused on three demands made by Tachihara's opponents: that the project be completed by finishing the Essays and Tables; that the name *Dai-Nihon shi* not be used; and that the Appraisals, written by Mito scholar Asaka Tanpaku (1656–1737), be expurgated.[28] I have dealt with the first of these demands above. Yūkoku made the second in a memorial to his colleagues in 1797. He argued in support of this demand that, in the past, Japan had been called "Nihon" (Nippon), or "Yamato," but never "Dai-Nihon." Second, it was inappropriate for a work carried on without the direct sponsorship of the court to be called a national history. Third, there was no need to use any country name at all in referring to a line of emperors unbroken by dynastic change, that is, the dynasty and the country were synonymous. And fourth, Mitsukuni himself never used the name "Dai-Nihon."[29] The second and third of these reasons, particularly, are based on taboos regarding the court, indicating that later Mito ideologues, such as Yūkoku, were even more sensitive than their earlier counterparts to any possible impropriety regarding the throne.

27. Ibid., p. 260.
28. Noguchi, *Edo no rekishika*, p. 253.
29. Ibid., p. 260.

Rectification and Myth

It is significant that the issue of the name of the work was resolved in 1809 when Mito daimyo Harutoshi asked for and received the court's approval for its use. That this should have immediately satisfied Yūkoku may be seen as marking, in itself, a new departure in Mito thinking regarding the throne. As Noguchi observes,

> If one wishes to make a distinction between Mitsukuni's preoccupation with the imperial court [*kōchōshugi*] and the reverence for the court [*sonnō shisō*] of the later period, one can take Yūkoku's attitude as a kind of index.... No matter how much Mitsukuni might have respected that institution, for him the historical legitimacy embodied in the court, and also the historical narrative that conveyed that legitimacy, had to be true regardless of the desires of the court itself.... For Yūkoku, on the other hand, a strong objection to the use of the name "Dai-Nihon shi" ... was dissolved easily through the logic of unconditional adherence to the pleasure of the court. At the risk of some exaggeration, one might interpret this as meaning that the will of the court now took precedence over all logic.[30]

Yūkoku's deference to the emperor who happened to be reigning at the time certainly reveals the heightened sense of historicity and active *involvement* in historical processes that differentiated the late Tokugawa thinkers from their seventeenth-century counterparts; it also exemplifies a process identified by H. D. Harootunian, in which the emperor was transformed from a historical "principle" into a political "principal."[31]

The issue of the Appraisals had been raised initially by Tsunaeda, Mitsukuni's successor. Mitsukuni had preferred to confine his moral judgments to the body of each chapter, where he used an encoded vocabulary to express either approval or disapproval through innuendo alone.[32] It was only after Mitsukuni's death that Tsunaeda turned back to Chinese practice by ordering Asaka to compile a separate set of Appraisals.

In the early nineteenth century, however, Tsunaeda's decision came under attack. The anti-Tachihara faction argued

---

30. Ibid., p. 262.
31. *Toward Restoration* (Berkeley and Los Angeles: University of California Press, 1970), p. 15.
32. Webb, "What is the *Dai Nihon Shi?*," pp. 138–39.

that, although such judgments might have been appropriate in China, where dynastic change was recognized, they would never be acceptable in Japan. That was because, unlike China where the history of a former dynasty was always compiled by members of a succeeding one—men eager to enumerate its faults as well as its merits—in Japan there could be no break in the dynastic line, and no history should include explicit evaluations of the reigning emperor's own ancestors.[33] This reformist policy signaled a new resistance to "Chinese" assumptions and marked a decisive departure from the philosophy of the earlier historians. Nevertheless, the policy prevailed, and the results of Asaka's labors were expunged from the work.

The factional struggle became increasingly politicized as Yūkoku, a low-ranking samurai of commoner origin, used the academic issues outlined above to present himself to the daimyo and improve his own position in the institute and the Mito house. But his seizure of power in the institute was not without setbacks. When his 1797 memorial, *Teishi fūji*, displeased the daimyo, Yūkoku was even sentenced to house arrest. As luck would have it, however, two years later Tachihara himself lost the trust of his lord, ostensibly for interfering in the domain's judicial process; as a result, Yūkoku seems to have been brought back into favor.[34] Tachihara finally resigned his post in 1803, and in 1807 Yūkoku himself was made co-director of the institute. In 1808, Yūkoku also became the provincial magistrate (*kōri bugyō*) of Hamada, a post that he held concurrently with the directorship.

Yūkoku's combination of offices suggests the strongly political and reformist thrust of his struggle as it was carried on both within and outside the historiographical organ itself. From this time forward—but, particularly from 1829, when Tokugawa Nariaki became daimyo, and the Shōkōkan was moved to Mito—the relationship between institute work and the administration of the domain became increasingly intimate and the reformist ideal of unity between scholarship and politics was substantially put into practice. However, the factional confrontation between the Fujita group (including Yūkoku, his son Tōko, and Aizawa

33. Bitō, "Mitogaku no tokushitsu," pp. 569–70.
34. Ibid., pp. 568–69.

Rectification and Myth

Seishisai) on the one hand, and the Tachihara group—now increasingly allied with Mito's high-ranking samurai elite (the so-called *monbatsu* faction)—on the other, was maintained and intensified throughout the years of reform under Nariaki and finally burst into a veritable Mito civil war in the 1860s.

RECTIFICATION OF NAMES

One of the earliest systematic attempts by a Mito samurai to come to terms with the crisis believed to be facing his domain and the nation was Fujita Yūkoku's 1791 essay, *Seimeiron* (On the rectification of names). In selecting such a title for his essay, of course, Yūkoku sought to draw on a rich variety of precedents for "rectifying names" in the Chinese philosophical and historiographical tradition. He begins his essay:

> How essential it is in a state [*tenka kokka*] that names and status distinctions [*meibun*] be correct and rigid. They must be as unchanging as Heaven-and-Earth itself! In the beginning there was Heaven-and-Earth, and then the ruler and his subjects. Sovereign and subject set the precedent for high and low in the social order. Once high and low were distinguished, there was a basis for rites and ceremonies.[35]

By linking ruler and subject to the precedence of Heaven over Earth, Yūkoku establishes from the outset the premise that both language and existing social hierarchies should be understood as aspects of a changeless, natural order.[36] However, he seems to deviate from the Chinese Confucian tradition in the first sentence by speaking of the rectification of "*names and status distinctions*" (*meibun*) rather than just of names. Bitō Masahide has suggested that Yūkoku emphasizes not only names, but "unchanging" distinctions in social status so he can sidestep much of the classical Confucian emphasis on the ruler's moral performance as the criterion for legitimacy. That is, Yūkoku deemphasizes the dimension of the rectification of

---

35. In Imai, Seya, and Bitō, eds., pp. 10–14.
36. Motoyama Yukihiko says Yūkoku "gives the hierarchical order of ruler and subject a basis in natural law" ("Kōki Mitogaku no hitobito," in Haga Tōru, Matsumoto Sannosuke, and Minamoto Ryōen, eds., *Edo no shisōka tachi* [Tokyo: Kenkyūsha, 1979], p. 223).

names that is presented most clearly in the Confucian *Analects:* "Let the ruler *be* a ruler, the minister *be* a minister, the father *be* a father, and the son *be* a son."[37] Rather than following Confucius in exhorting rulers and others in authority to perform in accord with the ethical demands of their office, Yūkoku prefers to call on the ruler to observe a rigidly prescribed hierarchy. His primary concern is to avoid the Chinese Confucian tradition of legitimate dynastic overthrow (*ekisei kakumei*), which was anathema in Japan because of taboos surrounding the unbroken imperial line.[38]

Yūkoku also raises the possibility of a disruption or overthrow of the natural order that would begin with disorderly nomenclature:

> If the names of sovereign and subject should be only slightly incorrect, and the relative status of high and low not always strictly observed, the positions of the respectable and the despicable would be reversed, the noble and the base would lose their places, the strong would despise the weak, the many violate the few, and collapse would not be far off.

He then cites a parallel selection from Confucius:

> Tzu-lu said, "The ruler of Wei is waiting for you to serve his administration. What will be your first measure?" Confucius said, "It will certainly concern the rectification of names. . . . If names are not rectified, then language will not be in accord with truth. If language is not in accord with truth, things cannot be accomplished. If things cannot be accomplished, then ceremonies and music will not flourish. If ceremonies and music do not flourish, then punishment will not be just. If punishments are not just, then the people will not know how to move hand or foot."[39]

Here, Confucius himself seems to be less concerned with performance than with the need to establish orderly relationships among names themselves. If the nomenclature is disorderly, he seems to be saying, there cannot be a proper status

---

37. The quote from the *Analects* is number 12:11; trans. from Wing-tsit Chan, ed., *A Source Book in Chinese Philosophy* (Princeton, N.J.: Princeton University Press, 1969), p. 39.
38. Bitō, "Mitogaku no tokushitsu," pp. 571–72.
39. Trans. from Chan, *A Source Book*, p. 40.

order in society. This quote, therefore, provides Yūkoku with a further opportunity to direct the problematic of rectification away from the issue of the ruler's moral practice, toward that of *what to call the ruler*. The problem of how to name the ruler had been a real one for Chinese historians beginning, apparently, with Confucius himself in the *Ch'un-ch'iu* (Spring and Autumn annals), because names, such as "emperor" or "traitor," were applied retrospectively and had strong moral implications. Conventions of naming established in China were also followed to some extent by Japanese historians of the seventeenth century.

However, Japanese historians had an additional terminological problem to confront. They had to adapt Chinese nomenclature to fit the anomalous duality of the postmedieval Japanese authority structure: the continuous existence of both emperor and shogun. Confucian theories of legitimacy had been premised on the assumption of a single legitimate ruler in whom all powers and prerogatives were vested. When the Japanese endeavored to write history on the basis of such theories, therefore, the apparent division of authority between emperor and shogun raised difficult questions of legitimacy. All the major historiographical Japanese schools of the seventeenth century—including those of Hayashi Gahō (1618–1680), Arai Hakuseki (1656–1725), and the Mito historians—were obliged to attempt in one way or another to resolve such questions. They all endeavored to demonstrate the legitimacy of the existing order according to classical Chinese practices and assumptions. Arai and the Mito historians also tried through their presentation of the historical record to remonstrate with the shogunate to be more benevolent and circumspect.[40]

The early Mito historians' approach to this task was to affirm the permanent legitimacy of the imperial line and then to deal with the shogunate by innovatively *redefining* the shogun's status. The problem was clear. Because the shogun was "appointed" by the emperor, he clearly could not be treated as the ruler in the Chinese sense; but, because he traditionally wielded all temporal power over the realm, he could not be treated as an ordinary courtier or other member of the population either. In

---

40. These efforts are explored in depth by Kate Wildman Nakai, "Tokugawa Confucian Historiography," in Peter Nosco, ed., pp. 62–91.

terms of Confucian historiographical categories, this meant that it was appropriate to write about the shoguns neither in the Annals (*hongi*), which dealt with rulers, nor in the Biographies (*retsuden*), where nonregnant figures were memorialized. The Mito solution to this dilemma was to create a new category called the Shogunal Biographies (*shogun-den*). A shogun's actions were now to be measured against a "name" that placed him in an ambivalent position between ruler and subject.[41] It was unclear whether this was to be taken as an affirmation of shogunal powers or as a criticism of them, and this ambiguity in the early Mito position might have been part of the reason for Yūkoku's renewed attempt to deal with the issue in *Seimeiron*.

Because placing the shoguns in a new historiographical category amounted to providing them with a new "name," this early Mito legitimating procedure is highly significant as a precedent for Yūkoku's own interpretation of rectification. That is, rather than accepting names as given, either by consistently applying a Chinese formula in the manner of Arai Hakuseki or inconsistently applying one in the style of Hayashi Gahō, the early Mito historians took the active route of constructing a new categorical "name." They sought to bring order to the world by rectifying names. We can take this innovation as evidence, therefore, for the early predominance in the Mito historiographical tradition of a constructivist approach to rectification similar to that which Yūkoku reapplied in the late Tokugawa context.

Yūkoku devotes the rest of *Seimeiron* to an exercise in the constructivist approach that was suggested to him by both Confucius and the Mito tradition. As noted above, his use of the term "names and status distinctions" rather than just "names" suggests that he is interested primarily in establishing an unassailable hierarchy in both nomenclature and institutions. Therefore, after listing a number of classical references to illustrate the degree to which the ancient sages supposedly respected "names and status distinctions," he reopens the question of how to name the shogun.

Yūkoku recounts Japan's sacred origins and the glory of the unbroken line of divinely born emperors, noting that it is the great achievement of maintaining that line that sets Japan above

---

41. Ibid., pp. 83–91.

all other nations in the strict preservation of names and status distinctions. Emperors are always emperors by birth; all others must resign themselves to lesser status. However, because "there is disorder as well as order in the world, and occasionally decline as well as prosperity," the Fujiwara set up their regency in the Heian period (794–1185) and since then military leaders had often been the actual rulers of Japan, carrying out the administration of government in the emperor's stead.

Yūkoku is frank enough to recognize that these military men ruled by force and, by this criterion, merit the unflattering name "hegemon" (*ha*). Nevertheless, Yūkoku notes that these "hegemons" established an important precedent in never attempting to usurp the emperor's imperial authority. Tokugawa Ieyasu, founder of the Tokugawa shogunate was, of course, no exception: "In correct preservation of the names of ruler and subject and the strict observation of distinctions between high and low, his virtue was not even exceeded by King Wen." Therefore, Ieyasu, particularly, behaved and ruled impeccably like a "king" (*ō*) in the Chinese tradition. Yūkoku resists the solution earlier adopted by Arai Hakuseki in his *Tokushi yoron* (Additional discussions on the explication of history) of 1712, which was to call the shoguns kings straightforwardly.[42] Instead, Yūkoku pays tribute to the Mito insistence on the sanctity of imperial authority, and also its constructivist approach to names, by concluding that the shogun should be called a "regent" (*sesshō*).

In addition to preserving for the emperor a unique claim to kingly authority, this solution had for Yūkoku the added merit of setting a good example for the populace. That is, the name regent placed the shogun in a status that implied formal reverence to the emperor, and therefore his position would provide an exemplar for those lower down in the social hierarchy. Yūkoku points out that even in China the ruler traditionally worshipped Heaven and his ancestors, but, because they were not personified, his reverence appeared to be focused on the empty sky. In Japan, however, the shogun worshipped the living emperor, thus providing the people with a much more compelling model of status distinction between sovereign and subject, superior and inferior. He says, "Just as the bakufu reveres the

---

42. Nakai, "Tokugawa Confucian Historiography," pp. 77–79.

emperor, the lords (daimyo) will revere the bakufu. And just as the lords revere the bakufu, the lesser lords and retainers will respect the lords."[43] As Kate Wildman Nakai points out: "[F]or the shogun, the effective ruler, to revere as sacrosanct the kingly authority inherent in the 'name' of emperor had a social value of its own. The respect for a fixed hierarchical order thus demonstrated by the shogun would set in motion a chain reaction of respect for superiors throughout society."[44]

Yūkoku concludes with a paraphrase of Confucius that again highlights the constructivist emphasis on the signifying power of language that characterized the Mito approach to rectification: "If names are rectified, will not language be in accord? And if names are rectified and language is in accord, rites and music will flourish. If rites and music flourish, the realm will be governed. How can it be called foolish for the ruler to rectify names?"[45]

NATURAL ORDER THROUGH ARTIFICE

The Confucian theory of rectification of names had been founded on the presumption of absolute norms that would make it possible to evaluate any particular historical circumstance. Accordingly, despite his constructivist approach to rectification, Yūkoku seems to have granted Confucian names an implicit ontological status as absolute moral standards. Even when he improvised a category or borrowed a name from a particular historical context, he probably assumed that its applicability was already latent in the order of things, needing only to be activated. He remained confident that, in principle, names were "as unchanging as Heaven-and-Earth."

However, other Tokugawa writings, including some from Mito, provide evidence that names were often considered to be merely forms or conventions, distinctly secondary to the Way, which was originally natural and therefore nameless. A notable example appears in *Kōdōkanki jutsugi*, written in 1846 by Yūkoku's son Tōko. Where Yūkoku had used the Confucian tradi-

---

43. Fujita, *Seimeiron*, p. 13.
44. Nakai, "Tokugawa Confucian Historiography," p. 91.
45. Fujita, *Seimeiron*, p. 14.

tion of rectifying names as the medium to clarify and represent the Way, Tōko chooses a mythical narrative of divine origins. That is, he presents us with a picture of what Japan had been like in antiquity, when the Way was practiced spontaneously. Underlying his choice, of course, is the willingness of late Tokugawa Mito historians to follow both the Kimon school and "restorationist" Shinto scholars, such as Motoori Norinaga, in treating Japan's creation myths as history.[46] But, aside from its significance as a reaffirmation of the Confucianized Shinto ideology formulated in the seventeenth century, Tōko's essay is also important as an indication of the ambivalent relationship in late Mito discourse between names and the Way. It begins:

> In antiquity, Japanese society was simple, and people were naive. There was no writing, and what we now call the Way had not yet been clearly articulated. Does that mean that the Way could not have originated in ancient Japan? No, why should it mean that? It means only that the *name* of the Way did not yet exist. As for *substance*, however, there is no aspect of the Way that did not originate [in Japan] with the Gods.[47]

Here, Tōko distinguishes between names and substance, placing names in a secondary role. He asserts that names are posterior to the Way, which is portrayed as an essence, beyond linguistic definition. This was by no means an original or even particularly unusual interpretation in seventeenth-century writings[48] or in the eighteenth century, when Motoori Norinaga wrote that "because the Way exists, there is no name for it, and though there is no name for it, the Way exists."[49] This interpretation is particularly significant in the context of late Mito discourse, however, not only because it seems to contradict the classical Confucian confidence in the ontological priority of names, but because it is entirely consistent with Yūkoku's earlier constructivist approach. Tōko goes on:

> What is called the Way is a broad thoroughfare. If [in antiquity] people followed it, never branching off, they would have no consciousness of it as a particular Way. When there is only one road

---

46. Fujita Tōko, *Kōdōkanki jutsugi*, in Seya, Imai and Bitō, eds., p. 263.
47. Ibid., p. 260. Emphasis added.
48. Ooms cites an example in the *Shintō denju* in *Tokugawa Ideology*, pp. 92–93.
49. Cited in Maruyama, *Studies*, p. 175.

with no branches, why should it be given a name? If there were no Way but this one since Heaven-and-Earth began, and if ruler and subject alike had rejoiced in and practiced it, without heterodoxy or blasphemy, is it so surprising that it should have no name?[50]

In other words, names serve no purpose but differentiation. Without a difference, names are superfluous.

Tōko goes on to make the argument, typical of the Kimon school of Confucianized Shinto, that the essence of Confucianism, the ethic of the Five Relationships, was already practiced naturally in Japan:

> It was only when scholars crossed over from Kudara [a country on the Korean peninsula from the fourth to seventh centuries] that Confucianism came to be known in Japan. Above all, Confucianism emphasized the Five Relationships. The Way of the Five Relationships, focusing on intimacy, duty, differentiation, precedence, and trust, was entirely indigenous to Japan. But the advanced theory of Confucianism amplified this natural Way, reinforcing the relationships between ruler and subject and father and son in our country, and adapting to our relationships between husband and wife, elder and younger, friend and friend. The essential purity of our Way did not thereby change.[51]

Tōko's focus on the Five Relationships recalls Chu Hsi's *Po-lu-tung shu-yüan chieh-shih* (Precepts of the White Deer Grotto Academy), a text especially prized by Yamazaki Ansai. According to Yamazaki's disciple Asami Keisai (1652–1711), these ethical qualities are the "innate Way," part of the natural endowment of all people.[52] Because the indigenous Japanese Way and the Confucian Way matched perfectly, they had merged without any "difference." Buddhism, however, was different. Buddhist teachings directly contradicted the social order of the Land of the Gods, and *when conflict ensued, it became necessary to devise names*, such as the Way of the Gods (Shinto), the Ancient Way, or the Way of the Ancient Kings, so as to differentiate the indigenous beliefs from Buddhism.

50. Fujita, *Kōdōkanki jutsugi*, p. 260.
51. Ibid., p. 261.
52. See Okada Takehiko, "Practical Learning in the Chu Hsi School," in de Bary and Bloom, eds., *Principle and Practicality*, p. 243; and Ryusaku Tsunoda, Wm. Theodore de Bary, and Donald Keene, eds., *Sources of Japanese Tradition* 1 (New York: Columbia University Press, 1958):356.

Rectification and Myth

In substance, the Way as presented by Yūkoku was coeval with the natural order of Heaven-and-Earth, rooted in human nature, and prior to all linguistic or other mediations. Names, on the other hand, were the products of human artifice, useful for making distinctions but redundant to the Way when it was functioning spontaneously in social and political relationships. Therefore, if one is curious about the Way, he says, one should look to substance rather than names.

The mythical mode of expressing the Way adopted by Tōko and, before him, other Mito writers, such as Aizawa Seishisai, led logically to a contrast between a mythical past, when the Way had been intuitively practiced without guile or artifice, and the historical past and present in which the Way had become obscure, distorted, or ignored. Therefore, this mode provided the Mito project with a strongly retrospective, restorationist aspect. Of course, the Way was still recognized as an inexhaustible potential, latent in every present. For the Mito thinkers, as for Yamazaki Ansai, "the beginnings of Heaven-and-Earth [were] today's beginnings."[53] But, in the more diachronic, mythic dimension focused on by Tōko, the Way was an archetype of natural order that had been manifest in pure form only in the age of the Gods. From that perspective, therefore, clarification of the Way always implied the possibility of reactivating or restoring the Way to natural spontaneity in the present.

Moreover, Tōko indicates paradoxically that although writing was an essential means in the project of clarifying the Way, writing itself was a major cause of the Way's increasing obscurity:

> In antiquity there was no writing. The meaning of the Way was conveyed through legend and song; preserved in manners and customs, politics and education; and retained in clan organizations, government offices, the names of things, and regulations of all kinds. But when it was written down in texts, no matter how carefully the recorder strove to preserve its original form, there is reason to fear that the true, original nature of the Way suffered.

The Way was further obscured when style became an end in itself: "The learned became enamored with the splendor of Chinese expression and dissatisfied with the simplicity of the Japanese Ancient Way. They devoted themselves to matters of form,

---

53. Ooms, *Tokugawa Ideology*, p. 223.

abandoning all that is unique to Japan and adhering to foreign mannerisms."[54]

As artifice, writing imposed arbitrary and sometimes even capricious forms on meaning, rendering it unnatural at best and often distortive. Nevertheless, for Tōko and his compatriots the written word remained essential to the task of clarifying the Way.[55] As a result, their works confront us with a paradox, analogous to that underlying the Mito approach to rectification of names, between ontological essence and constructive artifice. For Yūkoku, names whose normative force depended on continued belief in their ontological priority could, in fact, only be rectified through contrivance; and for Tōko, a Way whose natural substance was resistant to such formal media as writing could only be clarified through the use of these media.

The constructivist and restorationist paradoxes, which emerge so clearly from the Fujitas' approaches to names and to myth, were already firmly embedded not only in Tokugawa discourse, but in the Chinese Confucian tradition. Nevertheless, in order to understand the meaning of the Tenpō Reforms in Mito and the ideological and military mobilization that followed them, it is important to appreciate the fundamental role these elements played in the structure of Mito discourse. They are never described explicitly in Mito texts. Rather than assuming that they resulted from conscious commitment to a particular line of reasoning, it would be more accurate to see their syncretic coexistence as the de facto result of a series of exclusions. Theoretical works by Louis Althusser suggest that the epistemological framework of discourse is determined by exclusions or absences, rather than by manifest elements or themes.[56] With that insight in mind, we can conclude this preliminary summary of the structural premises of Mito discourse by suggesting some major contemporary tendencies excluded by that discourse.

Mito discourse excluded, in the first place, all hope that under contemporary conditions the Way could be understood immediately or intuitively. Mito texts, such as Tōko's, reveal a

---

54. Fujita, *Kōdōkanki jutsugi*, p. 322.
55. Ibid., pp. 318, 322.
56. Althusser and Etienne Balibar, *Reading Capital* (London: New Left Books, 1977), pp. 26–27.

great deal of nostalgia for such an understanding, but their apprehension of the Way in the present is always mediated by an assumption of the need for human construction, language, and, therefore, names. The views of Mito writers concerning nativists, such as Motoori Norinaga, are indicative. According to Tōko: "Their intricate studies all propound that the quintessence of the Way of Man is natural spontaneity [*shizen; jinen*], uncorrupted by human purpose [*jin'i*]. But this is merely a warmed-over version of the [Taoist] doctrines of Lao-tzu and Chuang-tzu."[57]

In this criticism of Taoist naturalism, Tōko might seem to be leaning toward Ogyū Sorai's view that the Way is "not the natural Way of Heaven-and-Earth."[58] Late Mito discourse owed a great deal to Ogyū, not only for reform proposals, but for his overall instrumentalist approach to the Way. On the other hand, Mito discourse also excluded, along with the pure naturalism of Motoori, the thorough sort of pragmatism that was associated with the Sorai school. Ogyū himself often approached nominalism in his effort to preserve within the bounds of the Way maximum breadth for the ruler to design laws and institutions to fit the needs of the time. He said, for example, that "The Way is an all-embracing term. . . . There is no such thing as the Way apart from rites, music, law enforcement, and political administration."[59]

Rather than following Ogyū here, however, Mito discourse leans toward the assumptions of Chu Hsi–oriented neo-Confucians like Yamazaki Ansai, who argued for the absolute validity of the Five Relationships as the essence of the Way. Tōko insists that: "No dimension of the Way supersedes the Five Relationships, and most important among them are the relationships between ruler and subject, father and child. Hence, loyalty and filial piety are the foundations of the doctrine of names and status distinctions."[60] Aizawa, also, says:

> The Way of ruler and subject, father and son, is the very apex of the Heavenly Way: affection and gratitude between father and son

57. Fujita, *Kōdōkanki jutsugi*, p. 323.
58. Ogyū Sorai, *Distinguishing the Way* [*Bendō*] (Tokyo: Sophia University, 1970), p. 24.
59. Ibid., p. 16.
60. Fujita, *Kōdōkanki jutsugi*, p. 324.

flourish within, the highest duty between subject and ruler is manifest without. Together they constitute the Way of loyalty and filial piety, which is the Great Way of Heaven and Man.[61]

And in *Tekiihen* (The way to proceed) Aizawa seems to contradict Ogyū directly: "That the prince employs his subjects, and the subjects serve their lord, is based on the fact that each is behaving righteously. *This is the great way of nature, it is not the invention of man.*"[62]

Rather than relying on Ogyū's abstract principle of creation, the content of which was historically mutable, the Mito writers make the Way morally substantive, natural, and eternal: "The manner of its expression might change, but its meaning is eternally the same."[63] Hence, they portrayed as immoral those, such as Kaiho Seiryō, who construed the Way in terms of a principle of self-interest. Aizawa, for example, berated them as "those who make intricate calculations, studying profit and daring to call it the art of governance."[64]

The above examples are meant to suggest that Mito discourse sought syncretically to incorporate elements of Motoori's nativist Shinto, Ogyū's *kogaku*, and the Chu Hsi/Shinto synthesis constructed by Yamazaki and others. But the particular field of vision the Mito writers mapped out on the basis of the urgent need to clarify and reactivate the Way tended to exclude any allegiance to the pure forms of "naturalism," "instrumentalism," and "moralism" that these schools represented. Mito discourse allowed elements of each of these perspectives an important role in the Mito project while blocking out any recognition that, if carried to their logical culmination, these elements would contradict each other.

The seemingly paradoxical juxtapositionings in Mito texts of elements of nativism, *kogaku*, and other doctrines of thought and action can be seen as merely the surface manifestations of a more profoundly contradictory relationship between commitments to a relativist concept of history, on the one hand, and to an eternal, natural order, on the other. At the level of action,

---

61. Aizawa, *Shinron*, p. 15.
62. Quoted in Masao Maruyama, *Studies*, p. 305.
63. Aizawa, *Shinron*, p. 55.
64. Ibid., p. 49.

Rectification and Myth

this pits a perceived need for timely and efficient instrumentality against confidence in the ritual reenactment of primal archetypes. Rather than attempt somehow to resolve these contradictions on behalf of the Mito writers, we must consider the possibility that contradiction constitutes the central organizing principle of discourse.[65]

If there is any dimension of Mito ideology in the late Tokugawa period that lies at its fountainhead, determining the form of its eruption and opening up the field within which its objects, strategies, and concepts are to be deployed, it is the contradiction between history and nature, action and ritual. For, in order to clarify the Way, it was necessary to objectify a "natural" state (the Way) through some form of "unnatural" (linguistic, instrumental, demonstrative) action. The object to be clarified and reactivated through human mediation was Heaven itself, not a temporary historical arrangement. Hence the inevitability of a paradox between human agency, which must operate in historical time by devising expedients, and the ultimate concern or purpose of action, which in the final analysis would admit only of permanence and universality.[66]

However, rather than perplexing or paralyzing the Mito writers, this contradiction seems to have goaded them on to reformist action. It appears that, when the Mito texts clarified the natural Way and thus dramatized its alienation from contemporary circumstance, men of high purpose were motivated to reactivate the Way through action. As ideology, Mito discourse affected the consciousness of human subjects and "qualified" them to act on Heaven's behalf.

---

65. Foucault, *The Archaeology of Knowledge*, p. 151.
66. According to J. G. A. Pocock, a similar contradiction was already latent in ancient Chinese philosophy ("Ritual, Language, Power," in Pocock, *Politics, Language and Time* [New York: Atheneum, 1973], pp. 45, 55).

2
THE NATIONAL ESSENCE

The occasion for Aizawa Seishisai's production of *Shinron* was the promulgation in early 1825 of the "Order to repel foreign ships" (*Ikokusen uchiharai-rei*). Aizawa indicates that his burst of activity was directly stimulated by the order, which encouraged him to hope that Japan's exclusionist policies would now be strictly enforced. Although ostensibly written solely for the inspiration and enlightenment of his teacher Fujita Yūkoku and his lord Tokugawa Narinobu (1797–1829), the book-length document soon "leaked out" and was widely disseminated in various versions by samurai activists.[1]

Aizawa was excited by the bakufu edict partially because he believed that the Western imperialists had aggressive designs on Japan. The visit by the Russian naval officer, Captain Adam Laxman, to Nemuro in 1792 had caused a flurry of concern in the coastal domain of Mito, and its impression on Aizawa, then 19, seems to have been profound.[2] He became a specialist on the territories to the north of Japan and in 1801 wrote a short history of eastern Russia. In the spring of 1824, twelve foreigners from an English whaler landed right in Mito, and Aizawa was

---

1. In a postscript to the version of *Shinron* published in 1857, Aizawa says:

I was employed in the Shōkōkan throughout the Bunsei era (1819–1829), so the seven chapters of *Shinron* were written as routine essays and sent to Tokugawa Narinobu by way of my teacher Fujita Yūkoku. Although we used them freely for discussion within the institute, they were not intended for general consumption. Therefore, we kept the texts hidden. Nevertheless, as time went on and I frequently discussed them with several of my colleagues, somehow the manuscripts were distributed broadly, and even some printed copies appeared. (In Imai, Seya, and Bitō, eds., p. 159)

2. For a study of Aizawa's early life and introduction to the problems of Western intrusions and knowledge, see Bob Tadashi Wakabayashi, "Aizawa Seishisai's Shinron and Western Learning, 1781–1828," Ph.D. dissertation, Princeton University, 1982, chap. 5.

engaged by the domain to carry on written communication with them. The experience seems to have intensified his anxiety over threats to Japan's security, particularly since this time the intruders were English rather than Russian. Thus his enthusiasm, when early the following year the bakufu seemed ready to take preventive action. He saw it as "one chance in a thousand years," now that "it has been made clear that the entire nation will treat them as enemies."[3]

Clearly Aizawa was genuinely concerned for the survival of the nation. On the other hand, the problem he formulated was not simply one of barbarian incursion. If Japan's domestic affairs had been in good order and the national morale in good health, there would have been little to fear. In fact, however, the foreign probes called attention to a deep-seated domestic malaise. The country was an invalid: "Japan is in a state similar to that of a patient who has barely escaped death from a usually fatal disease. It has not yet recovered full strength and does not know how to do so. Since it lacks a strong, inner constitution, it is easily susceptible to influences from without" (p. 51). Japan's predicament was serious because of chronic domestic weakness of a military sort, but economic and social as well.

HISTORY AS ENTROPY

A major objective of Aizawa's text is to explain, in light of a representation of original value, how the Japanese polity came to be in such a disorderly state. It is not to be wondered at that he found the roots of disorder in a particular concept of history. A sensitivity to historical process had been germinating in Mito ever since the mid-seventeenth century, when Tokugawa Mitsukuni initiated *Dai-Nihon shi*. Aizawa's mentor Fujita Yūkoku gained control of the project in 1807 by becoming president of the Shōkōkan, and Aizawa himself spent many years engaged in research and compilation under Yūkoku's direction. In respect to Aizawa's work, it is instructive to recall that, in the closing years of the eighteenth century, the project turned from an earlier preoccupation with moral judgment and historical biog-

---

3. Aizawa, *Shinron*, p. 41. Subsequent page references to *Shinron* are inserted in the text.

raphy in the Chinese tradition to a new concern with institutional studies. The latter emphasized indigenous Japanese developments and gave new credibility to the mythical themes that formed the nucleus of Aizawa's construct of *kokutai* (national essence).

Aizawa reviews Japanese history several times in *Shinron* in order to explain how the contemporary state of decadence arose and to compare it with historical precedents in the realm of political and economic structure, religion, military affairs, and foreign relations. Each historical survey culminates in the contemporary scene, bringing us back to the context in which he was led to set down his views.

For Aizawa, it goes without saying that the authority of the emperor had never been seriously challenged. No one had ever dared to seize the imperial regalia, and the sanctity of the imperial line remained forever undisturbed. Nevertheless, he says, there had been lapses in the actualization of imperial benevolence: "Nothing is ever perfect in the world, and defects are innumerable" (p. 31). Abuses seemed to fall in either of two categories: changes in the momentum of time (*jisei no hen*), or the evils of heresy (*jasetsu no gai*): "If we are to straighten the warped and revive what has declined, we must pay particular attention to these two."

Aizawa portrays the process of temporal fluctuation in Japanese history as a series of retrenchments, each followed eventually by a return to laxity or rebellion. It was the emperor Jinmu (legendary first emperor) who first pacified the realm and succeeded in establishing a decentralized form (*hōken*) of imperial rule over both land and people. His institutions atrophied after a while, however, and eventually there was rebellion. This time the uprisings were put down by the emperor Sujin (legendary tenth emperor), who set up tax systems and pacified the borders, initiating another long period of stability. Now, once again, "all the land was imperial land, and all the people the emperor's people; the popular will was unified, and the realm was well-governed" (p. 33).

Inevitably, however, the long period of peace initiated by Sujin led to indolence, and the court nobility began to seek personal gain. Land and people fell into private hands, and the realm was split up. The next hero to reconstitute the polity was the Emperor Tenchi (626–672), who carried out the Taika Reforms. Tenchi changed what had been a decentralized system into a centralized (*gunken*) regime with provincial governors. Land and people were again brought under imperial control.

The next period of disintegration followed the rise to power of the Fujiwara regents and the advent of the private estates (*shōen*). No sooner had the estates been formed than local warrior bands proceeded to bring villages under their own control and enslave the people, leading to the fractionalization of land among feuding barons. With the rise to power of Minamoto Yoritomo (1147–1199), all land and people came under the sway of the bakufu. Throughout the warrior rule of the Kamakura (1185–1334) and Muromachi (1338–1573) periods, the only warrant for authority was the ability to aggregate land and people through force, and the will of the court was generally spurned. Aizawa notes, as a sign of the degenerate times, that no one protested even when Shōgun Ashikaga Yoshimitsu (1358–1408) "got down on his knees and became a subject of the Ming dynasty" (p. 35). Aizawa says:

> When he who embodies supreme power in the realm comes to be known as a subject of a foreign country, our imperial court will be thought of as a provincial satrapy. Even though it involved immeasurable harm to the national essence, no one in the realm rose to question his act. Devotion to duty and fidelity to principle were dashed to the ground, and the overriding obligation of the subject to his sovereign was also abandoned. (pp. 35–37)

Nevertheless, "fluctuation between disorder and stability is the dynamic of politics (*tenka no jōsei*)" and so, "When Heaven had grown weary of disruption, heroes rose up in succession." First, Toyotomi Hideyoshi came up from lowly origins to become Kanpaku, unifying the land and people, and revering the emperor. Then Tokugawa Ieyasu emerged to "construct a foundation of loyalty and filial piety which brought two hundred years of peace." With the establishment of the Tokugawa shogunate, finally, "The land and people of the realm were all governed uniformly, and the entire country was unified. All paid respect to the benevolence of the imperial court and obeyed the just rule of the bakufu. Truly the realm was well governed" (p. 39).

Soon, however, because "after a long period of peace it is natural to become bored and lazy," the dynamic of political affairs again brought corruption and disintegration. The daimyo whiled away their time in idleness, making no provision for poor harvests or other emergencies; they did not attempt to regulate or eliminate wanderers, bandits, and others who disrupted life in the countryside; and they stood by unconcerned as foreign nations probed the shores of Japan. In effect, provincial leaders had abandoned both the land and those who worked it. The people themselves were little better, selfishly pursuing their own interests with no thought for loyalty to those above or service to the whole. They insulted their ancestors and ignored their fathers and rulers. Under such circumstances, how could "land and people be reunified and the national essence maintained?" (p. 39).

As explained above, Aizawa believed that the bakufu had already taken the first positive step toward a solution: the "Order to repel foreign ships" seemed to signify a new determination to assert Japan's isolationist policies. In his view, the decision represented a rare opportunity to forge a new unity in the nation and protect the polity from subversive influences.

It will be evident even from this brief summary that historical texts by Aizawa and other Mito writers follow the pattern elaborated primarily by Rai Sanyō (1780–1832), according to which history had to do less with the personal virtues and benevolent action of the ruler than with a relatively autonomous form of historical dynamism, usually expressed through some variant of the term *ikioi* (the *sei* component of Aizawa's term *jisei no hen*, meaning force, momentum, or tendency). The praise-and-blame historiography typical of the early stages of the *Dai-Nihon shi* project, which was based on classical Chinese models, gave way in the course of the Tokugawa period to a less moralistic, more holistic concept of change over time. Aspects of that transformation are a sense of politics and government that goes beyond the comportment of the ruler to encompass broad structural arrangements (the historicization of politics) and, conversely, a process of politicization by which history writing becomes a matter of characterizing structural change in government and society. Further concomitants of that new concept are what the historian Uete Michinari calls humanization, in which the role of human agency in history is given increased credibility, and a nascent recognition of the role in historical change of the social and economic power wielded by the masses (*minshū*).[4]

Aizawa's history writing also follows the common Tokugawa practice of adhering to a cyclical concept of change, often combined with the assumption that structures inevitably deteriorate over time (p. 65).[5] This degenerative concept of the historical process provides the framework for Aizawa's explanation of how the Japanese polity reached its contemporary state of disrepair.

The second major category of abuses plaguing the nation is the evil of heresy. Here again a process of degeneration is assumed to occur more or less cyclically, and an important role is assigned to human agency. Aizawa deals explicitly with the relationship between Shinto and Confucianism, and also discusses Buddhism, Christianity, shamanism, and so on. He begins, as usual, by evoking the origins of Japan's indigenous faith:

> In early times the gods based their teachings on Shinto and that method alone was used to bring the minds of the people together. . . . The spirit of service to Heaven and worship of ancestors was conveyed to later generations, and thus the meaning of showing gratitude to the origin and returning to the beginning was understood. (p. 41)[6]

Jinmu and Sujin contributed to the propagation and enhancement of the original faith both institutionally and by example, without entertaining any other beliefs. During the reign of Ōjin, however, the classics of Confucius were introduced. As Aizawa observed above, there is little to regret in that event:

---

4. Uete Michinari, "Edo jidai no rekishi ishiki," in Maruyama Masao, ed., *Rekishi shisō shū*, Nihon no shisō 6 (Tokyo: Chikuma Shobō, 1972), pp. 77–79.

5. Similarly, Ogyū Sorai wrote: "The succession of periods of peace and civil war is a part of the cyclical movements of the natural order but is implemented entirely through the medium of human action" (J. R. McEwan, *The Political Writings of Ogyū Sorai*, pp. 29–34).

6. A similar discussion of heresy in Japanese history may be found in Fujita Tōko, *Kōdōkanki jutsugi*, pp. 281–88.

> The land of China is next to Japan, and its climate and atmosphere are very similar to ours. The doctrines of Confucius are based on the mandate of Heaven and the mind of man; they clarify loyalty and filial piety, teach service to the emperor and worship of ancestors. Hence they are largely the same as the immortal doctrines of Amaterasu. (p. 43)

Confucianism per se is a constructive echo of Japan's native creed. On the other hand, "believers in magic, Buddhism, rigid and hidebound or vulgar forms of Confucianism, Christianity, and other belief systems which disrupt orthodox doctrines and public morality" are to be deplored, along with any who would make of indigenous beliefs a purely private, divisive pursuit:

> Amaterasu and her descendants consolidated the rites so that they, together with all the people of the realm, could serve Heaven and worship the ancestors. They are of universal import and applicability, without differentiation. Nevertheless, there are some archaic families that remain attached to particularistic creeds which have not been purged of error. In outlying regions and in private, they continue to worship false gods, concerning themselves only with prayers for good fortune and the pursuit of happiness. They know nothing of such basic principles as worshipping ancestors and serving Heaven. (pp. 43–45)

Religion, in other words, must serve the cause of unity and obedience to duly constituted authority if it is to find justification. Local rites and familistic practices must be integrated into a national system of religious beliefs and practice so that every act of piety, no matter how private, will serve public ends.

Buddhism was introduced to Japan through the perfidy of Soga no Umako (?–626) and Shōtoku Taishi (574–622). Taihō legislators had placed the Office of Deities (Jingikan) in a position superior to the Grand Council of State (Daijōkan), indicating that they still "knew the national essence." But Buddhism gained ground inexorably under the Emperor Shōmu (701–756) and the Empress Kōken (718–770). Then, with the establishment of the national temples (*kokubunji*), it became the state religion. As the masses followed suit, the Land of the Gods was "Indianized." "When people of their own accord become barbarians," he asks, "how could the national essence survive?" (p. 45).

Confucianists are not entirely above suspicion either. Aizawa castigates those who indulge in sophistry and distortion, particularly for their tendency to insult Japan's essence by referring to China, rather than Japan, as Chūgoku (the Middle Kingdom);[7] those who are swept up by the styles of the times, disturbing the correct status order and forgetting the supreme obligation to the emperor; those who deprecate the virtue of the emperor above and despise the justice of the shogun below; study profit and call it the art of governance; and affect the serious study of Sung Confucianism and austere manners but remain unmindful of the crisis facing the nation and hence fail to respond to the needs of the time. "None of these are loyal and none filial, nor do any follow the Way of Yao, Shun, and Confucius" (p. 49).

In addition to the evils and blasphemies propagated by their countrymen, the Japanese had to deal with heretical doctrines borne by the barbarians:

> Now we must cope with foreigners of the West, where every country upholds the law of Jesus and attempts therewith to subdue other countries. Everywhere they go they set fire to shrines and temples, deceive and delude the people, and then invade and seize the country. Their purpose is not realized until the ruler of the land is made a subject and the people of the land subservient. As they have gained momentum they have attempted to foist themselves on our Divine Land, as they have already done in Luzon and Java. The damaging effects of their heresies go far beyond anything done by those who attack from within our own land. (pp. 49–51)[8]

Among the evils from abroad was Rangaku (Dutch studies), a pursuit that did little harm in and of itself but could serve as a means of subversion if naive devotees were to become enthralled with the barbarous way of life followed in the West.

---

7. For treatment of the controversy among Tokugawa ideologues concerning the use of this term, see Nakai, "The Naturalization of Confucianism in Tokugawa Japan," *Harvard Journal of Asiatic Studies* 40, no. 1 (1980).

8. Trans. from Ryusaku Tsunoda, Wm. Theodore de Bary, and Donald Keene, eds., *Sources of Japanese Tradition* 2, p. 92.

Whereas changes in the momentum of time (*jisei no hen*) have to do with institutional relationships among land, people and authority, the issue of heresy (*jasetsu no gai*) focuses on the problem of religion. Yet the remedy for both must be sought in *kokutai* (the national essence).

ETERNAL RETURN THROUGH IMPERIAL RITUAL

In the introduction to *Shinron*, Aizawa states that, "First, in the chapter entitled 'Kokutai,' I will discuss how the gods founded the nation in accord with the principles of loyalty and filial piety, and then touch on their respect for the profession of arms and emphasis on the people's welfare" (p. 11). In truncated form, this statement provides an initial indication that Aizawa's concept of the Way is related closely to a Japanese essence. The "Kokutai" chapter itself is divided into three sections corresponding to the major elements of that statement: (1) the divine establishment of the nation in accord with the principles of loyalty and filial piety; (2) the respect of the gods for military arts; and (3) the concern of the gods for the popular welfare. When, in his final chapter, Aizawa reiterates these concepts in somewhat different terminology—"sufficient food, sufficient armaments, and the confidence of the people" (p. 221)—it is clear that he has adopted the three elements from Confucius:

> Tzu-kung asked about government. Confucius said, "Sufficient food, sufficient armament, and sufficient confidence of the people." Tzu-kung said, "Forced to give up one of these, which would you abandon first?" Confucius said, "I would abandon the armament." Tzu-kung said, "Forced to give up one of the remaining two, which would you abandon first? Confucius said, "I would abandon food. There have been deaths from time immemorial, but no state can exist without the confidence of the people."[9]

That Aizawa should borrow three political principles (or priorities) from the *Analects*, clothe them in the trappings of Japanese mythohistory, and install them as the foundation of Japan's national essence, provides a sure sign of the legacy of Confu-

---

9. Confucius, *Analects* 12:7; trans. from Chan, *A Source Book*, p. 39. The link to Confucius is identified in Imai, Seya, and Bitō, eds., p. 147.

The National Essence

cianized Shinto. He appeals not only to indigenous symbols, but to virtually the entire Confucian corpus in order to illustrate and legitimize his argument. It is already clear that the idea of *kokutai* had to do with the origins of the Japanese nation. Moreover, the form in which it is expressed suggests that it is also meant to encompass all the universality claimed by the Confucian tradition.

Aizawa's synthesis of a concept of the universal Way with a uniquely Japanese mythohistory is reinforced by his fervent belief in Japan's superiority: "Japan is by nature at the 'head' of the world and sets the standard for all other nations. The august authority and virtue of his imperial majesty radiate boundlessly to the ends of the earth" (p. 9).[10]

In an explanation of this anthropomorphic world model, Aizawa posits that all things, including the earth, have an original configuration. Although the globe may seem perfectly round in a physical sense, it nevertheless manifests clearly an organic differentiation among functional elements. Japan stands at the world's head for a distinct reason: the unprecedented continuity of its imperial line. Because the position of the imperial house has never been challenged domestically, its authority in the world is incontestable. On the other hand, Europeans are obviously unsuited to the maintenance of continuous relations of authority. They are adept only at traveling to the ends of the earth and therefore qualify as the world's "legs and feet."

Aizawa's organic metaphor indicates not only the symbolic importance of imperial continuity as the nucleus of Japan's national essence, but also its validity as a standard for the rest of the world.[11] With that in mind, it is not surprising that such values as loyalty and filial piety are considered by Aizawa to be both universal *and* originally Japanese. They are Chinese as well, but not in any prior or defining sense.

Similarly, Amaterasu Ōmikami is not presented as a peculiarly "Japanese" deity. Her position is identical with that of Heaven itself: "Long ago, when Amaterasu laid the foundation

---

10. Also cited by Fujita Yūkoku (*Teishi fūji*, p. 27).
11. Aizawa's presentation of the shape of the world is apparently not to be taken as his literal belief, because he was in possession of considerable geographical information (Wakabayashi, chap. 3).

of the nation, she acted as Heaven, her virtue was Heavenly virtue, and her deeds, Heavenly Deeds" (p. 9).[12] The imperial regalia—jewel, mirror and sword—that she bestowed on her earthly progeny symbolized their imperial status as rulers of the Japanese nation and their universal legitimacy as the representatives of Heaven on earth. In other words, the absolute universality of the Heavenly Way was transmuted once and for all into authority for a particular line of Japanese emperors.

In addition to serving as the living incarnation of both Amaterasu and universal principle, the imperial line also symbolizes a legacy of certain values, most importantly, the twin virtues of loyalty and filial piety mentioned by Aizawa in connection with the founding of the nation. The enshrinement of these two virtues in particular is consistent with the primacy granted to lineage. Whereas in the Chinese tradition the mandate of Heaven had in practice rested with anyone who could demonstrate an ability to rule successfully, in Japan kingship and ancestorship were to be united in a single manifestation. The imperial line would stand not only as the sole legitimate criterion of supreme authority, but also as the quintessential model of ancestor worship and filial piety. In the imperial succession itself, therefore, loyalty and filial piety would be unified in a single attitude of reverence. Also included in the legacy of values represented by the emperor was to be a certain ethos of rule summed up by Aizawa in the twin virtues of respect for the military arts and concern for the common welfare. In Tōko's *Kōdōkanki jutsugi*, these virtues are specified as valor (*yūbu*) and benevolence (*jin'i*).[13]

The first few pages of *Shinron*, then, provide a vivid impression of the significance of the national essence as a medium for representing the Way. As a fundamentally syncretic construct, it is universal and absolute in the manner of the Way as portrayed in the Confucian tradition and also capable of mobilizing the rich Shinto tradition of mythohistory. In concrete terms, it is manifested in the unbroken line of Japanese emperors. Each emperor exists as the living representative of Amaterasu Ōmi-

---

12. The significance of this passage is pointed out in Tsuyuguchi Takuya, "Bakumatsu ni okeru kokkateki rinen no sōshutsu," *Bunka shigaku* 31 (Dec. 1975):49.

13. Fujita, *Kōdōkanki jutsugi*, p. 286.

kami and, in a broader sense, of the divine genesis of the nation as symbolized in a legacy of particular values. The Way as national essence, in other words, may be defined as the political values that constitute the normative legacy of Japan's national origins.

By making lineage the only legitimate criterion for imperial authority, Aizawa's arrangement also made forever inviolable the distinction between the supreme ruler of the land and the ruled. Hence, the constant Mito compulsion to make such distinctions explicit—to "rectify names and statuses." But what about the practical danger of rebellion? Aizawa observes:

> It is not by intimidating the people, and forcing them into obedience for one dynasty at a time, that an imperial sovereign is able to pacify the four seas, govern in peace for extended periods, and preserve the realm in perfect tranquillity. His only bulwark is that the people should be of one mind, love their ruler, and harbor no desire to separate themselves from him. (p. 13)

It would be unthinkable for Japan's divine imperial house ever to be overturned. On the other hand, the ruler's "only bulwark is that the people should be of one mind," suggesting that the popular will plays a role in the maintenance of imperial continuity and, therefore, of the national essence.[14]

The emperor's ability to command the affection and support of his subjects is naturally latent in the very fact of his divine lineage, but that ability can be brought to full fruition only through the exercise of certain functions, the most important of which is sacred ritual. In other words, in addition to inhering in the person of the emperor, the divine origins of the nation may (indeed, must) be constantly reactualized through correct ceremonial practice. Aizawa devotes a considerable portion of his major text to the elaboration of a primary example of such ritual, the Daijōsai (Great Thanksgiving Festival).

In beginning to discuss that rite, Aizawa rhetorically evokes the pristine era, described by Tōko, when the Way was intuitively effective: "How is it that the doctrine of loyalty and filial

14. Wakabayashi argues that Aizawa perceived the Western nations as having succeeded in unifying the popular will through Christianity, and that he devised the concept of *kokutai* to describe the unity between religion and politics thus obtained ("Aizawa Seishisai's Shinron and Western Learning," pp. 254–85).

piety should exist without words and the people be unaware that they practice it daily?" (p. 15). He then makes it clear that a central element of such an ideal circumstance is the correct performance of ritual:

> The divine ancestor is in Heaven, shining forth across the land, while her Heavenly descendant on earth serves her by displaying a true and reverent heart toward his subjects below. Government and religion are one, the callings of governance and acting in Heaven's stead amount to service to the Heavenly ancestor. . . . Displays of filial piety on the part of successive emperors, such as worshipping at ancestral tombs and solemnly carrying out ceremonies and rites, reflect their efforts to exhaust the virtues of sincerity and reverence. Rites and ceremonies are abundant, but for showing gratitude to the origin and respect for ancestors the greatest among them is the Daijō [sai]. (pp. 15–16)

In other words, solemn ceremonies, such as the Daijōsai, are capable of unifying religion and government—mobilizing for purposes of governance the religious feeling devoted to gods and ancestors—and thus recapturing from the misty past a state in which objective representation of the Way was superfluous.

The rites of the Daijōsai are performed the first autumn following the ascension of a new emperor and consist basically in the offering of new grain to Amaterasu. The ceremonies all reenact mythical themes, particularly the founding of the nation and Amaterasu's benevolence:

> When Amaterasu received good seeds of grain, it occurred to her that by this means she could provide for the lives of her people, so she planted the seeds in fields. She also pulled threads from the silk cocoon she held in her mouth, and that was the beginning of silk cultivation. Thus, she provided the basis of clothing and food for the people at large. To her imperial descendants, she gave rice ears from the fields of the gods [yuniwa]. That is how we know that she placed great importance on the livelihood of the people and was anxious that they have good grain. Accordingly, the Daijōsai consists in cooking new grain and offering it in great quantities. (p. 17)

The ceremony is also believed by Aizawa to confer on the new emperor the mandate of Amaterasu. Indeed, as the rite's

The National Essence

climax, he envisions a mystical epiphany in which Amaterasu actually seems to appear as the symbol of unity and order:

> When the direct descendant of Amaterasu reverently carries out these rites in her honor, an indistinct image of Amaterasu's august countenance rises before the eyes of those present. None fails to sense her presence and become profoundly aware of her nearness to them. Therefore, as the officials respect and adore the emperor, they experience the spontaneous and irrepressible feeling that they are adoring Amaterasu herself. (pp. 19–20)[15]

In that liminal instant, a sacred community is consummated: despite wide differences in social station, all are minimally authenticated by the divine lineage. The ceremony reaffirms the secure compatibility of man and nature.

> Long ago, through the Daijōsai, the emperor together with the people of the realm worshipped with sincerity and reverence. When grain was cooked, there was invariably a ceremony of gratitude to the gods, and afterwards the emperor partook along with his subjects. The people of the realm were aware that the grain they ate originated in the seeds provided by Amaterasu. Hence they were in awe of the will of the heavenly progenetrix, and worked hard to develop the productive potential of the great earth. The minds of men were united with the mind of Heaven and Earth, and all shared wealth equally. (p. 79)

The emphasis on an ethic of economic interdependence founded on the primal concern of Amaterasu for the common welfare is clearly evident, associating the Daijōsai unmistakably with a conception of community in which labor and resources are equitably distributed.

The appearance of the Sun goddess recalls a similar passage in which Aizawa recounts the transmittal of the three imperial regalia to her earthly successor:

> When Amaterasu transferred the regalia, she took the mirror especially and said, "When you look into this mirror, it shall be as if you

---

15. For a description of preparations, dress, procedures, and other details related to the Daijōsai, see D. C. Holtom, *The Japanese Enthronement Ceremonies* (Tokyo and Kyoto: Kyo Bun Kwan, 1928). For a study of the Daijōsai from the perspective of theories of sacred kingship, see Robert S. Ellwood, *The Feast of Kingship* (Tokyo: Sophia University, 1973).

look upon me." Thus, down through the ages the mirror has been revered as the sacred body of Amaterasu Ōmikami, and as generation after generation of emperors have gazed into the mirror they have seen her form. Appearing in the mirror is none other than the emperor himself, who is of the same flesh and blood as the progenetrix, but in his own image he clearly perceives her face. When that occurs, at the instant of supplication there will be a mystical sense of mutual empathy between god and man. As a result, the emperor will inevitably display a heart of filiality in worshipping his ancestors and never rest in the pursuit of virtue. (p. 15)[16]

Most people, of course, can participate in the Daijōsai only vicariously, but the experiential basis of the national essence is meant to extend beyond that rite to encompass ancestral observances, and perhaps even such mundane rituals as gift-giving, which enable people to interrelate continuously in spontaneous, coordinated movement.[17]

Aizawa's juxtaposition of a form of historical entropy against a concept of the national essence as a constantly recoverable ideal recalls Mircea Eliade's description of an archaic mentality. For such a mentality, as for the Mito writers, time contaminates: "history . . . in proportion to and, by the mere fact of its duration, provokes an erosion of all forms by exhausting their ontological substance."[18] Therefore, one "tolerates 'history' with difficulty and attempts periodically to abolish it."[19]

The abolition of history is accomplished through the repetition of rites that reenact cosmogony: "myths serve as models for ceremonies that periodically reactualize the tremendous events that occurred at the beginning of time."[20] In the course of such ceremonies: "There is an abolition of time through the imitation of archetypes and the repetition of paradigmatic gestures,"[21] and thus archaic man is "free to be no longer what he was, free to annul his own history through periodic abolition of time and collective regeneration."[22]

16. This is also recounted in Fujita, *Kōdōkanki jutsugi*, p. 266.
17. See Herbert Fingarette, *Confucius* (Harper Torchbooks, 1972).
18. Eliade, *The Myth of the Eternal Return or, Cosmos and History* (Princeton, N.J.: Princeton University Press, 1971), p. 115.
19. Ibid., p. 36.
20. Ibid., p. xiv.
21. Ibid., p. 35.
22. Ibid., p. 157.

The National Essence 71

Clearly, Aizawa's strategy of representing the Way promises release from the determining constraints of recent history. As a return to the moment of creation *in illo tempore*, the Daijōsai symbolizes the eternal promise of renewal: the constant accessibility of sacred community as a potential latent in every historical context, regardless of how thoroughly it may have been obscured and distorted.

That Aizawa's view of the Daijōsai is idealized, of course, is beyond question. He virtually admits this himself toward the end of *Shinron* where, in the context of a discussion of the contemporary need for unity between religion and politics, he indicates that the Daijōsai observances themselves had fallen victim to the degenerative processes of time. In later ages, their scope had been limited largely to the vicinity of Kyoto and their symbolic, communal significance had declined (p. 227).

Aizawa goes on to describe in considerable detail how the ceremony should proceed. In line with Eliade's observation that the "archaic" mentality validates all human actions only by "their property of reproducing a primordial act,"[23] Aizawa illustrates a concept similar to ancestor worship but broader, that of "not forgetting the source" and "showing gratitude to the origin." Original utensils are preserved, participants are descendants of the original divine celebrants, and so on. But the central theme is ancestor worship. As the emperor honors his origins, the people who witness the ceremony are reminded of their own.

> The ancestors of the high officials who were present served Amaterasu and her imperial descendants, showed benevolence toward the people, and participated correctly in festive ceremonies.... In turn, the eldest sons under them gathered members of their clans together and led them in ritual worship. (pp. 19–21)

The ritual process symbolically transforms the entire population into relatives of the emperor and descendants of the gods:

> Inside they were filial to their own particular forebears, while outside they participated in the Daijōsai. In both cases they served their ancestors.... Once they drew themselves up straight in re-

---
23. Ibid., p. 4.

membrance of how their ancestors reverently served the emperor and the gods, how could they themselves ever neglect their forebears or feel like turning their backs on the emperor? That is how a spirit of filiality and sincerity is transmitted from father to child, child to descendants. The ancestral will is passed down for countless generations without the slightest change. (p. 21)

Aizawa's narrative then moves almost imperceptibly to a discussion of the political implications or uses of a pervasive spirit of filial piety. He goes on:

Filial piety gives rise to a spirit of loyalty to the sovereign, and loyalty is the result of following the will of one's ancestors. Hence loyalty and filial piety become one; the education of the people and the refinement of customs is accomplished without a word being spoken. Worship becomes government, and government has the effect of education; hence there is no essential difference between government and the indoctrination of the people. If the people just concentrate on revering Amaterasu and look up to her descendants, they will all face in the same direction and never go astray. Their intentions will converge, and Man will become one with Heaven. This is precisely what the sovereign relies upon in ruling the four seas, and is the final essence and ground upon which the founder established the nation. (pp. 21–23)

Here it is useful to remind ourselves that the national essence encompasses not only the origins of the Japanese people and the ritual recovery of the source of their community, but also universal truth as symbolized in the Way. The theme of unity through ritual can also be pursued from an angle that is more synchronic than diachronic, oriented more toward contemporary politico-religious space than linear inheritance from ancestors. So Aizawa further elaborates the political aspect of the pristine unity that characterized Japan in its original state and is still latent in every present, by turning to the vertical hierarchy of Heaven, Earth, and Man in an idiom of Confucianism.[24]

The transition is begun in the passage above, where the uniform reverence of the subjects for both Amaterasu and their

---

24. The distinction made here between diachronic and synchronic, horizontal and vertical, is analogous to that drawn by Ooms, in his discussion of seventeenth-century discourse, between mythological/narrative and deductive/argumentative modes of justification (p. 65 and passim).

The National Essence

own ancestors causes Heaven and Man to merge. He explains "Heaven and Man becoming one":

> All things originate in Heaven, and Man is born of his ancestors. He receives his body from his father, but his vitality is bestowed upon him by Heaven and Earth. Therefore, when there is talk of the spirits of Heaven and Earth, even simple men and women are moved to awe. When government, education, and laws all revere heaven and are consistent with gratitude to ancestors, the minds of the people will be unified. The human mind is of Heaven and Earth, and when the minds of men are unified, their vitality wells up. When people are of one mind, and the mind of Heaven and Earth is also collected together so that its vitality flourishes, the source of human vitality is filled to the brim. When people receive maximum vitality from that source at birth, the ethos of the nation will be warm and close-knit. That is called unity between Heaven and Man. (p. 23)

What emerges is a circular, mutually reinforcing arrangement between the unity of human minds and the vitality of the cosmos, which is the source of man's own vitality. This dynamism would seem to be self-supporting and perpetual. But what causes men to be of one mind in the first place? The answer provides the link between the linear, nativist appeal to origins and the spatial, Confucianist dynamic of Heaven, Earth, and Man: reverence for ancestors and loyalty to the descendants of Amaterasu. Aizawa implies that spontaneous gratitude for parental love leads to reverence for ancestors. The ancestors revered Amaterasu and the emperors, and, because the current emperor is always the lineal descendant of the divine progenetrix, each filial son must do likewise. If all people revere the emperor, they will be of one mind; they will then be one with Heaven, and the source of human vitality will flourish.

Although basically a manifestation of human nature, the cycle is effectively actualized through the power of example and correct ritual practice on both the private and public levels. The Confucian vision of unity between Heaven and Man is brought into play by the nativist reverence for origins; it is also the final completion of that reverence. The result, of course, is a polity in which force or other manipulation is superfluous—"not a word need be spoken."

In a long parenthetical insert, Aizawa appeals to the Confucian classics to further elaborate his religious concept of politics. His selections focus on the efficacy of ritual, particularly ancestor worship, in ordering relations between the ruler and the ruled, paralleling his early emphasis on the indigenous Daijōsai. From the *I ching*, he borrows the mystical imagery used to describe the trigram *Kwan:*

> "Kwan shows its subject like a worshipper who has washed his hands, but not (yet) presented his offerings:—with sincerity and an appearance of dignity (commanding reverent regard)":—(all) beneath look to him and are transformed....
>
> When we contemplate the spirit-like way of Heaven, we see how the four seasons proceed without error. The sages, in accordance with (this) spirit-like way, laid down their instructions, and all under Heaven yield submission to them.[25]
>
> (The trigram representing) the earth, and that for wind moving above it, form Kwan. The ancient kings, in accordance with this, examined the (different) regions (of the kingdom), to see the (ways of the) people, and set forth their instructions. (p. 23)[26]

In this trigram, Aizawa finds a cluster of symbolic evidence for the quintessential relationship between ruler and subjects. *Kwan* unifies the sincerity of a worshipper about to present his offering, on the one hand, with the supreme authority that proceeds naturally and inexorably like the seasons, on the other. The effect is to reinforce Aizawa's portrayal of an intimate relationship between ancestor worship and political order. He points out that the wind also symbolizes commands from above, sweeping over the land to bend uniformly everything in its path, penetrating everywhere. *Kwan* is also a sign of education (or indoctrination):

> For commands to be sent down from on high and for those below to obey them is the spirit-like way of Heaven. Those below watch their ruler and are deeply moved. Nothing is more sincere than the spirits of Heaven and Earth, and the precise moment when the worshipper has purified his hands and is about to make his offering is the height of communion between Man and the Gods. (p. 25)

---

25. Trans. from James Legge, trans., *The I Ching* (New York: Dover, 1963), p. 230.
26. Ibid., p. 292.

The National Essence

Among the references cited is also a passage from the *Chung yung* (Doctrine of the Mean):

> The ceremonies of sacrifices to Heaven and Earth are meant for the service of the Lord on High, and the ceremonies performed in the ancestral temple are meant for the service of ancestors. If one understands the ceremonies of the sacrifices to Heaven and Earth and the meaning of the grand sacrifice and the autumn sacrifice to ancestors, it would be as easy to govern a kingdom as to look at one's palm. (p. 25)[27]

Here is a classic statement of the doctrine of nonaction (*wu-wei*), according to which moral self-cultivation on the part of the ruler is adequate to the demands of benevolent government; institutions designed to manipulate behavior through reward and punishment are counterproductive. In tone, the statement refers us back to Aizawa's earlier discussion of the Daijōsai, which reinstates the archetypal unity of religion, government, and education in a single mood of reverence: "loyalty and filial piety become one; the education of the people . . . is accomplished without a word being spoken. . . . If the people just concentrate on revering Amaterasu and look up to her descendants they will all face in the same direction and never go astray."

Aizawa's concept of ritual derives ultimately from the classical Confucian idea, according to which rites are the actualization in social relations of the internal, mystical quality of *jen* (goodness, humaneness). In other words, ritual is the medium through which humaneness is extended and the inner and outer worlds are linked in a mode of moral practice. When that practice is effective, the realm will be well governed: "The Master said, Govern the people by regulations, keep order among them by chastisement, and they will flee from you, and lose all self-respect. Govern them by moral force, keep order among them by ritual, and they will keep their self-respect and come to you of their own accord."[28]

To summarize, in addition to serving as representation of the legacy of Japan's national origins, incarnate in the unbroken imperial line, the construct of national essence also symbolizes the

---

27. Trans. from Chan, *A Source Book*, p. 104.
28. *Analects* 2:3; in Arthur Waley, trans., *The Analects of Confucius* (New York: Vintage, 1938), p. 88.

eternal possibility of collective regeneration by means of ritual practice. Through ritual, it is possible to envision an escape from the corrosive effects of history into an original state of sacred community. Moreover, from Aizawa's perspective, *kokutai* in this formulation also stands for the political potential of religious ceremony. In other words, if the horizontal dimension of the national essence is symbolized in the imperial line, forever inviolable and pure, the vertical aspect is a principle of "magical" government, according to which the example of ancestral rites carried out by the emperor radiates downward and outward through correctly aligned "names and statuses," stimulating imitation and infusing the polity with a spirit of reverence.[29] In the order that results from that religious groundswell, loyalty and filial piety are unified, military morale is high, and nothing impedes the material abundance that is the inevitable product of the imperial benevolence.

The religio-political paradigm advanced by Aizawa was in many respects a restatement of the Confucianized Shinto ideology that had been gradually constructed in the seventeenth century and articulated in more or less final form by Yamazaki Ansai. Like Yamazaki, Aizawa not only grants the myths literal credence as history, but also finds in them allegorical traces of the universal Way of Heaven and Earth. In *Shinron*, too, myth, symbol, and, particularly, ritual exert powerful moral forces as they effectively "subject" the individual to prescribed forms of ethical practice. Finally, the construct of *kokutai* raises to new heights of sublimity the anagogical promise of a common national destiny.

However, Aizawa is not content merely to reiterate the seventeenth-century ideological orthodoxy. As the result of socioeconomic change and also a certain "ideological drift"[30] in the eighteenth century toward increased sensitivity to the inexorable forces of history, that orthodoxy now seemed to require something more than the "inner-worldly asceticism" that had served it during the first half of the Tokugawa period.[31] Al-

---

29. The term magical is borrowed from Fingarette: "By 'magic' I mean the power of a specific person to accomplish his will directly and effortlessly through ritual gesture and incantation" (*Confucius*, p. 3).
30. Therborn, *The Ideology of Power*, pp. 124–25.
31. Ooms, *Tokugawa Ideology*, p. 160.

The National Essence

though an attitude of "reverence" was still essential, the recovery of "Tokugawa ideology" now also seemed to require vigorous action. If the seventeenth-century ideology had allowed man to be a "source of initiative" only for action that confirmed the order postulated in its discourse,[32] in the nineteenth century that confirmation had to be premised on action that radically reformed existence. In continuing his essay, therefore, Aizawa turns from ideological reconstruction to a form of ideological mobilization.[33]

THE NEED FOR ACTION

In his treatment of the military system and the economy, Aizawa focuses attention more closely on the need for action in the present. As he addresses the contemporary milieu, against the background of his sensitivity to the significance of historical flux, he comes directly to grips with the need for flexible adaptation to current trends. The particular demands of each specific context must be noted, and the response must be swift and practical. In a format similar to his treatment of "changes in the momentum of time" and "the evils of heresy," he first posits the ideal legacy for military and economic affairs that was bestowed by Amaterasu's primal creative act, and then recounts the historical exigencies that have led to the present state.

Respect for the martial arts is one of the three important dimensions of the national essence, and it is clear that military exploits should provide an opportunity for what Eliade would call the repetition of a primordial archetype:

> The country was established through military force, and since antiquity arms have been maintained in order to conquer surrounding territory. Bows and lances were already in use in the Age of the Gods, and the sword is one of the three imperial regalia. Hence, Japan was known as Kuwashi-hokochitaru-no-kuni, the land of fine weaponry. (p. 55)

It is also significant that, in their pristine form, military affairs reflected the communal unity of politics and religion:

32. Ibid., p. 95.
33. Therborn, *The Ideology of Power*, p. 116.

> In ancient times weapons were kept in the shrine, and on the occasion of a military campaign the Gods were invariably consulted. Even the Son of Heaven did not rashly take matters into his own hands, but rather always sought the mandate of the Gods prior to military action. Therefore, people were of one mind, and there was no dispersion of power. The army consisted of soldiers of the Gods. (p. 59)

Indeed, unity among gods, warriors, and the land is the standard against which all later regimes are to be judged: "When the warriors are on the land, and the emperor receives the mandate of the Gods (before military action), then Heaven, land, and people are one body" (p. 61). Of course, Buddhism disrupted that unity early in Japan's written history, but unity between warriors and the land was particularly problematical in the Tokugawa period.

Hideyoshi was the first to force loyal daimyo to reside in Osaka, and then Tokugawa Ieyasu pursued an even grander policy of strengthening the center at the expense of the periphery. According to Aizawa, the removal of the samurai from the land to the castle towns did not result immediately in a significant weakening of military capabilities, because morale remained high. Eventually, however, the inevitable process of degeneration set in:

> Once a system was established to support the warriors with taxes in kind, wealth tended to concentrate in the vicinity of the warriors [in the castle towns]. Of course, where wealth has collected, merchants also tend to swarm. And merchants are always caught up in the fashions of the moment. Forever in pursuit of outrageous profit, they are constantly in search of the strange and unusual. That is fine if the purpose of government is to make brave and dashing warriors forget war and enjoy a period of perpetual peace. But, as their bad habits continued, they developed opulent lifestyles which were inconsistent with social status. As they became slaves of desire, they soon forgot propriety and righteousness. (p. 63)

As a result, the erstwhile warriors abandoned their rustic past to become soft, pampered, and fat, skilled at repartee in the parlor, but unable to withstand privation.

Aizawa's solution was to return the samurai to the land. Ieyasu's grand strategy of pacification had worked well as an antidote to generations of war and rebellion; there was much to be learned from his emphasis on strengthening the center. Now, however, it was also necessary to bolster the periphery. Indeed, the bakufu should be given credit for having recognized the problem: "To make the people ignorant and the soldiers weak may be a clever plan from the point of view of politics. But, where there is benefit, there is also damage, so that strategy must now be reformed" (p. 71).

It was necessary, however, that the transformation be carried out with the utmost flexibility. There is a certain logic to the affairs of the world that requires that, when one point tightens up, another be loosened, and vice versa:

> There are ways to make ad hoc decisions on when to tighten and when to loosen, when to use and when to set aside, and there comes a time when those ways should be put into practice. It is impossible to deal with such matters as the number of alternate residences in Edo . . . according to hard and fast rules. *The secret of preventing the spread of resentment among the people is an ability to seize the moment.* (p. 75; emphasis added)

To act flexibly and swiftly in response to events as they occur was not inconsistent with respect for the accomplishments of Tokugawa Ieyasu in unifying and pacifying the country:

> Long ago Ieyasu respected arms in order to build a foundation, and he rendered the people ignorant and weak in order to allow the realm to rest. In other words, he tightened up and then allowed leeway. At the present time, the barbarians are waging war day after day, setting their minds on aggression and alternately probing our borders. Our situation is like Ieyasu, when the Oda, the Takeda and the Hōjō surrounded his headquarters in Hamamatsu. Since it was no time for slackness, he had to tighten what had formerly lain loose. Therefore, his intention of laying the foundation for the nation should continue to be honored, but there is no need to follow the precedent of rendering the realm ignorant and weak. This is a good example of changing times. (pp. 75–77)

Here Aizawa explicitly advocates flexible practicality as the best policy in a world of incessant change. It is the spirit of rational choice and adaptability displayed by such heroes as Tokugawa

Ieyasu that is to be emulated, not their specific laws, rules, and institutional mechanisms. Of course the ultimate end of expedient and adaptive measures must always be reconstitution of the original order:

> A foundation for administration should be laid, doctrine should be clarified, and soldiers should invariably receive the command of the Gods; Heaven and Man should be unified, the multitude be of one mind, the virtue of the ancestors be made manifest and their meritorious deeds sung; the glory of the nation should be expanded across the seas, the barbarians expelled, and the homeland reclaimed. Only then can the profound meaning of the oracle of Amaterasu and the great achievements of her imperial descendants be fully actualized. (p. 77)

Aizawa's proposal that the samurai should be returned to the land is only suggestive of the wide-ranging institutional reforms outlined in *Shinron* and other Mito texts. Clearly instrumental innovation and adaptation in the tradition of the political invention (*sakui*) advocated by Ogyū Sorai was at least necessary, if not sufficient, to realize the "magical" government of ritual idealized in the *Chung yung*. Once a mystical, ritualistic concept of the national essence was juxtaposed against the degenerative force inherent in the passage of time, it became abundantly clear that men must act on Heaven's behalf. In other words, by presenting the Mito activists with an apparent contradiction between historical decline, on the one hand, and the vision of an original archetype of ritualized order, on the other, the Mito problematic opened a discursive space that could be filled only by a broad range of human effort. Hence, it is impossible to understand Mito ideology as a matter solely of language in texts. As expressed in the perceived need to rectify names and statuses constructively, the Mito program demanded not only linguistic clarification, but the fabrication of exemplary institutions and the active demonstration of moral and political principles, that is, Mito discourse was always "in action." Moreover, in functioning to make action possible and at the same time subjecting that action to the problematic of discourse, it was profoundly ideological.

3
REFORM AS REPRESENTATION

The young samurai who followed Fujita Yūkoku and Aizawa Seishisai were not the only reformers in Mito at the beginning of the Tenpō period. When Tokugawa Nariaki became daimyo in 1829, he in fact had the support of two renovationist groups: the Fujita faction, whose concept of reform was embedded in the discourse on rectification, myth, and ritual, and the more pragmatically oriented Tachihara faction, led by Yūkoku's erstwhile rival in the Shōkōkan, Tachihara Suiken. The membership for these factions overlapped somewhat and shifted over time. It is also hazardous to assume a direct equivalency between the academic and political manifestations of the two groups.[1] Nevertheless, it is possible to identify in the writings and actions of the leading participants two contending paradigms for reform. My focus is primarily on the Fujita paradigm, which was politically dominant, but, for contrastive purposes, it is useful to describe some aspects of the rival view.

The two paradigms differ most strikingly with respect to economic policy. As is well known, the urbanization of the *bushi* during the Tokugawa period had created an essential and lucrative role for the despised merchant class and led eventually to widespread commercialization, economic imbalances, and the relative impoverishment of the ruling class. Therefore, the major reforms carried out by the bakufu in the Kyōhō and Kansei periods focused on economic issues from the perspective of the ruling class and sought to improve its economic prospects. Typical measures were efforts to reduce expenditures through sumptuary regulations and retrenchment; attempts to increase tax yield by encouraging the development of new fields

---

1. Suzuki Fusako, "Mito-han Tenpō kaikaku no ichi kōsatsu," *Ochanomizu shigaku* 15 (1972): 64–68.

and modifying collection methods; and a variety of other devices, including forced loans from daimyo, cancellation of debts, controls on merchant guilds, currency debasement and reform, and price controls.

Measures such as these were also proposed frequently by the Tachihara faction and actually played a role in the Tenpō Reforms in Mito. Luxury was prohibited, and Nariaki set an example by dressing simply and eating frugally. Loans were forcibly extracted from retainer stipends, and trade was promoted. Indeed, one of the first new institutions constructed under Nariaki was a system by which the domainal administration took monopoly control over the promotion and marketing of local products. In 1830 an office in charge of Mito-han production was established in the Mito mansion in Edo, with authority to collect from the domain such products as paper and tobacco and facilitate their marketing in Edo. Later Nariaki sent men to Kyoto and elsewhere to study pottery production and had a kiln constructed in Mito to promote that industry. He also attempted to encourage the production of glass, tea, lacquer, and silk.[2]

Nevertheless, relatively little attention was devoted to these economic measures in the context of the reforms as a whole, and none was very successful. Historian Seya Yoshihiko suggests that this relative neglect was partly because the Fujita reform faction did not include a single expert on economic or financial affairs.[3] It is also significant that the Fujita faction itself did not, in fact, actively support these innovations. From the beginning of the reform period, the Fujita group, now led primarily by Tōko following the death of Yūkoku in 1826, had advocated a comprehensive cadastral survey as the only way to rebuild the tax structure and provide a long-range, structural solution to the domain's economic difficulties. It was only because such a radical measure seemed premature in the early years of the reforms that Tachihara-faction proposals like the *han* products monopoly were instituted.[4]

These contrasting views on economics are an initial indication of how the Tachihara paradigm differed from that of the

2. Seya and Toyosaki, *Ibaraki-ken no rekishi*, p. 158.
3. Ibid.
4. Suzuki, "Mito-han Tenpō kaikaku no ichi kōsatsu," p. 72.

Fujitas. Tachihara lieutenants like Komiyama Fūken were apparently anxious to follow the recommendations of Ogyū Sorai's disciple Dazai Shundai.[5] In an iconoclastic extension of Ogyū's philosophy, Dazai had suggested to the daimyo that they abandon the traditional piety that a rice economy was the only legitimate basis of wealth and turn to the active promotion and exploitation of trade. The Fujita faction members, on the other hand, generally abhorred the commercial money economy and sought to solve economic problems by reconstituting the economic basis for natural order. Although they were willing to compromise at the level of means in order to facilitate this reconstruction, their ends went beyond piecemeal economic benefits. Moreover, the Fujita faction still operated out of a discourse on rectification, which prescribed nomenclature and status order deductively, from the top down; if the form (names and statuses) were correct, Yūkoku believed, its normative force would cause ethical content to follow spontaneously. The Tachihara faction, on the other hand, sought to address specific problems in an inductive fashion in order to bring discrete, measurable results.

The difference between the factions is also illustrated in their contrasting approaches to the problem of depopulation. Komiyama, a leading member of the Tachihara faction, set down his views on this issue in some detail. For him, depopulation was primarily the result of informal population controls, particularly infanticide (*mabiki*), and had to be attacked directly at the family level. Therefore, he proposed a practical policy that combined a prohibition of infanticide with monetary incentives for live births. Komiyama's proposal was not opposed by the Fujita faction and was instituted for a time, beginning in 1832. But there is little evidence that Tōko or any member of his faction ever addressed the issues of infanticide or population as such. Rather, as with the issue of finances, they focused their efforts on the need for a survey based on the assumption that depopulation was the result of unequal land distribution and therefore that a rectification of landholding would provide the only lasting solution.[6]

The major elements of the Tenpō Reforms in Mito, including

---

5. Dazai Shundai, "Keizairokushūi," in Rai Tsutomu, ed., *Soraigakuha*, Nihon shisō taikei 37 (Tokyo: Iwanami Shoten, 1972): 45–56.
6. Suzuki, "Mito-han Tenpō kaikaku no ichi kōsatsu," pp. 74–75.

the cadastral survey, the return of samurai to the land, and the new domainal academy, conformed closely to the Fujita-faction paradigm. They were aspects of a formal, structural rectification designed to approximate the contours of an archetypal order. As in the cases of economic and depopulation policy, each of these measures was contested by Komiyama and others associated with the Tachihara faction. Komiyama's proposals were always pragmatic, gradualist, and often meticulously inductive in their intent to achieve piecemeal results through the use of existing institutions and practices. In contrast, the Fujita program was more schematic than practical, radical rather than gradualist, and even formalistic in the sense that it gave top priority to the replication of institutional and religious archetypes. The reformists under Fujita believed that, once names and institutions were rectified and ideals were brought into alignment with actualities, "it would be as easy to govern a kingdom as to look at one's palm."

The Fujita concept of reform might be summed up by saying that rather than *merely* means to other ends, such as profits, stable population, or increased tax receipts, the institutional configurations they established had to be justifiable as ends in themselves. They were justifiable in that way because they represented the authority of Shinto myth and the persuasiveness of neo-Confucian arguments for the possibility of spontaneous resonance between human minds and the Mind of Heaven-and-Earth. Therefore, although the reforms can to some extent be *explained* teleologically, as means to other ends, they can and should also be treated as semiotic and symbolic events that are meaningful and therefore able to be *interpreted* alongside linguistic texts for the meaning they contain.[7] Indeed, by attempting to read their acts as texts, we are only complying with the Mito writers' own dictum that "letters and military arts do not conflict; scholarship and practical enterprise are the same in effect."[8] If writing can be considered continuous with practical action, then perhaps practical action can be considered as a

---

7. Ricoeur says, "All significant events and deeds are, in this way, opened to a kind of practical interpretation through present *praxis*. Human action, too, is opened to anybody who *can read*. In the same way that the meaning of an event is the sense of its forthcoming intepretations, the interpretation by contemporaries has no particular privilege in this process" ("The Model of the Text," pp. 545–46).

8. *Kōdōkanki*, in Imai, Seya, and Bitō, eds., p. 231.

form of writing: the inscription in human affairs of a representation of the Way.

DEMARCATING THE LAND

In 1837 (Tenpō 8) Tokugawa Nariaki announced a list of four reforms that would receive top priority: *keikai no gi*—a comprehensive cadastral survey; *dochaku no gi*—the return of samurai to the land; *gakkō no gi*—establishment of a domainal academy and regional schools; and *sōkōtai no gi*—termination of the practice of maintaining a permanent staff in Edo.[9] With the exception of the last, which in practice merged with the general problem of attaching samurai to the land, these items provide convenient, although by no means exhaustive, focal points for an analysis of the Tenpō reforms in Mito.

The discrepancy between "name" and "reality" that obsessed Mito activists was nowhere more pronounced than in the area of land registry and taxation. In the Tenpō period, taxes were still levied on the basis of documents compiled in 1641, nearly two hundred years before, when surveys had been carried out under the auspices of the shogunate in the Kan'ei era.[10] However, the buying, selling and pawning of land that had occurred since that time, along with natural disasters of one kind or another, had resulted in vast changes in land boundaries and ownership, not all of which were accurately reflected, even in local records. The classification of fields on the basis of yield (*kokudaka*) was often far removed from their actual quality and productivity, tax inequities were glaring, and a small rural elite had often benefited from official confusion by aggregating ever-larger plots of land on which they paid relatively little tax. Those who were dispossessed sometimes left their homes, resulting in steady losses of rural population.

In his 1791 treatise on rural problems, *Kannō wakumon* (Questions and answers concerning the promotion of agriculture), Fujita Yūkoku had reaffirmed that there was nothing particularly new or unique about such problems. According to Yūkoku, the

9. Mito-shi Shi Hensan Iinkai, ed., *Mito-shi shi* (hereafter cited as *Mss*), II/3, p. 60.
10. This was not a situation peculiar to Mito. See Thomas C. Smith, "The Land Tax in the Tokugawa Period," in John W. Hall and Marius B. Jansen, eds., *Studies in the Institutional History of Early Modern Japan* (Princeton, N.J.: Princeton University Press, 1968), pp. 284–85.

earliest Mito lords, Yorifusa and Mitsukuni, had erected institutional structures that gave proper attention to agriculture, stimulated high productivity, and contributed to the development of new land. From the Genroku period (1688–1703), however, the administration had become corrupt. Ill-considered laws were passed, and, when taxes were raised gratuitously, a peasant rebellion ensued in Hōei 6 (1709). Peasants abandoned their land and drifted to other domains, so in 1712 a program of "*hitogaeshi*" was put into effect to bring them back. It was unsuccessful, and failed to stem a drop in population of some 30,000 people between 1726 and 1747. This trend continued, so that, whereas in 1726 the population of Mito *han* had been 318,475, by 1798 it numbered only 229,239.[11] For Yūkoku these figures symbolized not only a disastrous decline in tax revenues, but a failure of policy and the degeneration of popular morality. He believed that a comprehensive land survey was necessary to correct such anomalies, and it is for that reason that the "correction of boundaries" (*keikai*) headed Nariaki's list of priority reforms. Yūkoku writes that "First, the land and people must be properly arranged." He also cites Mencius' dictum that "Benevolent government must begin with land demarcation."[12] Indeed, although Yūkoku does not quote at greater length, the remainder of the passage in the *Mencius* concerning the ancient well-field system seems to provide a useful introduction to the meaning of a cadastral survey in the context of the Mito problematic:

> When boundaries are not properly drawn, the division of land according to the well-field system and the yield of grain used for paying officials cannot be equitable. For this reason, despotic rulers and corrupt officials always neglect the boundaries. Once the boundaries are correctly fixed, there will be no difficulty in settling the distribution of land and the determination of emolument.[13]

Here order and clarity are linked with equity and benevolence, a combination that goes to the heart of the Mito concern for *meibun* (the proper delineation of names and statuses). A survey

---

11. *Kannō wakumon*, in Takasu Yoshijirō, ed., *Mitogaku taikei* 3 (Tokyo: Mitogaku Taikei Kankōkai, 1941): 12, 2–3.
12. Ibid., pp. 21, 120.
13. D. C. Lau, trans., *Mencius* (London: Penguin Books, 1970), p. 99.

would bring normative borders in line with actual ones and so eliminate ambiguity. In a somewhat less obvious sense, it also would actualize the transcendental imperative of benevolent government (*jinsei*), making manifest in the relative, historically circumscribed world the absolute principle of the Way. The restorationist meaning of the survey in that sense is highlighted by Yūkoku's discussion of the well-field system as recommended by Mencius.

The term "well-field" refers to the arrangement of nine fields in such a way that they resemble the Chinese character for "well" (*ching*). As Mencius describes that system:

> A *ching* is a piece of land measuring 1 *li* square, and each *ching* consists of 900 *mu*. Of these, the central plot of 100 *mu* belongs to the state, while the other eight plots of 100 *mu* each are held by eight families who share the duty of caring for the plot owned by the state. Only when they have done this duty dare they turn to their own affairs. This is what sets the common people apart.[14]

The result of the arrangement from the viewpoint of the state, of course, is a 1-to-9 tax/land ratio. Mencius says, "I suggest that in the country the tax should be 1 in 9, using the method of *chu*, but in the capital it should be 1 in 10, to be levied in kind."[15]

Having paid obeisance, as had Ogyū Sorai and others before him, to the nearly divine authority of the well-field system as the archetype of benevolence in the countryside, Yūkoku is immediately faced with the problem of its inapplicability in practice. He himself suggested a tax ratio of 1 to 3 based on assessed productivity, and at times actual ratios far exceeded that figure.[16] Obviously, adherence to the letter of the Mencian ratio of 1 to 9 would have been disastrous for the samurai class. He admonishes:

> Some arbitrarily regard the reduction of taxes alone as comprising benevolence. Oblivious to changes in institutional structure between long ago and the present, they advocate that the laws of the sages providing for a tax of 1 in 10 should be instituted right now. This is the corrupt advice of bogus Confucians.[17]

---

14. Ibid., p. 100.
15. Ibid., p. 99.
16. At times they averaged 60% (Seya and Toyosaki, *Ibaraki-ken*, p. 134).
17. Fujita, *Kannō wakumon*, p. 17.

Moreover, as Yūkoku points out, at the time the well-field system was actually employed, a landowner's freedom to dispose of his land was circumscribed. Only at the hands of the state could "land be equalized, manpower measured and fields parceled out at will." But:

> In more recent times the system changed so that fields became the private property of the peasant and came to vary widely in size. An owner now has few obligations to the government [*kōgi*] besides payment of taxes in kind. When land is the exclusive property of the peasant, it is no longer subject to free allocation by the authorities.[18]

In sum, "the well-field system should not be instituted at the present time." Nevertheless,

> Its intentions should be observed for ten thousand generations. Reforms will surely fail if they do not include [efforts to] eliminate differences among fields as to size and productivity, narrow the gap between rich and poor, promote a frugal and diligent public morality, and admonish peasants away from extravagance and sloth in accord with the intentions bequeathed by the sages.[19]

Yūkoku's debt to Ogyū Sorai is unmistakable. The role of the ruler is not to imitate slavishly the ancient sages in the specifics of their rules and practices, but to follow their example in *devising* equivalent laws in accordance with the demands of his own time. Indeed, Yūkoku makes quite explicit his view that

> laws are tools for ruling the people and cannot be replaced even by the virtue of sages and wise men. Certainly those who employ laws must exercise great care. But in the end laws are like implements, and it is up to people to make them good. Therefore, no matter how worthy a law may be inherently, if the individual employing it is not capable, he will be like the poor workman who despite high-quality tools is unable to produce fine craftsmanship.[20]

Moreover, time constantly changes the environment in which laws work: "The laws laid down by the founder were certainly good originally, and if at the present time they do not always accord with the sentiments (*ninjō*) of the people that is not the fault of the laws themselves. It is merely because evils have

---

18. Ibid., pp. 16–17.
19. Ibid., p. 17.
20. Ibid., p. 74.

emerged in the specifics of their application (*matsu*)." It is important that the ruler respond to such difficulties in the proper manner. Rather than taking into account only immediate exigencies and tinkering with regulations and ordinances so that they proliferate endlessly, he should return to the "essence" (*moto*) of the original law and then modify its details as necessary in order to accommodate the needs and special circumstances of the time.[21] In the final analysis, laws must unify past (as archetype) and present (as history) in a dynamic, creative adaptation: "If [on the one hand] the laws prior to the Genroku period are studied and Yorifusa and Mitsukuni are held up as our models, and [on the other] the present situation and atmosphere are taken into consideration and skillfully employed, no one within our borders will fail to submit willingly." Such are the principles of a "restorationist" administration.[22]

Yūkoku divides the evils that had beset the domain since the days of Yorifusa and Mitsukuni into five categories—dissipation (*shida*), aggregation of land (*kenpei*), forced labor (*rikieki*), extortion (*ōren*), and petty harassment (*hanjō*).

Shida meant that "the people are extravagant and deceitful." They "spurn simple manners and crave elegance, hate hard work and delight in relaxation."[23] Such tendencies marked a process of degeneration from the system established by Tokugawa Ieyasu according to which "Peasants were ruled in such a way that they experienced neither surplus nor insufficiency."[24] Now, however, a world had developed where "with money one can do anything." The tendency toward luxury and ostentation had begun with the great merchants and local rich and then gradually filtered down to the poor peasants. The latter "no longer devote themselves to agriculture as they once did, and produce relatively little grain; while former tax levels have been maintained, the material demands of the peasants are now five or even ten times as great, so [relative] poverty daily becomes more severe."[25] In other words, the domain suffers a revolution of rising expectations.

In order to correct the debilitating effects of a pervasive taste

21. Ibid., pp. 19, 74.
22. Ibid., p. 21.
23. Ibid., p. 23.
24. Ibid., p. 24.
25. Ibid., p. 25.

for luxury, Yūkoku proposes that class distinctions among samurai, peasants, artisans, and merchants be strictly enforced. Marriage between peasants and townsmen should be prohibited; merchant activities in the villages should be regulated. Once accomplished, such measures would insulate the peasants from corrosive merchant values and help restore the moral integrity and industriousness that was their natural heritage.

The second evil, land accumulation by the rich, relates closely to the dissemination of urban values in the sense that peasants forced off their land tended to migrate to the castle towns. In discussing dissipation, Yūkoku had bemoaned the fact that money raised through commercial activities enabled a prosperous few to buy up much of the good land. Having established themselves in the countryside, they would purchase the status of rural samurai (*gōshi*) for 500 to 1,000 *ryō* and live the life of country aristocrats.[26] Meanwhile, those forced by circumstances to sell their land turned to liquor, gambling, and villainy. Eventually, they ended up as servants, day laborers, or street vendors in the city, where life was easier but far less virtuous and productive than in the villages. At the same time, the social standing of ordinary peasants had suffered. Despised as "dirt farmers" (*dobyakushō*), they had fallen lower than merchants and townsmen.[27]

Land had been aggregated into large plots so that "the rich get richer and the poor poorer," a trend counter to the demands of the Way: "While it is commonly said that the presence in the villages of an affluent elite brings glory to the domain, those who are schooled in administration know that it actually causes great harm. In Japan and China where the Way prevails no effort is spared to eliminate it."[28] Moreover, the problem

26. Shibahara Takuji doubts that there was actually much rural commercialism in the relatively poor and backward Mito countryside, and he attributes Yūkoku's concern about aggregation of land to a "rigid Confucian aversion to commerce and support for hegemony by independent farmers (*honbyakushō*)." His partial data indicate that accumulations of more than 15 *koku* were quite rare in areas like Naka-gun in the north, but quite evident around Ushibori in southern Namekata-gun. Shibahara observes, however, that in most cases the few who amassed land seemed to use the surplus to elevate their status in a traditional manner to *ōjōya* (regional headman), often by purchasing the requisite approval (*Meiji ishin no kenryoku kiban* [Tokyo: Ochanomizu Shobō, 1965], pp. 120–23).
27. Fujita, *Kannō wakumon*, pp. 25–28.
28. Ibid., p. 39.

went beyond aggregation per se. In fact, transactions were often carried out in such a way that the rich obtained land on which little or no taxes were assessed, while the poor were left with high assessments but little good land. According to one practice, a 10-*tan* plot would be divided in such a way that the buyer would receive 7 *tan* with a tax assessment of only 3 *koku* while the seller was left with only 3 *tan* of land on which 7 *koku* of tax must be paid.[29] Such abuses were not often reflected accurately in land registers and tax rolls, and the domain lost revenue when the poor defaulted.

To correct such disorderly inequities, Yūkoku proposed an equivalency law (*kinden no hō*), according to which land dimensions entered in the ledger would be corrected to reflect actual ownership and eliminate hidden sources of wealth, and a field regulation law (*genden no hō*), by which land accumulation would be limited directly and a peasant allowed no more land than he could work together with his own family. As noted above, he also proposed that a tax of one-third on the total productivity of land be retained as the norm.

It is instructive here to refer back to Yūkoku's theory on the rectification of names. Rather than offering an interpretation that concentrated on making behavior adhere more closely to the form inherent in a name, Yūkoku focused on the prescriptive need to reorganize and assign names. If we substitute laws for names, it becomes clear that Yūkoku's policy recommendations generally adhere to his theoretical principle. That is, he chooses to rectify *names* (laws) instead of behavior, which, he implies, will follow naturally if the laws are appropriate. Yūkoku's specific solution, therefore, is a new framework of laws.

The "evil of forced labor" referred to the excessive and often arbitrarily exacted corvée. Prior to the Genroku period, corvée had been levied on the basis of population. Later, however, duties came to be based on tax assessment and allocated to entire villages in such a way that the labor of a given number of ablebodied men would be required for each hundred *koku* of rice tax a village paid. In Yūkoku's view, the latter system was oppressive and arbitrary, and to correct it he proposes an "equal

---

29. Ibid., p. 48. (A *tan* equals .245 acres.)

duties law" (*kin'eki no hō*), which would include a return to assessments per individual.

The evil of extortion referred to a variety of extra tax levies that Yūkoku proposed be eliminated. "Petty harassment" consisted of tedious reporting and petitioning procedures, often laid down by incompetent local officials, which took the time of village leaders and detracted from the prestige of local government. Yūkoku called here for a higher level of competence (*jinzai*) among lower officials, more delegation of authority to the lower levels, and fairness in meting out corrections and punishments.

A cadastral survey was still viewed as fundamental, however. According to Yūkoku it should consist in the innovative adaptation of an original archetype to the needs of administration at the beginning of the nineteenth century. As such, it would bring actualities into accord with a prescriptive design and actualize the Way in its political manifestation as the ruler's calling to provide a benevolent order (*jinsei*). It was this concept of the meaning of cadastral order that fueled the efforts of Mito reformists in the 1830s and 1840s.

Toward the end of 1838, magistrates of each district (*kōri bugyō*) were informed that the survey, or what Nariaki now called "land reform" (*tochikata kaisei*), would begin immediately if crop conditions were found to be adequate the following autumn (which, as it turned out, they were).[30] In the meantime, personnel changes were made as necessary to consolidate a domainal leadership committed to action. Yūkoku's son, Fujita Tōko, was one of those given staff responsibilities for the survey. The following New Year's, an announcement was sent out to district offices outlining the projected magnitude of the task. A survey of the domain's rice land was to take four years and require a budget of 13,799 *ryō*, and a basic law governing survey policy and procedures (*kenchi jōmoku*) was promulgated in April 1839.[31]

The danger of peasant uprisings in response to the survey

30. *Mss* II/3, p. 775.
31. A detailed breakdown of projected survey costs may be found in ibid., pp. 776–79. A complete text of the law may be found in *Mito-han shiryō* (Tokyo: Yoshikawa Kōbunkan, 1915), *bekki ge*, no. 18. For a thorough description of the survey, see Inui Hiromi, "Mito-han tōsō no ichi kōsatsu," *Rekishigaku kenkyū* 232 (Aug. 1959).

had always been a practical concern for reformists and presented a major obstacle to their plans. Serious crop failures had occurred in 1833, 1836, and again in 1838, straining relations with peasants and heightening the danger of disorder. A minor rebellion regarding food distribution had broken out in Ōzu village in 1833, and news of the 1837 rebellion led by Ōshio Heihachirō in Osaka spread alarm among Mito samurai.[32] They were keenly aware that, during an incident in Mito at the time of the Kan'ei survey, peasants had carried out "forcible petitioning" (gōso), which had resulted in the suicide of two survey commissioners. Such fears had effectively frustrated progress during Nariaki's first visit to Mito in 1833.

In 1836, however, Nariaki successfully laid down emergency sumptuary laws, built a storehouse for grain, and carried out several other reforms. Then in August, during a conference on measures to deal with crop failure and famine, he called for an immediate cadastral survey. Some advisers agreed, but many others, including Tōko himself, still felt the time was not ripe. Tōko counseled that, because the people had not yet had time to develop firm confidence in Nariaki, the latter should spend some time preparing the way for a survey with tangible signs of benevolence.[33]

Ironically, it seems to have been the disastrous crop conditions that offered Nariaki the opportunity to display his "benevolence." Relief measures of one kind or another instituted by his administration between autumn 1836 and spring 1837 reportedly created an environment of cooperation between officials and the masses and catalyzed an atmosphere of submissiveness among the people.[34] According to Tōko, Nariaki was even inspired to take money previously earmarked for reconstruction of the roof of the Mito mansion in Koishikawa, Edo, and donate it to the district magistrates for relief work.[35]

Nariaki's personal displays of asceticism and firm enforce-

32. *Mss* II/3, p. 56; and Fujita Tōko, *Kaiten shishi*, in Takasu, ed., *Fujita Tōko zenshū* 1:161. On the rebellion, see Tetsuo Najita, "Ōshio Heihachirō (1793–1837)," in Albert M. Craig and Donald H. Shively, eds., *Personality in Japanese History* (Berkeley and Los Angeles: University of California Press, 1970).
33. *Mss* II/3, p. 773; also see Fujita, *Hitachi obi*, in Takasu Yoshijirō, ed., *Fujita Tōko zenshū* 1:461.
34. *Mss* II/3, p. 773.
35. Fujita, *Hitachi obi*, p. 461.

ment of sumptuary legislation may also have helped. By midsummer of 1837, at any rate, Tōko and the others had come around to aggressive support for an immediate cadastral survey. Fujita Tōko describes the survey process:

> The domain was divided into four districts, named East, West, South and North (these are not the original designations, but have been applied only recently; at one time in the past, however, the domain was divided into three districts called South, North, and Central), and each was governed by a district magistrate. Those four districts, in turn, were each split into four regions so that they numbered sixteen in all.
>
> Two competent samurai were chosen as survey team commissioners [*nawa bugyō*] in each region, for a total complement of thirty-two (actually, considering personnel changes over the entire five years of the survey, the team leaders numbered about fifty in all). To the pair of leaders who jointly carried out their functions were added two or three officials in charge of district administration. Honest individuals were also selected from among the rustic samurai, headmen, and neighborhood leaders, along with another independent individual—one who was very familiar with agriculture—called the "peasant elder" [*rōnō*]. In conjunction with the various pole-holders and rope-takers they directed, each such group comprised one survey team.
>
> The teams went to each field, measured its length and breadth, and entered the figures in the register [*daichō*]. When an estimate of the quality of the field was reported to the district magistrate, he and the finance commissioner [*kanjō bugyō*] would go to the fields with their retinues and classify the fields as good, average or poor. Moreover, from time to time the elders would go around encouraging the teams, making judgments in cases where there was disagreement, and so on. With all these officials combining their efforts, it took about five years to complete the job.[36]

The task advanced in three stages. First, each village charted and graded its own land in a process called preparation (*shitagumi*). This stage was considered essential in order to create an aura of fairness and give credence to a village's own intimate knowledge of the fields within its boundaries. Next, the officials mentioned by Tōko scrutinized the data reported by each vil-

---

36. Ibid., pp. 464–66.

lage and made a judgment on their accuracy. Called *naichō*, the second stage began in the autumn of 1840. Finally, the actual measuring (*nawauchi*) was carried out.

The procedures and policies outlined in the basic survey law included a number of departures from the way the task had been carried out in 1641. As Yūkoku had cautioned in *Kannō wakumon*, reformers were obliged to take the atmosphere (*ninjō*) of the time into account. The absolute could only be represented through the material offered by the historical moment. For example, in the earlier survey, quality ratings had been determined more or less dictatorially by the survey officials. Now, largely out of fear of rebellion, they were generally assigned by the villagers themselves. A district magistrate observed:

> It appears that, during the Bunroku, Keichō and Kan'ei surveys, land was not rated as to quality before it was measured. At that time the people were naive and manipulable [*sunao*], and rating procedures were generally accurate, so survey officials merely looked over the soil quality and configuration, made an overall determination of grade, and proceeded with measurement. Now *people are no longer so docile*, and it is necessary to follow a policy of scrutinizing quality ratings several times over. The preliminary stage is followed by adjudication, and then reviewed more than once before actual measurement commences.[37]

Moreover, whereas in earlier surveys the land of an entire village had been rated as a unit, now there was a so-called *torikado* system, according to which tax rates were allowed to vary even within each village. The system was instituted because of the obvious variation within villages in terms of access to water, soil quality, and so on, and also in order to give official sanction to a de facto system of land grades that had evolved in many villages in the preceding two centuries.[38] Rating procedures and guidelines had also changed. Such circumstances as sunlight exposure, distance from residence, and other elements were to be taken into consideration in addition to more readily apparent factors, such as soil fertility. The survey law stipulated that: "If a village is energetic and highspirited, a difficult choice between

---

37. Kaneko Kyōkō (Magojirō), *Megumi no kiri*, quoted in *Mss* II/3, p. 803. Emphasis added.
38. *Mss* II/3, pp. 789–90.

'good' and 'medium' is to be resolved on the side of 'good' . . . where that is not the case, such an issue is to be resolved on the side of 'medium.'"[39]

In the Kan'ei era only four grades had been used (good, medium, poor, and very poor), but in the Tenpō survey another was added so that a field could be rated as good, medium-good, medium, poor, or very poor. The new system of finer gradations was instituted to make up for the impracticality of the Kan'ei practice of discretion (*nawa gokoro*), by which the surveyors on their own responsibility would measure leniently what seemed to be poorer fields and treat relatively rich ones more strictly. Given what were perceived by reformist samurai to be the suspicious natures of late Tokugawa villagers, such discretion was bound to be interpreted as inequity, so the new system was established in its place.[40]

The Tenpō reformists also modified the units of measurement. Ropes were usually used for measuring, but they were sometimes combined with rods, particularly of 1 *ken* in length. A *ken* had been interpreted to mean anything from 6 *shaku* (1.82 meters) to 6 *shaku* 5 *sun* (about 1.97 meters) in various parts of Japan at various times, but in the Kan'ei survey the *ken* had been pegged at a strict 6 *shaku*. Because the survey prior to Kan'ei had used 6 *shaku* 3 *sun* and reduction of the standard naturally resulted in larger dimensions and, therefore, greater expectations of yield as a basis for taxation, it had been said that the Kan'ei survey "snatched sixty-days worth of rice from the peasant."[41] Against that background, the Tenpō officials found it difficult to agree on what length to use this time. Disagreement was not resolved until 1840, when an earlier decision in favor of the strict use of 6 *shaku* was overturned by those who favored a more lenient policy of 6 *shaku* 5 *sun*. The discretionary leniency of the measuring officials had been eliminated, but they apparently decided that the peasants should be given full benefit of the doubt, even though domainal revenues would surely suffer.

Largely because of the above procedures, the survey resulted in a 24 percent drop in domainal resources (*kokudaka*), from the

39. Ibid., p. 787.
40. Ibid., pp. 788–89.
41. Ibid., p. 791.

418,394 *koku* that had been reported to the bakufu in 1835 to a new official level of only 317,086. Indeed, there is some evidence to suggest that the new total was actually closer to 289,000 *koku*, and that the 317,086 figure reported to the bakufu was a misrepresentation. It was apparently not uncommon for domains to *underestimate* their capacity to the bakufu in order to keep down their military and other obligations, which were scaled according to domain size as measured by number of *koku*. The reason for Mito's *overestimation* is therefore obscure but probably has to do with the traditional Mito desire to rank equally in *kokudaka* to the other Tokugawa collateral houses, Owari and Kii.[42]

Nevertheless, the vast reduction in tax revenue was probably more than balanced by other financial manipulations, most notably a doubling of the exchange rate used to determine the amount of the tax payments due in cash for dry-field rice. Until this reform, the rate had remained at the level set in 1637, of 1 *ryō* as the equivalent to 2 *koku* 5 *to* of rice. This reflected market conditions at the time, but over the 200-odd years separating the Kan'ei and Tenpō periods it had been overtaken by rises in the price of rice. Now the exchange rate was officially doubled, so that 1 *ryō* would be the equivalent of only 1 *koku* 2 *to* 5 *shō*.

In addition, stricter enforcement of uniformity in the domain-wide system of taxation rates may have affected many farmers adversely. It appears that, prior to the reform, two different systems had been employed: the *kemi* system, under which the percentage of the crop to be taken as tax was determined annually by inspecting fields and estimating probable harvest levels, and the *jōmen* system, by which a standard amount of tax was fixed for a period of several years. Samurai agricultural theorists had often criticized the *kemi* system for taking too much time and trouble; for encouraging duplicity on the part of peasants who had an incentive to make prospective harvests appear poorer than they were; and for not including the extra work incentive supposedly built into the *jōmen* system, which allowed the cultivator to keep whatever he was able to produce over the fixed tax amount. Thus, as part of the Tenpō Reforms the entire domain was placed under the *jōmen* system of fixed rates. But, though the system was to be uniform, actual

42. Ibid., pp. 835–37.

tax rates appear to have differed from place to place, and a special effort was made to take a wide variety of factors into account in determining the rate appropriate to a given plot of land or village.

Other changes were, on balance, more favorable to most cultivators, particularly those made in the area that Fujita Yūkoku had called "extortion" (ōren). Miscellaneous taxes had long been particularly draconian in Mito, but one practice in particular had been subjected to increasing criticism. According to that practice, fixed amounts of three "miscellaneous grains" had to be sold to the domain at inordinately low prices. The amounts, for every 100 *koku* of dry fields, were 5 *koku* of soy beans, 3 *koku* of millet, and 1 *koku* 2 *to* of other beans (*jin*). These products were then sold back to the peasant consumers at highly inflated prices, the profits going to the domain government as a kind of tax. Moreover, the amounts had periodically become inflated far above the levels set in the original law, causing undue hardship. This practice was entirely abolished in the reforms.[43]

The results of the survey and accompanying reforms seem to have been mixed. Although reports issued after the project's completion suggested that, on balance, the survey would actually reduce revenue for the domainal government, albeit by a mere 1,000 *ryō*, current research indicates that in fact a small overall increase was more likely to have been the outcome of the reforms.[44] More important, perhaps, is the impact of the survey on those against whom, according to Yūkoku, it was principally directed: the rich landlords and other locals whose wealth had increased enormously in some areas at the expense of ordinary farmers. There is, in fact, some reason to believe that the survey succeeded in increasing the land assessments and thus the basis for taxing the true wealth of these local magnates. A rich farmer named Suda, in the southern region of the domain, found that his total *kokudaka* assessment rose as a result of the survey from roughly 92 to 131 *koku*, an increase of 42 percent. Other examples of increase are less spectacular, but apparently not particularly rare.[45]

43. Ibid., pp. 856–59. (1 *koku* = 180 liters; 1 *to* = 18 liters; 1 *shō* = 1.8 liters.)
44. Ibid., p. 881.
45. Ibid., pp. 849–51; Shibahara, *Meiji ishin*, p. 142. On the Suda, see chap. 6.

Reform as Representation

Although the survey and accompanying reforms may have been long-term financial successes, they did not seem at the time to have been so effective politically. An "intelligence report" (*kenbunsho*) submitted to Nariaki in 1844 (Kōka 1) observed that "many peasants are complaining of excessive taxes."[46] Tōko, too, opined that no one was really overjoyed about the results of the project: "The rich peasants are bitter, the poor peasants are not particularly happy, and the overall resources of the domain have been reduced." To Tōko, however, that was not of primary importance. The main point was achievement of "benevolent rule":

> Even if the fruits of benevolent government are not immediately visible, as the days go by they always tend to increase. Surely it is the height of benevolence to have gone into every last corner of the domain to measure the boundaries of fields which had become scrambled to the point of incomprehensibility, to judge the quality of the land, equalize the assets of the peasants, and correct imbalance in the stipends of samurai.... Now that we have long been at peace, in a world where those at the top as well as at the bottom of society pursue selfish profits, it has become extremely difficult to carry out land reform. The domain of Mito admittedly is small, but to have completed such a major enterprise without the slightest resistance on the part of tens of thousands of people bears witness of the depth to which my lord's virtue has penetrated the hearts of the people.[47]

Tōko's allusion to resistance provides a reminder that the survey was carried out in the face of considerable opposition. As the reforms were pressed forward by Nariaki and his supporters, discourse and action joined forces to systematically exclude other viewpoints regarding Mito's agricultural doldrums. The group loyal to Tachihara Suiken advocated rural development centering on the village elite.[48] The leading spokesman for that group, Komiyama Fūken, believed that differences in wealth among peasants generally reflected disparities in diligence and industriousness. Therefore, he argued, execution of Yūkoku's

---

46. *Mss* II/3, p. 860.
47. Fujita, *Hitachi obi*, pp. 469, 470–71.
48. See Inui Hiromi and Inoue Katsuo, "Chōshū-han to Mito-han," *Iwanami kōza Nihon rekishi* 12 (Tokyo: Iwanami Shoten, 1976), p. 310.

policy of "land equivalency" by means of a systematic cadastral survey would cause a decline in productivity. Moreover, a new demarcation of land against the interests of the rural elite might well lead to rebellion. A safer and more practical policy would be to support the existing elite and work through them in order to raise morale and generate new productive energy.

Komiyama suggested that district magistrates should reside in their region of responsibility and have the authority to select their own intermediate-level officials. Once the magistrates had established intimate relations with local residents, they should disseminate moral and practical knowledge, carry out research on agricultural problems, and keep themselves well informed regarding local developments. Such proposals conflicted with the reformist faction's decision in 1831 to unify rural policy by converting from seven districts to four and eliminating local garrisons.[49]

Although generally faultless in his understanding of rural circumstances and his ability to conceptualize practical solutions, Komiyama lacked the restorationist consciousness of Tōko and his faction. When Komiyama's views on rural policy were combined with other devices, such as the practice of conferring samurai status on commoners willing and able to pay a high price, his position seems to have represented a strong residual tendency in Mito toward social "piecemeal engineering."

In contrast, the reformists emphasized the holistic restructuring of institutions in such a way as to represent archetypical paradigms in historical context. That is not to say, of course, that the reformists were impractical. Timely instrumentality remained a central value, as represented vividly in Aizawa's *Shinron* and other major texts. Their efforts to adapt original paradigms to historical circumstances sometimes even led to measures that would have been criticized as unprincipled if suggested by conservatives.[50] On the other hand, unbridled utilitarianism and opportunism, along with the opposite extreme of "Taoist" naturalism, were among the negative poles against

---

49. Suzuki Fusako, "Mito-han Tenpō kaikaku no ichi kōsatsu," pp. 74–78. Shibahara Takuji sees the roots of bureaucratic centralization in such policies as the conversion from seven to four districts (*Meiji ishin*, p. 149).

50. Inui and Inoue, "Chōshū-han to Mito-han," pp. 313, 316–17.

which the reformists defined their own position. For them, practical action had always to be directed toward the end value of reconstituting a natural order, and natural order always required practical action to become manifest.

In its broadest and most fundamental meaning, the Tenpō land survey was an attempt to reduce the lacunae between history and an eternal archetype of order. The Mito reformers repeatedly compromised to accommodate the popular attitudes and other circumstances they perceived, but nothing was allowed for long to impede the imperative of creating order, of "inscribing" in the demarcation and contours of the land itself the overriding absolute of the Way. Such a conclusion in no way contradicts the obvious, practical implications of such reforms. As historians such as Tōyama, Shibahara, and others have observed, the samurai were responding to a pervasive crisis, which seemed to threaten the foundations of their existence as a privileged, managerial class. Rather, what is in question here is the manner in which the Mito samurai understood their situation and how they perceived the crisis primarily as an erosion of order and responded with action designed to reestablish control. The need for control, however, presented itself as a demand for rectification. Therefore, they used the means presented to them by history—the language and institutions which, through proliferation and corruption, had been responsible for obscuring the true Way—and, by redefining, purifying, and manipulating those media, sought to render them transparent again to the dictates of Heaven.

GROUNDING THE ARISTOCRACY

Once the reformists had restored order to the land through the proper definition of boundaries, their next priority was to rectify the relationship between the land and its hereditary rulers and protectors: the samurai. Here too the restorationist problematic provided original archetypes for emulation: concepts of the true nature of the samurai and of the unity of Heaven, land, and Man in "one body": "The original function of the samurai is to defend the land; that of the land to support the samurai. The two are by their very nature inseparable. When they are split apart, the land becomes barren, the samurai few and weak. That is the course of nature."[51] The samurai need the land as a practical matter as well, because without it they dissipate:

> Today's warriors live only in the castle towns. All they talk about is women, eating and drinking, actors and dramatic productions, gardening and floral arrangement, bird-catching and fishing. Their fencing practice and lance work are only for personal vendettas; their study of archery and gunnery are solely for show; their riding just for ceremonies.[52]

Not only do their own numbers dwindle in the cities, but they are no longer able to support and train the manpower necessary for war: "The original purpose in providing the samurai with a stipend is so that he might employ attendants.... [Nevertheless] When the samurai leave the land ... they get by with the services of unemployed city dwellers, setting them to a wide variety of tasks. Such idlers fill the castle towns, but they would be of no use at all if it ever came to war."[53] Conversely, the land needs the samurai for defense, of course, and also for economic reasons. When the warrior bureaucrats congregate in the cities, so does the rice from the countryside and with it the nation's wealth:

> When the samurai live in the cities ... instead of storing their rice in a frugal manner they dump it all on the market for cash.... Obviously a daily increase in those who sell their rice means a daily decrease in the amount of rice available to support the people: moreover, corresponding to that decrease is a constant increase in the volume of rice brought to the cities. In other words, people suffer shortages because the cities have a surfeit.[54]

Moreover, since the market is controlled by the merchants, "the life of the people is now in the hands of the townsmen."[55] All this is the result of the policy, begun by Hideyoshi and expanded by Tokugawa Ieyasu, of separating the samurai from the land.

51. Aizawa, *Shinron*, p. 67.
52. Ibid., pp. 63–65.
53. Ibid., pp. 67, 81.
54. Ibid., p. 85.
55. Ibid., pp. 89–91.

Reform as Representation

Hideyoshi and Ieyasu had contrived to bring order by strengthening the "trunk" at the expense of the "branches." That was a timely policy, well suited to the overriding necessity of pacifying the country, but now times had changed and priorities were different. The spirit of Ieyasu's instrumentality and decisiveness was worthy of imitation, but the content of his policy did not have to be slavishly retained:

> To allow the daimyo to develop strong armies within their domains, and to let retainers cultivate their own troops on their fief, thereby putting samurai and land back together again, is a policy of strengthening the branches. When both trunk and branches are strong, both warriors and weapons will be abundant and a spirit of dutifulness will overflow among the people. The national essence will be saved from disgrace only if domestic strength is completely mobilized in an expeditionary force, if our land and seas are swept clean of foreign barbarians, and if they dare not ever again approach our borders.[56]

In the case of Mito domain, the issue of *dochaku* (the return of samurai to the land) seems to have arisen primarily in relation to serious and enduring financial problems and secondarily as an answer to needs in the realms of defense, morale, and order in the countryside. Of course, proposals that the samurai be returned to the land were anything but novel in the Tokugawa period. Political commentators as various as Kumazawa Banzan and Ogyū Sorai had made similar recommendations much earlier, and (despite important differences between Ogyū and Kumazawa) had justified them in much the same socioeconomic and restorationist terms as Aizawa and Fujita. Lacking in those earlier treatises, however, is Aizawa's strong concern for coastal defense as a major concrete objective of the reform. Also peculiar to Mito is a more radical sense of crisis occasioned not only by the imminence of a foreign threat, but also by the presence in Mito discourse of a much sharper contradiction at the level of epistemology between confidence in a natural order rooted in the past and a poignant awareness of historical indeterminacy.

In Mito as in most domains, the ideal of the *hōken* (decentral-

---

56. Ibid., p. 71.

ized) system had been seriously diluted with a strong dose of centralization in the early stages of the Tokugawa period. According to the ideals of the decentralized system, the retainer receives a fief from the overlord and, in exchange for fealty, preserves the right to govern land and people within that fief, free from external interference. In fact, however, retainers had lost most of their police, judicial, and other discretionary powers early in the Tokugawa period, leaving them basically able only to collect taxes and exact corvée. As time went on, even the prerogative of collecting taxes was often transmuted into little more than the privilege of receiving from the daimyo a salary equivalent to the yield of a given amount of land.

That transformation was by no means uniform, however, and even in the early nineteenth century it was possible to distinguish two basic forms of relationship between samurai and the land. In the first, the retainer continued despite his limited powers to be granted a specific parcel of land rated at a given yield of rice (*kokudaka*). He was entitled to taxes from that land at a determinate rate. Of course, the real income he received varied from year to year, depending on harvest conditions. This was generally termed the fief system (*jikata chigyō*). The second was the result of measures taken in most domains to stabilize samurai incomes. According to this system, the retainer was paid annually from domainal coffers an amount of cash equivalent to the yield of a fief, which was now purely notional. Hence, the retainer became virtually a salaried employee of the daimyo. This cash-equivalent system was called *kuramae* or *mononari chigyō*.

In Mito, following the first land survey, completed in the Kan'ei era (1624–1644), most retainers seem to have collected taxes in kind directly from their own land, according to the fief system. Then, accompanying a general transition toward a money economy between the Genroku (1688–1703) and Kyōhō (1716–1736) periods, there was a shift away from the fief to the cash-equivalent system. One factor in that transition was the institution, in conformity with bakufu practice in the Kyōhō Reforms, of a system of supplementary stipends (*tashibun*) and accounts (*yakuryō*) attached to each position in the bureaucracy. Another was the increasing number of officials who for communication and administrative purposes lived permanently in Edo and were therefore more easily paid in currency than rice.[57]

In addition to putting pressure on domainal finances, the conversion from fief to cash-equivalent involved a major revolution in the allocation of land. In the Kan'ei era, the land under the direct jurisdiction of domainal authorities, termed *kurairichi*, had amounted to only 5,000 *koku*, compared to the 230,000 devoted to the fiefs of retainers (*kyūchi*). By the Tenpō period that ratio had nearly reversed.[58]

Fujita Tōko indicates that, to some extent, the transfer to cash-equivalent had been the intended result of domainal policy. In the early years the tax rate had been 50 percent for fiefs but only 40 for the cash-equivalent,[59] so the authorities apparently found it financially advantageous to increase the cash-equivalent portion. On the other hand, the extra prestige of the fief system, in addition to its higher tax rate, made it more desirable from the standpoint of retainers.

From the mid-Tokugawa on, however, harvests were poor, and actual tax receipts decreased. Samurai on the fief system saw their incomes fall measurably, while the rate according to which the cash stipends were determined remained the same. Therefore, despite the accompanying loss in prestige, many retainers now requested transfers to cash. The strain on domainal budgets increased as such transfers were granted, and even a reduction in the cash-equivalency rate from 40 to 38 percent failed to provide sufficient relief.[60] On the eve of the Tenpō Reforms, therefore, a policy of comprehensive reversion to fiefs enjoyed considerable financial as well as philosophical justification.

One of the most detailed proposals for such a reform is Tōko's memorial, *Jōge fuyū no gi* (The need for prosperity at all levels), submitted in 1837. Taking note of the economic dilemma facing the domain, he begins by laying down major principles. Finances must be based on a doctrine of agrarianism, because "silver and gold are secondary to goods, and goods all come

---

57. *Mss* II/3, pp. 127–28.
58. Ibid., p. 130; and Fujita Tōko, *Jōge fuyū no gi*, in Takasu, ed., *Fujita Tōko zenshū* 6:241.
59. Fujita, *Jōge fuyū no gi*, p. 241.
60. *Mss* II/3, p. 130.

from the land."⁶¹ Budgetary policy, in turn, must be based on the principle of "living within one's income" (*iru o hakatte izuru o nasu*), even though that was "often difficult in practice." Tōko then points out the inequities among the stipends of retainers resulting from the difference between the fief and cash-equivalent forms of support: "Those on the cash system receive a rate of 38 percent regardless of the quality of the harvest. Contrary to former times, that is quite a bit better than the rate at which taxes are actually collected. . . . It amounts, in fact, to a subsidy." Such injustices had to be rectified. Moreover, because "apportioning military duties in accord with the size of a samurai's stipend is like collecting taxes in accord with the harvest reaped by the peasants," something had to be done to make sure that retainers fulfilled their obligation by maintaining military capability. Tōko estimates that in an emergency the domain would be hard-pressed to mobilize a thousand troops out of a total retainer wealth of 160,000 *koku* and speculates that the number could be doubled if the size of the staff each samurai must maintain were pegged to the number of *koku* he was entitled to as a stipend.⁶²

In addition to proposing a set ratio between militarily capable attendants and stipend size, Tōko advances proposals to solve the problems of inequities in samurai income. In principle, he says, it would be best to transfer all Mito retainers presently on the cash system back to specific fiefs. In fact, however, he is afraid that those on the lower levels of the samurai hierarchy will resist out of the belief that someone above was trying to make a profit at their expense. Also, it would be difficult because, though 70 to 80 percent of the samurai on the cash-equivalent system were of undistinguished pedigree, the same percentage of the fief-system group were old and proud. Therefore, they would no doubt be offended to have the "new" families given the same status as they. In a manner comparable to Yūkoku's proposal for a cadastral survey, Tōko argues that the true principles of the fief system must be retained in devising a policy that will also be "in accord with the times [*jisei*]."⁶³

61. Fujita, *Jōge fuyū no gi*, p. 210.
62. Ibid., pp. 212, 222, 223–24, 226–27.
63. Ibid., pp. 242, 243.

In that spirit, Tōko proposes, first, that the fiefs of those still on the traditional system should be rearranged so that each is a coherent parcel rather than scattered across a number of villages. Second, all those on cash who were entitled to a stipend of more than 150 *koku* should be transferred back to the fief system. Third, the rate of payment for those still on the cash-equivalent system should equal the rate actually received from peasants, thereby ending their subsidy.[64]

In another memorial, entitled *Bushi dochaku no gi* (The need to return samurai to the land), Tōko discusses problems involved in the restoration of natural relationships between samurai and the land and makes several concrete proposals to actualize that ideal. Here, too, he distinguishes between principle, based on the archetypal symbiosis between warriors and the land, and historical realities, which seldom allow immediate and thorough replication of the archetype. Although "the ancients often discussed the evils of life in castle towns and the virtues of rooting the warriors on the land," nevertheless, "it is foolish under present circumstances to favor execution of such a policy to the letter of perfection."[65]

Among the difficulties were the attitudes of erstwhile warriors who had never experienced anything but city life and such economic factors as housing and transportation costs. Indeed, "if even in the age of Mitsukuni it had been impossible to overcome the evils of city life by placing all mounted samurai on the land, how much more difficult would such an accomplishment be under present circumstances." Nevertheless, the idea should certainly not be abandoned: "If [differences between the] trends and institutional frameworks of long ago and those of today are taken carefully into account and we proceed gradually, it should be quite feasible."[66]

Tōko also invokes the classical alternatives by which systems of rule and therefore the relationship among rulers, land, and people were most often discussed: the decentralized ("feudal") system (*hōken no sekai*) and the centralized system (*gunken no sekai*).[67] China was decentralized up to the Chou period (1122–

---

64. Ibid., p. 245.
65. Fujita Tōko, *Bushi dochaku no gi*, in Takasu, ed., *Fujita Tōko zenshū* 6:258.
66. Ibid., p. 266.
67. Ibid., p. 268.

256 B.C.) but then centralized. In Japan as well, the early system of provincial governors (*kuni no miyatsuko*) was a form of decentralization, and later a more centralized system was established in imitation of the T'ang dynasty. But, contrary to the Chinese experience, the Japanese middle ages again brought a trend toward decentralization, as warriors and their bands took to the land. Finally, at the beginning of the Tokugawa period in the early seventeenth century, the samurai were pulled in to the castle towns.

In Tōko's view, however, only the Chou-period form of decentralization was applicable to Japan in the nineteenth century. The basic difference between decentralization (*hōken*) in the ordinary sense and that of the Chou was that in the latter "the warriors were not mixed in with the people," so there was less danger of their "planning great rebellions under the command of local lords." Therefore, "under present circumstances return to the land should be discussed on the basis of the principle of decentralization, but with reference primarily to the Chou system." If that were the case, it would be possible to avoid both the urban phenomenon of "potted-plant warriors" (samurai who live in the city away from their natural element, the land) and also the danger of rebellion against central authority.[68]

In line with such premises, Tōko makes the following proposals: (1) Retainers with stipends in excess of 150 *koku* should be placed on fiefs within 2 *ri* of the castle so they would be able to commute to their jobs there. Those of less than 150 *koku* should continue to reside in the castle town; (2) Only retainers with stipends of more than 500 *koku* should be allowed to maintain large residences in the castle town, whereas those with more than 1,000 *koku* would be free to establish residences as far away as they liked; (3) The area near the castle in which small fiefs were located should be divided into four or five sectors (*kumi*), and a prominent individual should be put in charge of each to facilitate communication; (4) Samurai with fiefs should be allowed to own their fields and cultivate them independently, but sale and purchase of land should be restricted; (5) An academy (*gakkō*) should be constructed in the

---

68. Ibid., pp. 271, 272.

castle town, and local schools (*kyōkō*) in each sector; (6) The castle town should be reduced in size to the equivalent of a district (*kōri*); and (7) Thirty or so retainers should be moved to their new fiefs each year. Because the samurai above 150 *koku* numbered 300, the transition was to take ten years.[69]

Tōko's proposals were eventually instituted in substance. In the meantime, they met with considerable opposition from those whose lives would be directly affected. It was only after completion of the land survey that further progress could be made with regard to samurai reversion to the land and reform of the stipend system. Paralleling those issues, however, were the problems of reducing the staff in Edo and providing for defense by stationing military forces along the coast. Here Nariaki and the reformists had their way more readily.

Mito was a collateral house particularly close to the bakufu, and of all the domains was the only one exempted from the *sankin kōtai* system by which daimyo and their retinues were required to alternate their residence between Edo and their castle town. The Mito daimyo lived permanently in Edo. Although this circumstance conferred some extra prestige, it also entailed a number of problems, not the least of which was the financial strain of maintaining parallel staffs. Hence, Mito had instituted its own system of alternate attendance, according to which samurai officials worked a year in Edo and a year in Mito. Gradually, however, only a certain group tended to stay in Edo, and they vigorously resisted any suggestion that they should abandon their cosmopolitan life for the provinces. Their manner of life and thought diverged from that of the Mito contingent, and they required a large budget for maintenance.

After a number of proposals and controversies, Nariaki finally decided in spring 1836 to institute a new austerity program and return a large contingent of officials and their families to Mito. This was the repeal of permanent residency, which had constituted one of Nariaki's four major priorities. Tōko quotes Nariaki's announcement:

> All the other daimyo, including those of the other two collateral houses [Kii and Owari], must alternate their residence between the

---

69. Ibid., pp. 278–86; *Mss* II/3, p. 133. A *ri* equals 3.93 km.

castle and Edo in order to protect the shogun's house and prepare for an emergency. While in their case the retainers of the daimyo are also obliged to travel back and forth . . . [which they do] unstintingly, you have forgotten your original orders and made of your temporary garrison a permanent home. Should an emergency arise under such circumstances, women and children would be crying and yelling as they try to transport household effects. That would hinder you in the loyal performance of your duty. However, when we have tried to move some of you—who have now become lifetime residents of Edo—back to Mito one or two at a time, there has been no end to the agitation and upset. Hence I have now made up my mind to send a large contingent of samurai back to Mito all at once.[70]

By autumn, about two hundred samurai, their families and attendants had returned to Mito, where massive confusion apparently ensued for the remainder of the year as they sought housing, reimbursement for expenses, and so on.[71]

The transfer back to Mito at this stage involved little more than a move from a large city to a considerably smaller one, but it was consistent with the spirit of return to the land as discussed in Tōko's memorials.

In January and May of the same year (1836), two genuine forms of return were carried out. In January two Mito retainers of 200 *koku* each were granted fiefs in Ōnuma and Tomobe near the coast where they were expected to live permanently and maintain coastal defense garrisons. In May, moreover, in a measure much more momentous in scale and implication, Nariaki created the post of Coastal Defense Commander (*kaibō sōshi*) for the 10,000-*koku* retainer Yamanobe Yoshitsune and located him in the coastal village of Sukegawa (in modern times, the city of Hitachi). Once appropriations for the construction of residences and other facilities were secure (over the opposition of conservatives in the upper reaches of the domainal hierarchy), Yamanobe, his 28 samurai retainers, 87 foot-soldiers and attendants, and 132 others made the trek to their new home. Yamanobe assumed command of the Tomobe and Ōnuma garrisons in addition to establishing his own, built gun emplace-

70. Fujita, *Hitachi obi*, p. 338.
71. *Mss* II/3, p. 137.

ments, and advanced Mito's defense preparations to a new level.[72]

Finally, after completion of the land survey, work was begun to reform the stipend system and return retainers to the fief system. Reformists began to parcel out land in spring 1843 and in midsummer announced the impending transfer from cash-equivalent back to fiefs. In the autumn, they cancelled all existing fiefs and placed land under the control of district commissioners to be inspected and put in order.

Preparations were complete by the third month of the following year, and on the ninth day of that month all samurai with stipends of more than 100 *koku* gathered in the castle to receive their new fiefs. As Tōko describes the occasion:

> Each was personally handed a certificate on which were recorded the number of *koku* at which he was rated, the names of villages in his fief, the number of peasant households each contained, and other details. All were stamped with the vermilion seal [*goshuin*]. All retainers ranking above those with so-called ordinary dress [*yoriai* and below] gathered for their presentation in the "white library," those above the rank of *monogashira* in the "black library," and those in the very lowest ranks in the great hall. It was pointed out to Nariaki that the number of those from Yamanobe on down with fiefs of more than 100 *koku* was very large, and to spare him the tiring process of presenting all the certificates it was suggested that the elders [*toshiyori*] handle distribution to the lower ranks. Nariaki replied, "Is there anything more enjoyable for a sovereign than bestowing fiefs on his retainers? I want to complete the task." So he handed them out to all. The presentations to Nakayama Bizen-no-kami and the others who lived permanently in Edo were made by Nariaki's heir, Yoshiatsu.[73]

Appended to each certificate were detailed provisions governing control of the fiefs and the collection of taxes. Based on these documents, it appears that the main points of the reform were as follows.[74] All samurai above 100 *koku* were converted to the fief system, and in accord with Tōko's proposal in *Bushi dochaku no gi*, most retainers were located near the castle town,

---

72. Ibid., pp. 218–19, 221–23.
73. Fujita, *Hitachi obi*, pp. 465–66.
74. *Mss* II/3, pp. 885–87.

rather than "mixed in with the people." Low-stipended samurai were given villages nearest the castle, and the higher the stipend the farther away they were positioned. One of each retainer's villages was always within 4 or 5 *ri*. Villages within 1 *ri* of the castle and those with large markets or other peculiarities were excluded. Samurai ranking between 100 and 150 *koku* received two villages, those with 200 to 300 *koku* got three, those between 300 and 600 *koku* got four, 700 to 900 got five, over 1,000 received five or six, and those above 5,000 *koku* got twelve or thirteen.

An effort was made to combine both productive and relatively unproductive villages in each fief so as to avoid the widespread disparities in yield experienced in the past even among samurai of equal rank.

Clear specifications were issued detailing which households in each village would belong to a given retainer steward (*jitō*). This procedure was designed to rectify an earlier situation in which fiefs had been spread over a number of villages, and a given peasant might be nominally subordinate to two or three stewards. Under such circumstances, it was impossible for close bonds to develop between lord and peasant. As Tōko observed, under the previous system empathy (*ninjō*) between fief-holder and peasant had been precluded. It had also been difficult to mobilize peasants for military duty, and there had even been cases in which villagers were abused by the stewards or their representatives. Now, however:

> Each peasant definitely has only one steward as lord, and tax collection is carried out only by officials. Therefore, not only do the fief stewards no longer worry about inequities in yield, but stewards and peasants can form close relationships, and the peasants no longer are set upon by many different authorities. While this may not seem consistent with the original meaning of *chigyō* [fief], it is a good law that has reformed all the evils of the era in a single stroke. If our descendants carry out its provisions faithfully in accord with the intentions of our lord [Nariaki], it will allow them to deepen relations of mutual respect and obligation [*ongi*] between fief-holders and peasants, and to augment military strength.[75]

---

75. Fujita, *Hitachi obi*, p. 468.

Reform as Representation

For each 100 *koku* of rank, a retainer received eight units of mountain, forest, or other nonagricultural land for lumber, fuel, and feed for horses. The purpose was primarily to strengthen their capacity for military mobilization.

The number of *koku* at which each samurai was rated was maintained, even though the total resources of the domain had been reduced as a result of the land survey. Moreover, the actual percentage they received in taxes each year was equalized to the rate in effect for domainal lands (*kurairibun*), so that in an average year a 100-*koku* rating would provide the equivalent of seventy bags of unhulled rice and 8 *ryō* in cash. For those of 150 *koku* or less, two extra bags of rice were added on. Then, in years when the unhulled rice gathered as tax in kind (*nengu*) was in excess of the standard amount, those bags were deposited to the domainal account; when it was less, the difference was made up by adding bags from the domainal account. Hence, the retainers' income was stabilized, and parity was maintained between the domainal land and the portion devoted to retainer fiefs.

A retainer collected unhulled rice from his fief directly, and cash payments for dry-field rice were collected by the district magistrate's office. Strict regulations were to govern the collection of taxes in kind, and the entire process was supposed to be controlled at the provincial level. Corvée and other matters affecting the peasants were also regulated. The standard corvée for each 100 *koku* was the labor of one individual per household and two horses; anything more required the assent of the provincial magistrate.

As with other reforms instituted in the Tenpō period, the realignment between samurai and the land arose out of a continuing political struggle, in the course of which other concrete alternatives were offered to solve some of the problems. Komiyama Fūken, for example, espoused a vision of return to the land that was quite inconsistent with Tōko's. His definition of the problem also differed. Komiyama's immediate concerns focused on defense and rural renewal, and he was less worried than Tōko about where samurai lived and how they were paid. From Komiyama's point of view, the wholesale return of samurai to the land meant that they would have to commute to their jobs in the castle, and that was likely to increase the burdens placed on rural residents along the routes. Rather than focusing on the samurai, Komiyama argued, it would be best to begin by arming a few able villagers who already had horses and commanded the trust of their peers. They could continue to farm, while remaining ready to perform military functions in time of crisis. Then, high-ranking samurai without bureaucratic positions, third and fourth sons of warrior households without hereditary stipends, and samurai who were anxious to move to the land could gradually be returned to rural environments in the future as this seemed advantageous.[76]

Just as in the case of the land survey, Fujita and the other reformists rejected Komiyama's approach at the time it was proffered. Ironically, however, in the Ansei period (1854–1860) the Fujita faction itself became involved in an effort to arm and provide training for rural elites through the provincial schools.

SPREADING THE WAY

Following demarcation of land boundaries and adjustment of the nexus between land and society, the third major element of Nariaki's reformist vision was the ordering of thought and action through education. In concrete terms, this involved two major projects: construction of a domainal academy (*hankō*) to train samurai, and establishment of district schools (*kyōkō*) to provide practical and moral training to local elites.

It was essential to construct institutions to propagate the Way because, as *Shinron* and other texts made clear, the truly natural Way had been obscured and distorted by foreign doctrines. Because people no longer acted spontaneously in accordance with the Way, it was necessary to teach them to follow their own natures and the Great Way of Heaven-and-Earth. Nowhere was this made more clear than in *Kōdōkanki* (The manifesto of Mito Academy).

In mid-1837, Tokugawa Nariaki ordered Fujita Tōko to draft an inscription as the conceptual basis for the establishment of a domainal academy. Tōko's draft was then sent to Aizawa Sei-

---

76. Suzuki Fusako, "Mito-han Tenpō kaikaku no ichi kōsatsu," pp. 78–79.

shisai and Aoyama Nobuyuki (1776–1843) for their criticisms and additions, and also submitted to Satō Issai (1772–1859) who was then teaching at the bakufu academy in Edo. Once his advisers had made their contributions, Nariaki approved a final version, which was then published under his name in March 1838. At that time the document was merely called the *Gakkō gohimon* (School inscription), and a name had not yet been chosen for the academy itself. The names Kōdōkan for the school and *Kōdōkanki* for the manifesto were apparently decided upon only after long deliberation, ultimately by adopting the first two characters used in Tōko's draft.[77]

The first few sentences of the *Kōdōkanki* encapsulate the fundamental paradox of the Mito problematic. Tōko says: "What does *kōdō* mean? It means that people spread the Way. What is the Way? It is the great principle of Heaven-and-Earth, from which people are never separated even for an instant." Combining phrases from the *Analects* and the *Chung yung*, the passage indicates that the Way is an inseparable aspect of the eternal order of Heaven-and-Earth. It is inherent in society as well, and hence people can never be alienated from it in any ultimate sense. On the other hand, human mediation is essential to its propagation: it can only be actualized by people acting, as it were, on Heaven's behalf. The Way is not created by man, but, even as a natural principle, it requires their effort for its realization.

The document then elaborates further on the relations among the Way, history, and human action. The Way is eternal and absolute because of its origins in divine cosmogony:

> I reverently submit that the divine sages of old erected the eternal Way and passed it down to their imperial descendants. Thus, Heaven and Earth were in their place, and all things gained life. [The imperial descendants] rule over Heaven and Earth by virtue of their dependence on the Way in all things. The imperial throne is eternal in [its reliance on] the Way; the national essence is sanctified by the Way; the people are made peaceful by the Way; the foreign barbarians are subjugated by the Way.

---

77. *Mss* II/3, pp. 166–70.

Through the virtue and constant good works of the line of emperors, "the Way gradually expands and becomes clearer without any augmentation." Historically, however, events occurred that impeded such natural processes. Since the middle ages,

> heretical doctrines have deluded the people and bewildered the world. Vulgar Confucians and opportunistic scholars have forgotten Japan and followed China. The imperial authority has declined. Incidents and rebellions have occurred repeatedly. For an exceedingly long time, the Great Way of Heaven-and-Earth has been unclear.

Then, in the early seventeenth century, Tokugawa Ieyasu "quelled disorder and restored the correct Way." Tokugawa Yorifusa and Mitsukuni played an analogous role on the level of the Mito domain. To the present day, therefore, the people have "basked in the virtue" of the Mito daimyos who have followed the founders. Accordingly, "their humble successor [Nariaki] is deeply conscious of the need to spread the Way and exalt the virtues of his ancestors." This is the purpose of the academy.

Having distinguished the original, ontological primacy of the Way from the disruptive effects of history on the phenomenal level, and having explained the need for action in order to represent the Way in human affairs, the *Kōdōkanki* turns to a brief enunciation of educational doctrine. Here it pays major attention to the unities that, if perfectly realized, would represent the fundamental identity of Heaven-and-Earth and therefore actualize the original, self-regulating order of the Way. First, the unity of Shinto and Confucianism is explained in terms of the worship of the Shinto god Takemi-katsuchi-no-kami and Confucius:

> Why is it that Takemi-katsuchi-no-kami was originally worshipped? Because that deity aided Amaterasu Ōmikami in her great deeds in the age of the gods and its spirit came to rest in Hitachi. Therefore, we worship that deity to memorialize the origin of the Way, to honor the deity's divine virtue, and to make the people aware of the Way's origin.

Takemi-katsuchi-no-kami was enshrined at Kashima Shrine, and when the Kōdōkan was built a branch shrine was established on the grounds of that institution. The other major shrine of the Kōdōkan was the Kōshi-rō (Confucius Hall): "Why do we construct a shrine to Confucius in the Kōdōkan? Confucius synthesized the Way of the Three Kingdoms and we therefore love his virtue, study his teachings, and seek to show the people that it is no accident that his Way grows ever broader and clearer."

Therefore, the people of Mito "serve the Ancient Way of Japan and supplement it with the Confucianism of China." Also, "The gods are revered and Confucianism is respected without inclining one-sidedly to either." Other unities are merely listed: "Loyalty and filial piety are undivided; letters (*bun*) and military arts (*bu*) do not conflict; scholarship and practical enterprise (*jigyō*) are the same in effect."[78] And, of course, the very establishment of the academy symbolized the unity of government and education. As Tōko observes in his commentary on the document, it is precisely the historical division of government from learning that necessitates the establishment of educational institutions: "Government and education are not united, scholarship and politics are split apart. That is why the Great Way is unclear."[79]

Once all such unities are consummated, the minds of the people will also be unified, and present realities will finally accord with an original archetype: "If the thoughts of the people are unified and their strength mobilized to begin to repay their infinite obligations to the realm, the intentions of Yorifusa and Mitsukuni will be preserved forever and the spirits of the divine emperors in Heaven will shine forth unimpeded."[80]

Actual construction of the academy did not begin for another two years after publication of the *Kōdōkanki*, and the academy was not opened until midsummer 1841. Even then it was only provisional, because most of the buildings were still incomplete.

The need for such a facility had been contemplated since the beginning of the Tenpō period in 1830, but plans were not actually made until Nariaki's first visit to the domain in May and

---

78. The text of the *Kōdōkanki* is reproduced with notes in Imai, Seya, and Bitō, eds., pp. 230–32.
79. Fujita Tōko, *Kōdōkanki jutsugi* in Imai, Seya, and Bitō, eds., pp. 236–37.
80. *Kōdōkanki*, p. 232.

June 1833. Despite Nariaki's determination, the project met with obstacles from the beginning. The major factor was a series of poor harvests, which resulted in famine, financial doldrums, and popular unrest. A contributing factor, obviously exacerbated by economic instability, was the strong opposition of leading officials in the domainal government. Komiyama Fūken and others argued from the experience of other domains that schools were related only tangentially to practical utility and in the end amounted to little more than ostentation. Therefore, particularly under the present circumstances, the domain should content itself with the historiographical institute (Shōkōkan) as a scholarly establishment. The high-ranking domainal official Fujita Teisei (1774–1846) agreed but was rebuked by Nariaki for resting content with such inadequacy.[81] Backed by reformists such as Fujita Tōko, Toda Tadahisa (1804–1855), and Yamaguchi Tokumasa (1783–1842), the daimyo persisted and eventually succeeded in arranging a special grant from the bakufu, which he devoted to the project.

Despite the continued delay of construction plans as a result of bad harvests, Nariaki decided in 1839 that the academy should be located at the site where twelve high-ranking retainers had their mansions. They were subsequently forced to move. Nariaki also went ahead and named Aizawa Seishisai and Aoyama Nobuyuki as "head professors" (*kyōju tōshu*) and Sugiyama Chūryō (1801–1845) and Aoyama Nobumitsu (1808–1871) as professors (*kyōju*) of the future institution. Actual construction finally began in 1840 during Nariaki's second sojourn in Mito. The preliminary opening ceremonies held in August 1841 were attended by a crowd of about 3,000 individuals, including samurai, Shinto priests, mountain ascetics (*yamabushi*) who practiced the discipline of Shugendō, rustic samurai, and low-ranking retainers. Events included lectures by Aizawa on the *Hsiao ching* (Classic of filial piety) and Aoyama Nobuyuki on the early historical account, the *Nihon shoki*. Classes were begun soon after the preliminary opening, and it was not long before several hundred students were reportedly enrolled. At that time there were twenty-two faculty members in Mito and nine in Edo;

---

81. *Mss* II/3, pp. 163–65.

Reform as Representation 119

at the peak of activity in the Keiō period (1865–1867), however, these numbers rose to fifty-two and twenty-two, respectively.[82]

Apparently to reinforce the impression, created by such major construction, that reforms were proceeding at a lively pace, in early autumn Nariaki held a military exercise, called the Oitorigari, for his retainers on the outskirts of the castle town.

The final complex measured 178,200 square meters and was easily the largest such facility in Tokugawa Japan. At the time of the provisional opening, however, only a small part of the facility was completed, and operations proceeded on an ad hoc basis. Neither the branch of Kashima Jingū to enshrine Takemikatsuchi-no-kami nor the Kōshi-rō to enshrine Confucius had been installed. Once constructed, the two facilities were to be located in the central portion of the complex and would together form the spiritual and religious focal point of the whole.[83]

In addition to the *Kōdōkanki*, educational philosophy was outlined in the *Kōdōkan gakusoku* (Rules of Mito Academy) written by Aizawa and Aoyama and then revised and officially authored by Nariaki. Consisting of nine articles, the document admonished students to read for profound meaning and to think about what they read; to study widely but concentrate their efforts on Japanese history from the ancient chronicles and strive to understand the Great Way of the Divine Sages (*shinsei no ōdō*); to follow the Way of liberal and military arts, rather than contenting themselves solely with technical proficiency; to practice the meaning of unity between learning and practical action (*jigyō*); to avoid the dangers of biased or rigid scholarship; and to cultivate a state of mind suitable to the reading of the classics and national histories. Finally, students should "reverently follow the calling of discipleship, associate with each other courteously, encourage each other in loyalty and filial piety, cleave to the shadows in pursuing their studies, and become useful resources."[84]

Like all students, of course, the elite offspring of samurai who attended the academy were not always model disciples in

---

82. Ibid., pp. 171, 1121.
83. Ibid., p. 171.
84. Ibid., pp. 1120–21. The complete text of the *Kōdōkan gakusoku* is in Takasu, ed., *Mitogaku taikei* 5 : 183–88.

the mold cast by Nariaki. In a memorial of 1856, a number of instructors complained that students not only were often lazy, but tended to focus their energies on either the liberal or the military arts rather than paying equal attention to each. They also were likely to emphasize the Chinese classics over native Japanese texts.[85]

Attendance was obligatory for samurai, but the number of required school-days per month increased with rank. Eldest sons of retainers rated at 300 *koku* and above, for example, had to attend fifteen days; the sons of ordinary samurai (*heishi*) attended only about ten days. Exceptions were made so that those in official positions could attend only half-time, and those over 40 years of age were exempted. Once the final opening of the institution had taken place in 1857, the training schedule prescribed liberal arts (*bun*) in the morning (9:00–12:00) and military arts (*bu*) in the afternoon until about 4:00 P.M. On entering the grounds in the morning, a student would submit his name card to serve as the basis for attendance records. Annual reports on student attendance and discipline were made by the school to the inspector (*metsuke*) who meted out rewards and punishments accordingly.[86]

Admission to the military arts portion of the training was open without examination, but the liberal arts portion required an examination on the *Analects* and the *Hsiao ching*. Those who were not able to pass the examination by age 15 were sent to the military library and made to read works on strategy and tactics written in the simple Japanese syllabary. After 1857, when the final opening ceremonies took place, those who failed to complete their studies by age 20 were admitted to a special program in the academy's liberal arts section where they were schooled in military affairs and history through the use of syllabic texts.[87]

An aspirant was called a lecture student (*kōshūsei*) once he gained admission to the liberal arts course. He was placed in one of several smaller groups (*kumi*) and taught through a combination of lectures and group reading (*kaidoku*) sessions. As his understanding of the texts increased, he could become an oral presentation student (*rinkōsei*). At this level, he would periodi-

---

85. *Mss* II/3, pp. 1134–36.
86. Ibid., p. 1125.
87. Ibid., p. 1118.

Reform as Representation 121

cally take his turn in giving oral interpretations of texts that he had studied under the guidance of an assistant professor (*jokyō*) or instructor (*kundō*). Usually he would begin with the *Analects*, pass from there to the *Mencius*, and then advance to the *Ch'un-ch'iu*. If examinations revealed him to be a superior learner, he could become a student in residence (*kyogakusei*). He would then receive a small private room for his studies, be allowed to attend lectures delivered by the professors, and also be qualified to take the major examinations offered annually in the autumn. The student in residence pursued his study under the tutelage of a professor or head professor, and each month submitted for their criticism two essays (one in Japanese [*wabun*], the other in Chinese [*kanbun*]), and a poem.[88]

The call in the *Kōdōkanki* for unification of the minds of the people required more than just an academy for Mito samurai. An important dimension of the Tenpō reforms was the effort to clarify and rectify relationships not only among samurai themselves and between them and their lord, but also between samurai and the people. Similarly, in the realm of education, a commitment was made to local schools and the dissemination of moral and practical learning among local elites, which included rich peasants, rustic samurai, village leaders, Shinto priests, and other non-Buddhist religious practitioners, such as mountain ascetics.

As early as 1830, Aizawa Seishisai had set forth the system of the Chinese Chou dynasty as a paradigm for education. As outlined in the *Chou li* (Rites of Chou) and the *Li chi* (Book of rites), that system provided for "higher schools" (*daigaku*) and for three varieties of "lower schools" (*shōgaku*), including a local institution (*kyōkō*) for every 12,500 households. Noting that adequate education was difficult to enforce under the existing Japanese system of heredity rank and stipend, he opined that adoption of a program modeled on that of the Chou would enable talent and ability to be cultivated at all levels of the social hierarchy:

> If the ancient decentralized system [*hōken no sei*] is clarified, and the trends of the times [*jisei*] taken into account in a way consistent with the intentions of the ancient sages; if higher and lower schools are

88. Ibid., pp. 1124–25.

established in consideration of different cultural conditions; and if the sons of retainers are educated in such a manner; it will be only a matter of time until manners and morals are refined and the domain flourishes.[89]

Similarly Tōko, in commenting on the injunction in the *Kōdōkanki* that the minds of the people must be unified, observes in a manner reminiscent of Ogyū Sorai that, though the role of the subject is to cultivate virtue, practice the Way, and serve the sovereign, that of the sovereign is to aggregate the thoughts and activate the collective strengths of his subjects. As a result, sovereign and subjects form a single body, and the Way is actualized.[90] Such a vision of the role of the ruler implies the unity of education and government, and requires the establishment of institutions through which the talents and practical skills of the people can be identified and cultivated: "The Sages devoted particular attention to schools for the people, emphasizing particularly filial piety and service to elders."[91]

Education, like the rectification of land boundaries and the return of samurai to the land, was oriented to the actualization in special historical circumstances of an original state in which virtue and obedience emerged spontaneously in a self-regulating polity. Noting that education was often combined in ancient times with rewards and punishments to enforce compliance, Tōko adds the caveat that most likely such instruments were used only on those who were incapable of being educated. Because the *Shih ching* (Book of odes) says the "people observe the unchanging Way and love virtue," there must have been circumstances in which law was rendered superfluous by the education and natural virtue of the people. In later ages, however:

> Education of the common people was no longer considered very important, filial piety and respect for the aged were no longer emphasized, and when those ignorant of the teachings committed crimes they were punished immediately. . . . It is not surprising that the people now thought, "if one does not run afoul of the law he has no reason to feel he has done anything wrong."[92]

---

89. Ibid., p. 1113.
90. Fujita *Kōdōkanki jutsugi*, pp. 334–35. Also see Shibahara, *Meiji ishin*, pp. 148–49.
91. Imai, Seya, and Bitō, eds., p. 336.
92. Ibid.

Tokō's ideal is for administration to be carried out in such a manner that rewards and punishments are unnecessary. Partial and expedient measures, in other words, are poor substitutes for an archetypal unity between ruler and subject fostered through truly benevolent government, religion, and education.

Nevertheless, historical forces not only were capable of disrupting such an ideal polity, but had to be taken fully into account when means were devised to reactualize the natural order. Economic conditions, the resistance offered by powerful political forces in the domain, and Japan's particular cultural tradition made the mechanical transplanting of Chou-period models impractical. As with all other reforms, the problem was how to restore the spirit of education and politics that informed those original archetypes, while taking account of historical exigencies. The establishment in the Tenpō period of three district schools (*kyōkō*) and the planning of a fourth exemplify such an effort.

Schools actually constructed in the Tenpō period were the Keigyōkan in Minato-mura in 1835, the Ekishūkan in Ōtamura in 1837 and the Kōgeikan (later Kashūkan) in Ōkubo-mura in 1839. They were in the south, north, and east districts (*kōri*), respectively. The fourth (Jiyōkan) was planned for the western district but not actually constructed until 1850. It is obvious from the systematic manner in which they were planned and established that guidance and initiative came from domainal authorities in Mito, including Nariaki himself.[93] Only two local schools had been established earlier, without central guidance from the Mito authorities. The Keiikan had been built in 1804 in the southern village of Ogawa as a training center for medical practitioners. Nobukata Gakkō, on the other hand, was set up in 1807 by district magistrate Komiyama Fūken for the purpose of providing moral instruction to peasants. It was aimed, therefore, at a lower stratum of the population than were the Keiikan and the Tenpō-period schools.[94]

93. *Mss* II/3, p. 200. Local schools of this sort were by no means unique to Mito. According to Herbert Passin, the first *kyōkō* (Passin employs the reading *gōkō*) were established in Okayama in 1667 and proliferated throughout many domains in the first half of the nineteenth century. (*Society and Education in Japan* [Tokyo: Kodansha, 1982], pp. 37–40).

94. See Seya Yoshihiko, "Kinsei kyōiku no chihōteki tenkai" in Chihōshi Kenkyū Kyōgikai, eds., *Ibaraki-ken no shisō bunka no rekishiteki kiban* (Tokyo: Yūzankaku, 1978), p. 163.

In the case of the Keigyōkan, Nariaki pressed forward with land purchase and other plans during his visit to the domain in 1833 and 1834, and it appears that domainal involvement in the project increased following the actual construction in 1835. The actual building and equipping of the facility, however, were carried out largely through local participation. Rural notables who contributed money, books, and time were often rewarded with official recognition or posts in school administration or instruction.

The collection of money and materials for the Ekishūkan began as soon as construction plans were made, and, according to one inventory, 4,953 books were contributed by locals for the library. Similarly, surviving documents indicate that the Kashūkan at one time maintained a library of 3,700 volumes, most of which were probably contributed by locals or purchased with local funds. In content, the latter were primarily Chinese classics, with a large number of nativist classics and medical books thrown in.[95] Letters of thanks from the district magistrate's office were sent to major donors, and, in some cases, such tokens as serving trays embossed with the Mito crest were presented.[96]

The actual administration of programs was carried out by the school director (*kanmori*), who in the case of Ekishūkan received an annual salary of 5 *ryō* in four installments. The directors were often local luminaries or reformist samurai who had displayed an interest and a high level of capability in scholarly pursuits.

The major portion of the instruction offered in the district schools constructed in the Tenpō period was devoted to medical training. Indeed, there is some evidence that Nariaki explicitly rejected a focus on popular moral education. Although he was to change his views by the Ansei period of 1854–1860, during the Tenpō Reforms Nariaki appears to have felt that education was wasted on peasants, who should be encouraged to spend their time on agriculture. His highest priority appears to have been medical education.[97]

95. Seya Yoshihiko, *Mito-han kyōkō no shiteki kenkyū* (Tokyo: Yamakawa Shuppansha, 1976), p. 199. A complete list is in ibid., pp. 192–98.
96. Ibid., p. 182.
97. Seya, "Kinsei kyōiku no chihōteki tenkai," pp. 164–166.

Local doctors were required to attend instructional sessions at the school once a month or so and were reprimanded by district authorities if they failed to attend with a spirit of cooperation. Sessions at Ekishūkan focused not only on medical practice and technology, but on problems of medical ethics as well. Used in that connection was an early text by Nariaki, apparently devoted to certain lamentable tendencies in the medical profession.[98]

THE DOMAIN AS MICROCOSM

The reform of institutions in Mito during the Tenpō period dramatizes what has been referred to as secession: the propensity of various occupational groups, religious communities, administrative units, and other elements to withdraw, in spirit, from the Tokugawa order. Although, for the past two centuries, they had accepted their role as parts in a larger system, they now reconstituted themselves as more or less autonomous entities. Indeed, each sought to stand as a microcosm in relation to the whole.[99]

For Mito reformists, of course, it was the domain (*han*) that symbolically retained the capacity to stand on its own; that capacity was proven in the reforms outlined above. The reforms demonstrated, in other words, that institutional patterns authenticated by their association with the divine origins of the nation and the universal imperative of the Way could be adequately represented within the temporal and spatial confines of the domain. Archetypal unities among land, the polity, and Heaven itself could be actualized by a "restorationist" daimyo to provide a model of how the national essence might be brought to full fruition in the nation as a whole.

Nariaki reveals the degree of his concern for the integrity of the *han* or house (*ie*) of the daimyo, in his *Kokushi-hen* (Exhortation):

> As it is written in the *Hsiao ching*, each person from the Son of Heaven down to the average man performs filial duties in accord

---

98. Seya, *Mito-han kyōkō*, pp. 180, 179.
99. Harootunian, "Ideology as Conflict," in Najita and Koschmann, eds., pp. 23, 39.

with his station. Similarly when, in an attempt to repay their obligations to Amaterasu or Tokugawa Ieyasu, people mistakenly ignore their immediate overlord or father and instead discharge loyalty directly to the court or the bakufu, it is difficult to avoid the sin of "improper attention to status ranking" [*senran*].[100]

Here Nariaki is expressing a sentiment that, according to Tahara Tsuguo, formed an indispensable, if covert, element of what he calls the Tokugawa ideology. From the perspective of the Tokugawa bakufu, the political order was legitimized by a principle of "benevolent government" (*jinsei*) by which the daimyo were subordinated to the Tokugawa in a form of "patrimonialism." Tahara summarizes the characteristics of that ideology as follows:

> In the first place, it portrays the bakuhan order as a political organization designed to provide peace and security to the people, that is, as a civil government. Second, within that political organization, the shogun, backed by the transcendental and omnipotent presence of Heaven, exercises overwhelming superiority as commander and supervisor of the daimyo, who in turn bear direct responsibility for civil government. In other words, power is concentrated in the position of the shogun. The shogun himself is theoretically responsible for the vast area of bakufu lands. Thirdly, the function of the daimyo is limited to civil government, and of course he must defer to the shogun and remain receptive to the shogun's command and supervision. He is essentially a regional administrator, liable to unilateral transfer at the convenience of the shogun.[101]

From the perspective of Nariaki and other daimyo, on the other hand, the political order could also be visualized as a "domainal lord system" (*daimyō ryōkokusei*), modeled on the structure of the Muromachi period. In that system, the daimyo was a "relatively independent, landed aristocrat, or feudal lord, who treated his fief as his personal estate and controlled his warriors as members of his own house." The daimyo maintained strict equality among themselves, and each "reserved to himself the right of military force, i.e., the right of self-help; should the shogun's control ever become ineffective, he would exercise that

---

100. Tokugawa Nariaki, *Kokushihen*, in Imai, Seya, and Bitō, eds., *Mitogaku*, p. 212.
101. Tahara Tsuguo, "'Jinsei' no shisō to 'oie' no shisō," *Shisō*, no. 633 (March 1977):71.

Reform as Representation   127

right as a means of conflict resolution." More important to Nariaki, the daimyo's retainers were "bound to the house in life and death": "No authority supersedes the daimyo in his capacity as sovereign of the house. Even though the daimyo himself owes allegiance to a higher sovereign lord, his own lord is not his retainer's lord."[102]

Of course, the incumbents of the Tokugawa's three collateral houses of Mito, Owari, and Kii, traditionally had considered themselves more "equal" than their peers, and it was as one of those three that Nariaki asserted his own autonomy and offered the Mito reforms as an object lesson for the bakufu as a whole. His memorials to the shogun were unprecedented in their comprehensiveness and earned him the enmity of bakufu conservatives. As the historian Inui Hiromi observes:

> Regardless of whether Nariaki and the other reformist leaders intended it to be so, as long as administrative reforms in the Tenpō period were aimed at the sloganized objective of *fukoku kyōhei* (wealthy domain, strong army) on the domainal level, they were bound to result in a degree of relative autonomy ... from the bakufu.[103]

During the Tenpō period, in other words, the Mito reformists revived the ideology of the feudal "house" and reified the domain as more than a mere aspect of the bakuhan system. They made it into an autonomous whole capable of achieving universal authenticity as the embodiment of natural order.

Latent in such a pretense, of course, was the assumption of immediate access to the timeless archetype of origins that was the national essence. Indeed, it was only as a representation of the national essence that the domain could claim authenticity as a microcosm of natural order. Such an assumption seems at first to contradict the Fujita faction's concern with preserving the proper order of names and statuses (*meibun*) and its specific professions of support for the bakufu. As indicated, Fujita Yūkoku theorized that: "When the bakufu reveres the emperor, the lords will worship the bakufu; when lords worship the bakufu, the lesser lords and stewards will respect the lords."[104] Similarly,

102. Ibid., pp. 66, 72, 74.
103. Inui and Inoue, "Chōshū-han to Mito-han," p. 321.
104. Fujita, *Seimeiron*, p. 13.

Aizawa, in *Shinron* and *Tekiihen*, made no secret of his belief that the bakufu should be revered and obeyed:

> The emperor, representing the activities of Heaven, spreads the deeds of Heaven. The bakufu aids the imperial court and governs the whole country. The local rulers are all supporters of the imperial court and promulgate the decrees of the bakufu throughout their provinces. That is why the people who obey the commands of the local daimyo are in effect obeying the decrees of the bakufu, and this is precisely the way to revere the imperial court and repay one's debt to the heavenly ancestors. The principle is simple, and the way is clear. The subjects of today are the descendants of those who were favored by the benevolence of the heavenly ancestors and heavenly descendants. They must obey the decrees of the bakufu and the local daimyo.[105]

Maruyama Masao concludes on the basis of the above passages that "Seishisai's *sonnō* (royalist) philosophy is not only not in contradiction with the feudal hierarchy but, on the contrary, supports it." He further notes, "By placing the relations between the imperial family and its subjects on the same plane as the relations between feudal lord and subject, Seishisai sought to extend the former's eternal immutability to the latter."[106]

However, Aizawa's stance toward the bakufu was not unambiguous. The intention to foster loyalty and service to the bakufu is unmistakable in statements such as those above, but they do not place the bakufu at anywhere near the same level as the court. The bakufu "aids the imperial court." Moreover, in the sections of *Shinron* quoted in chapter 2, the bakufu invariably enters in as a manifestation of history rather than archetype. Ieyasu was a great restorationist leader but even his "pax Tokugawa" emerged in the context of contending historical forces and presumably could never transcend its conditional status. Indeed, Aizawa's sense of crisis is rooted in the belief that the system established by Ieyasu had in fact declined to the point that the nation now faced grave danger.

It would appear, then, that the support of Mito activists for the bakufu should not be overemphasized. The bakufu could only be seen as a limited and conditional authority in com-

---

105. Quoted in Maruyama, *Studies*, p. 305. Italics in the original have been removed.
106. Ibid., pp. 305, 306.

parison with the court. Moreover, insofar as it remained an historical structure, the bakufu had no absolute, qualitative superiority over Mito domain. Indeed, it was perhaps less able in its contemporary state to stand as a representation of the national essence than was the domain itself.

The character of the reforms as outlined above suggests that Mito discourse was always already "in action" as ideology. That discourse made action possible by providing a framework for intentionality, and at the same time reached its own full clarity and persuasiveness only as it was represented in practice. When "read" in and through action, therefore, ideology appears not as the source or cause of human activity so much as the integral standard of its coherence.

That is not to say that there were no difficulties among the various media by which the discourse found expression. Language, institutions, and demonstrative gesture each "qualified" the discursive problematic and manifested it historically in different ways. That is nowhere more evident than in the transition from samurai to commoner, instrumentality to demonstration, and domain to nation that took place in the 1850s and 1860s.

4
RECRUITMENT OF COMMONERS

The Tenpō Reforms in Mito were directed against such symptoms of disorder as peasant rebellion, a market economy, and social fluidity. Yet these specific concerns seem to have been apprehended from the perspective of what Mircea Eliade has called the "terror of history." Mito activists were virtually obsessed, haunted by the possibility that historical change might finally emerge as a primary determining force or mode of being.

In late Tokugawa Mito, the importance of history as the major intervening variable between contemporary circumstances and a normative order was undeniable. The deleterious effects of history were all too apparent, and, though history provided the only available context for action in service to original archetypes, it also inevitably constrained that action through its recalcitrant forces of flux and uncertainty. The temporal relativity implied by such forces was sufficiently abhorrent to the Mito ideologues to completely shut out any thought of "internalizing" the historical process. The historical particularity of the Mito ideology consisted precisely in the enormous effort expended to avoid such a "historicized" existence. As we have seen, land and society were thoroughly reorganized in order somehow to prevent historical change from becoming a way of life.

The final paradox attendant on a profoundly paradoxical discourse, however, is that even action to escape from history has its historical consequences. Like all ideology, as described by Althusser, Mito discourse was "a system of representations"—not only images, myths, or concepts, but actions as well—"endowed with a historical existence and role within a given society."[1] As such it constituted a "material force," indispensable

---

1. Althusser, *For Marx*, p. 231.

"if men are to be formed, transformed and equipped to respond to the demands of their conditions of existence."[2] In short, Mito discourse was ideological to the extent that it provided certain segments of late Tokugawa society with a coherent world view, adequate to the performance of political, social, and economic roles.

THE TENPŌ LEGACY

Reformist practice in Mito initially re-qualified as historical actors the managerial class of samurai, whose ascriptive privilege to think and act in the public realm helped them to maintain control in threatening circumstances. Problems, such as the accumulation of wealth by merchants and rich peasants, maldistribution of resources, social dislocation, and peasant rebellion, were perceived as symptoms of the recent failure of the managerial aristocracy to perform adequately.

Such perceptions led to the Tenpō Reforms, which, in the course of rectifying institutions and human minds, inevitably drew on the practical energies of a certain class of historical subjects. Moreover, not only did the reformist assault on history have historical implications for the way institutions would henceforth be shaped and operate, but it also set in motion new human relationships—among samurai themselves and between samurai and the local elites they sought to transform and rule. Eventually, those relationships, and the new sets of expectations and aspirations they occasioned, contributed to the subjection and qualification of new groups of historical actors who were implicated with, but remained distinct from, the samurai reformists. The expansion of the subject of action to include commoners was largely a post-Ansei phenomenon but had to some extent been envisioned in the philosophies of earlier Mito writers, such as Aizawa and Fujita Tōko. Tōko, for example, says that: "The job of a ruler is to pacify the people and rule the land, not by employing the abilities (*chiryoku*) of one man but rather by aggregating and making use of the abilities of all the people." Tōko's debt to Ogyū Sorai here is unmistakable.[3]

Perhaps the most important force precipitating new possibili-

2. Ibid., p. 235.
3. See Shibahara, *Meiji ishin*, p. 148.

ties for alliance and action was the land survey. Planning for the survey was from the beginning accompanied by anxiety regarding possible negative reactions from peasants. Pains were taken to create an atmosphere of fairness and cooperation between survey officials and local cultivators. Each village was allowed to perform a preliminary survey of its own land and to participate in the determination of quality ratings. More importantly, local leaders, such as headmen, rural samurai, and trusted elders, were coopted as members of survey teams. Such practices appear to have significantly affected relations between the reformist administration under Nariaki and local luminaries, providing the latter with an opportunity for further advances in status over their peers.

Concern to maintain order in the countryside also led the samurai reformers to bestow on selected local leaders who had cooperated in the survey the surnames, swords, and clothing of rural samurai (*gōshi*). An understanding of the full implications of that measure requires some background. The practice of allowing certain samurai to remain on the land began in Mito, as it did in Tosa domain also, as a means of pacifying local regions at a time of transition in political power.[4]

When Tokugawa Yorifusa assumed control of Mito in 1619, already in place were a number of powerful, local families whose cooperation was essential to the preservation of order. One means adopted to bring their leaders under Yorifusa's sway was to name them *gōshi*, provide them with a stipend, and leave them in place as a stabilizing force. Yorifusa seems to have adopted this procedure in only four major cases, but his successors, Mitsukuni and Tsunaeda, continued the practice in some fourteen more. Most received stipends of either 25 or 50 *koku* and other allowances. It is interesting to note that the earliest rural samurai in Mito, who came to be called the *kyūke* (old families), were not granted fiefs but were instead provided with stipend rice from domainal coffers in accordance with the *mononari* system (discussed in chapter 3). In their local existence, they appear to have remained farmers rather than landed warriors.[5]

The next stage in the history of the *gōshi* system in Mito fol-

4. See Marius B. Jansen, "Tosa in the Seventeenth Century: The Establishment of Yamauchi Rule," in Hall and Jansen, eds., p. 125.
5. Seya, *Mito-han kyōkō*, pp. 257–63.

lowed decades of financial woes. During the term of the daimyo Harumori, which included among other disasters the great famine of the Tenmei period and the Mito peasant rebellions of 1771 and 1774, such difficulties reached crisis proportions. Countermeasures now included, in addition to the practice of withholding a percentage of retainers' stipends, a new policy of making rural-samurai status available for a price.[6] Standard prices appear to have been 500 *ryō* in exchange for 25-*koku* status and 1,000 *ryō* for 50-*koku* status, including, in most cases, the right to be armed and assume a surname. During Harumori's tenure (1766–1805), two large landlords purchased the status of 150 *koku*, one individual obtained 100 *koku*, six got 50 *koku*, four got 25, and a number of others were able to buy lesser *gōshi* status. The numbers were even larger for the Bunsei era of 1818–1829.[7]

During the era of Nariaki and the Tenpō Reforms, however, the practice of exchanging rural-samurai status for money was strictly prohibited. Yūkoku, Tōko, Aizawa, and other reformers were unanimous in their disdain for the practice. Even when wealthy families acted on their own initiative to donate money and grain for famine relief in the Tenpō period, Nariaki's administration made no move to reward them in any tangible way.[8]

Nevertheless, the reformists were sufficiently concerned about the success of the land survey and related reforms to grant samurai status (without emoluments) to the locals who were most cooperative. According to existing records, thirteen were rewarded in this manner for their performance during the survey, and eleven more for their cooperation with religious reforms.[9] As historian Shibahara Takuji suggests, this treatment not only allowed certain local landlords, village headmen, and other notables to rise in status relative to their peers (even though the survey may have cost them increased taxes), but perhaps also infused their class generally with a sense of indebtedness that played a significant role in the extension of Mito loyalism to a new group of historical subjects.

Shibahara also suggests that, in addition to elevating certain

6. Such practices were by no means unique to Mito (Smith, *Agrarian Origins*, p. 177.).
7. Seya, *Mito-han kyōkō*, pp. 267, 270.
8. Ibid., p. 275.
9. Ibid., p. 276.

segments of the rural elite to new social heights, the survey probably also helped ameliorate peasant discontent that, elsewhere in the late Tokugawa period, was often expressed in destructive outbreaks of "world renewal" (*yonaoshi*).[10] Reformist ideology relied heavily on pronouncements concerning the "leveling" and "equalization" of conditions for rich and poor alike. Following Yūkoku, Tōko, and others, Nariaki himself had announced at the time of the reforms that "wealthy commoners are the source of the realm's decline."[11] Moreover, the survey did result in significantly higher taxes for certain wealthy peasant landholders, with the possible effect that some poorer families experienced a proportionate lessening of their own burden. Shibahara postulates that the Tenpō Reforms had the important ideological effect of raising self-consciousness among peasants and increasing their level of "trust" in the domainal administration.[12] Under certain circumstances, as in the Ansei and later periods, the legacy of the land survey may have been influential in allowing loyalist samurai to mobilize local leaders and ordinary peasants as well.

Policies of reorganization pursued under the rubric of "grounding" the samurai may also have been effective in some cases in establishing firmer connections between samurai fiefholders and villagers. Close relationships between samurai land stewards and peasants, including those of a military nature, were among the explicit objectives informing the return to the fief system. Once the lines of responsibility and loyalty between samurai and cultivators were clarified, it was hoped that samurai could effectively mobilize peasant soldiers in time of emergency and thus extend in a limited sense the prerogatives of military duty to an entirely new constituency. The full implications of such a policy would not become apparent until the Ansei period.

In sum, the Tenpō Reforms in Mito revealed their ideological

10. Shibahara, *Meiji ishin*, p. 143. On *yonaoshi*, see Winston Davis, "Pilgrimage and World Renewal . . . Part I," *History of Religions* 23, no. 2 (Nov. 1983), and "Pilgrimage and World Renewal . . . Part II," ibid. 23, no. 3 (Feb. 1984). Also refer to essays by Stephen Vlastos, Hashimoto Mitsuru, and George Wilson, in Najita and Koschmann, eds.
11. Seya, *Mito-han kyōkō*, p. 274.
12. *Meiji ishin*, p. 143.

potency by reconstituting the restorationist subjectivity of talented samurai and at the same time providing an initial opening for rural non-samurai to participate in moral and political action. The process by which a rural elite became increasingly self-conscious and active politically as a result of the reforms is typified by a family called the Suda, of the region of Itako in the southern part of Mito domain.[13] The Suda were an old and prosperous line: village records from 1687 indicate that the household, numbering sixteen members, held land yielding 24 *koku*. At that time, the villages of Ushibori and Nagayama included some 148 households, of which only 4 held land producing more than 20 *koku*. Hence, the Suda were among the two or three most prominent families in the area.

However, even the Suda were not immune to the effects of bad weather, crop failures, and the reductions in population that resulted from starvation and migration. Population began to fall in Mito in the early eighteenth century, and marginal land was sometimes left uncultivated. Many small holders went bankrupt, and it was not unusual for such large farmers as the Suda to be reduced to poverty. By 1716 the Suda holdings had been reduced to only 7 *koku*, and it looked as if harder times were ahead. In the 1760s, however, the household received a series of adopted heirs and other aid from a stronger family, in a neighboring village, named the Imai. This support enabled the household to survive the great famine of the Tenmei period, and by 1790 the Suda had employed two servants (*genin*) and begun to reaccumulate a little extra land. By the turn of the nineteenth century, the family had obtained a great deal more land, which now was let to tenants; when the Mito reformists under Nariaki carried out the Tenpō land survey, the Suda were found to own a total of 131 *koku*. Prior to the survey, the Suda holdings had been estimated at about 92 *koku*, so it is clear that by making official the Suda ownership of some 39 *koku* of land that had formerly been attributed to others, the survey increased that family's tax liability substantially.[14]

It is important to note that the pattern followed by the Suda

---

13. Inui Hiromi, "Gōnō shisō no tenkai," in Hayashiya Tatsusaburō, ed., *Bakumatsu bunka no kenkyū* (Tokyo: Iwanami Shoten, 1978).
14. See chap. 3, and Inui Hiromi, "Mito-han tōsō no ichi kōsatsu," p. 18.

family was a common one in the Kantō plain and elsewhere.[15] Large households tended in the seventeenth century to farm extensive plots with a combination of kin (or fictive kin) and servant labor. But, when famine destroyed or drove away the poor families whose offspring provided servant labor for large holders, this traditional method of farming became impractical. If such formerly prosperous households managed to survive into the eighteenth century, they tended to change their management style, first by hiring short-term labor at peak periods, and then finally by letting land to tenants, rather than continuing to farm it themselves. Hence, the Bunka and Bunsei periods of the early nineteenth century saw the rise of a new set of large landowners like the Suda who took advantage of hard times to accumulate land and then let it to tenants.

The head of the Suda family at the time of the Tenpō Reforms was Gennosuke, a learned gentleman in his late fifties. Gennosuke had used his wealth and leisure to take advantage of the increased circulation of written materials, expanded opportunities for travel, and general cultural sophistication of the early nineteenth century to become a prominent rural *bunjin*, or man of culture. He collected a substantial library and pursued such avocations as poetry, tea ceremony, and flower arrangement. Through an investigation of records of the hand-copied books Gennosuke acquired over the years, the historian Inui Hiromi has found that, in general, the titles suggest a gradual transition in subject matter from local to national concerns, from historical settings to contemporary ones, and from geography to politics.[16] This raises the possibility that Gennosuke and others like him were already moving toward an intellectual engagement with contemporary political issues. If that was the case, for Gennosuke that trend was certainly accelerated by Nariaki's Tenpō Reforms. When, as part of those reforms, domainal administration was reorganized and all village heads (*shōya*) and regional headmen (*ōyamamori*) were replaced, Gennosuke was made regional headman responsible for Itako's sixteen villages and their overall productivity of about 10,000 *koku*. His office made him accountable not only for forest lands

---

15. Inui, "Gōnō shisō," in Hayashiya, ed., p. 337.
16. Ibid., p. 340.

and waterworks, but also for rural improvement and public morals. Gennosuke had been placed on the front lines of reformist politics.

Suda Gennosuke was by no means an active supporter of the reformist program. He wrote a number of memorials on problems of rural organization and administration, and was particularly critical of plans for a comprehensive land survey. Like Komiyama Fūken, Gennosuke was flexibly receptive to "changing times" (*jisei*)—including aspects of the commercialization of agriculture—and apparently was suspicious of the zealots' urge to recapture the purity of original archetypes. Inequalities among peasants, for example, were for Gennosuke primarily a matter of individual attributes, such as attitude: If poor peasants would just change their ways, work hard, and be frugal, their fortunes would improve. He was opposed, therefore, to any attempt by means of a land survey to "equalize" landholdings. Such opinions are perhaps entirely explainable as expressions of Gennosuke's own material interests as a wealthy landowner, but, as Inui points out, he seems to have genuinely believed in the desirability of upward mobility in accordance with effort.[17]

Gennosuke also differed from the reformist samurai in his view of land, which he was content to employ as a source of wealth, to be bought, sold, and rented much like any other commodity. At the same time, he supported other reformist measures, such as sumptuary legislation, restrictions on pawning, and lower prices for the services of artisans.

More significant than Gennosuke's generally anti-reformist views, however, was his willingness to adopt an activist stance in a time of political turmoil. He was astute in the ways and means of power, aware of the complexities of policy, and willing to take positions that were partisan and perhaps dangerous. In these ways, he well exemplifies the late Tokugawa tendency of peasant elites to aspire culturally and politically beyond their formal social status, which remained frozen at an inferior level. Reformist samurai, such as those who took over domainal administration under Nariaki in the 1830s, provided opportuni-

---

17. Ibid., p. 344.

ties for such men to express themselves politically and to act in a public arena formerly reserved for warrior aristocrats.

However, the tendency of the Tenpō Reforms to catalyze new ties between radical samurai and commoners and to infuse lower levels of society with new ideological perspectives is best illustrated not in Gennosuke's own life, but in the activities of his son Mojūrō. The younger Suda, born as Gennosuke's first son in 1810, grew up as the family was rapidly expanding its wealth and was just in his twenties during the Tenpō Reforms. As a result partly of his father's position and partly of mere circumstance, Mojūrō performed some local surveys at the behest of the district magistrate responsible for Mito's southern region, Yoshinari Mataemon (1797–1850). A loyalist radical and leader of Mito reformists, Yoshinari seems to have continued to patronize Mojūrō and in 1837 even appointed him headman of the Ushibori and Nagayama villages. When the land survey was carried out in 1840, the elder Suda was named as one of the officials in the Itako region who would inspect measurements (*naichō*) on behalf of the domainal administration; the actual work, however, was performed by Mojūrō, and as a result Yoshinari awarded him hereditary *gōshi* status and the temporary rank of regional headman, making him equal in rank to his father.

Mojūrō also had occasion to set down his views on policy issues, and the divergence from his father's position is striking. Mojūrō supported the land survey enthusiastically and agreed with the reformists' insistence on strict accuracy with no "discretion" on the part of survey officials. He disapproved of the excessive accumulation of land by households such as his own, and, in direct opposition to his father, openly supported measures to limit such accumulation. Thus, perhaps as a result of his relationship with Yoshinari and the atmosphere of iconoclasm that pervaded reformist circles, the young heir to the Suda holdings subordinated his own interests to the need for "rectification" in the context of a broader political community.

Gennosuke turned the family leadership over to Mojūrō in 1844, the same year that Nariaki was censured by the bakufu. As noted below, reformist samurai who had not themselves been purged responded to Nariaki's discomfiture with an "exoneration movement." One of the organizers of the movement was Yoshinari Mataemon; when Yoshinari went to Edo to protest, Mojūrō went along. On this occasion, therefore, Mojūrō was able to translate his reformist idealism and fervent "*han* patriotism" into radical action on behalf of the Mito lord, and to do so in close association with a member of the military caste. As Inui suggests, the relationship between Yoshinari and Suda might be viewed as a microcosm of the "alliance" between rich landlords (*gōnō*) and low-ranking samurai that twentieth-century Marxist historians have claimed to find beneath the late Tokugawa events. But, rather than an alliance between equal and autonomous parties, this relationship is better viewed as part of the process of ideological hegemony that sometimes allowed non-samurai to become involved in certain aspects of reformist politics.[18]

The reforms, in this case particularly the land survey, brought local interests into the vortex of the domainal power struggle. The result was to subject local leaders to new constraints and also to qualify them by placing them in positions of authority in relation to certain public issues. Moreover, because of Mito's collateral ties to the Tokugawa house, Nariaki's role in bakufu politics, and the threat posed by certain of the reforms to conservative elements in the domain and in the bakufu itself, participation in domainal politics also meant an involvement, directly or indirectly, in "national" political controversy, and a certain qualification (as in the case of Mojūrō) to intervene in bakufu affairs as well. It was through such links, which fostered a process of simultaneous empowerment and subordination, that thought had its impact as ideology.

THE INTRUSION OF NATIONAL POLITICS

Reformist activity in Mito came temporarily to a halt in 1844, when Mito elder (*karō*) Nakayama Bizen-no-kami was interrogated by bakufu senior councillor Abe Masahiro. Abe expressed official displeasure concerning some aspects of the Tenpō Reforms in Mito, mentioning the initiation of heavy construction projects, such as the Kōdōkan, despite Mito's financial distress;

---

18. Ibid., p. 355.

the conversion of the Tokiwayama Tōshōgū shrine from Shinbutsu Ryōbu (a Shinto-Buddhist synthesis) to Yuiitsu Shinto (Unity Shinto); the desecration of Buddhist temples; the collection of firearms; and the hiring of masterless samurai from outside the domain. Nariaki was subsequently punished with confinement at the Mito mansion at Komagome, and household leadership devolved to his son Yoshiatsu (1832–1868). Because of Yoshiatsu's youth, however, actual power was given to three other daimyo: Matsudaira Yoritane of Takamatsu, Matsudaira Yorimasa of Fuchū, and Matsudaira Yorinori of Moriyama. Mito reformist leaders, such as Fujita Tōko, Yamanobe Yoshitsune, and Toda Tadahisa, were also relieved of their duties and confined, effectively putting an end to the Tenpō Reforms in Mito.

Nariaki's punishment provided one of the earliest occasions on which new relationships between locals and reformist administrators were expressed in direct political intervention. Not only samurai, but commoners as well joined in a movement to exonerate Nariaki and to secure his return to Mito. Groups of "zealots" (*gimin*), led by village headmen, rural samurai, and Shinto priests, traveled to Edo where they presented petitions at the mansions of the other two Tokugawa collateral houses (Owari and Kii) and at the residences of the three daimyo named to oversee Mito politics. Nariaki's samurai retainers also protested, of course. Reformist divisional commander Takeda Kōunsai (1803–1865) and provincial commissioner Yoshinari Mataemon presented petitions to bakufu senior councillors Mizuno Tadakuni and Makino Tadayuki, and were imprisoned for their trouble.[19] Rai Mikisaburō (1825–1859), son of the great historian Rai Sanyō, also reportedly petitioned at the Makino mansion.[20] Although Nariaki's confinement was lifted later the same year, he was still excluded from domainal politics, and the daimyo overseers retained power. Moreover, anti-reformist policies remained in effect, and by 1845 most participants in the exoneration movement had been jailed.

The several years following Nariaki's incarceration saw the stagnation or reversal of many of the reforms carried out dur-

19. Katsuta-shi Shi Hensan Iinkai, ed., *Katsuta-shi shi* (Katsuta: Katsuta Shiyakusho, 1978), pp. 1012–13.
20. Suifu-mura Shi Hensan Iinkai, ed., *Suifu-mura shi* (Suifu: Ron Shobō, 1977), p. 238.

ing the Tenpō period. Moreover, there arose greater concern about foreign incursions, climaxing with the political furor over Commodore Matthew Perry's arrival in 1853. Perry's visit occurred after a period of gradual reconciliation between Abe Masahiro and Nariaki and eventually resulted in an appointment for the former Mito daimyo as bakufu defense adviser.[21] Before his resignation from bakufu service the following year, Nariaki seems to have had considerable impact on bakufu policy in response to Perry's demands. He recommended thorough defense preparations, including military production and the mobilization and training of peasant militia.[22]

In the years following Nariaki's punishment by the bakufu in 1844, Mito was split into hostile factions by three major issues: shogunal succession, the signing of a commercial treaty between the United States and Japan, and the Bogo secret imperial decree.[23] Mito's candidate as successor to the heirless and ailing thirteenth shogun Iesada was Nariaki's seventh son, Hitotsubashi Keiki (Tokugawa Yoshinobu, 1837–1913). Keiki had studied with Aizawa in Mito as a child, and then succeeded to the house of Hitotsubashi, which like Mito was supposed to supply a shogunal heir when needed. On the other side was the so-called Kishū faction, which supported the young daimyo of Kii, Tokugawa Yoshitomi (1846–1866). Leading the Kishū faction was the Hikone daimyo Ii Naosuke, who was destined to be killed by Mito swordsmen at the Sakurada Gate.

Mito radicals also confronted both Ii and conservatives in Mito over Western demands for commercial treaties. Chief senior councillor Hotta Masayoshi (1810–1864) had failed to get a decree from Emperor Kōmei (1831–1867) supporting such treaties, and pro-imperial radicals stubbornly opposed them. But soon after, Ii became *tairō* (great elder), the highest post in the bakufu administration. In mid-1858, he signed a treaty with American representative Townsend Harris and had Yoshitomi

---

21. For a detailed analysis of this event, see Conrad Totman, "Political Reconciliation in the Tokugawa Bakufu," in Craig and Shively, eds., pp. 180–208.
22. Nariaki's memorial on defense, *Kaibō guzon*, is translated into English in W. G. Beasley, *Select Documents on Japanese Foreign Policy, 1853–1868* (London: Oxford University Press, 1955), pp. 102–7.
23. This interpretation is suggested in Seya and Toyosaki, *Ibaraki-ken no rekishi*, pp. 172–76.

(fourteenth shogun Iemochi) named heir-apparent. It was to protest that chain of events that Nariaki defied confinement orders by taking his son, the incumbent daimyo of Mito, to Edo. In mid-1858 Nariaki was again confined, this time to the Mito mansion in the Komagome section of Edo, stimulating another "exoneration movement" on the part of his reformist supporters in Mito.

The third issue of contention involved the so-called Bogo imperial rescript. The Mito representative at court, Ugai Yoshizaemon (1797–1859), had surreptitiously been given this rescript, along with a particularly explicit attachment, in August 1858 by radical partisans in court. Ugai's son then secretly delivered the documents to the Mito mansion in Edo; in the meantime another copy, without the attachment, was delivered from the court through regular channels to the bakufu. The message implied that bakufu actions had been inadequate for a time of national crisis and also criticized bakufu officials for punishing Nariaki. By way of recommendation, it suggested that the bakufu should attempt to stabilize the situation by moving toward a policy of *kōbu gattai* (accommodation between court and bakufu) in cooperation with the collateral houses of Owari, Kii, and Mito. Afraid that Mito would leak the document to the other domains, Ii Naosuke ordered that Mito's copy be returned to the bakufu. Heightened bakufu suspicions eventually led to the execution of a number of Mito activists, including Ugai and his son, as part of the Ansei purge.

Ii Naosuke's demand that the rescript be returned to the bakufu fomented a split in Mito between conservatives and reformists and among the reformists themselves. The extreme positions were those of the conservatives, who favored return of the document to the bakufu, and the radicals, who advocated its dissemination to the other major domains. Between, or at least circumventing the two extremes, however, was a moderate reformist group led by Aizawa Seishisai, which insisted that the document should neither be disseminated nor relinquished, but rather sent back to the court where it originated.

The radicals resolved to resist by force, and, in late December 1859, when they feared that the conservatives might attempt secretly to transport the document to Edo, they blocked the Mitsukaidō, which was the main highway between Mito and Edo. In an action that came to be known as the *Nagaoka tonshū* (Nagaoka occupation), they set up camp and searched all southbound travelers. The incident marked a turning point in the Mito loyalist movement, in that it separated radicals clearly from moderates and neutrals and brought together a force of hundreds, including peasants as well as samurai. In a negative sense, it fostered unity between reformist moderates and conservatives, who now joined in a pacification campaign against the radicals. Despite repeated calls for dissolution by domainal authorities, the occupation lasted until the middle of the following February.

EDUCATION AS IDEOLOGY

Despite the ideological potency of the land survey, it was probably the district schools in Mito that were the most effective of the reform measures in qualifying and subjecting to ideological precepts a new set of rural political actors. The schools were controlled and administered by the district magistrates, and domainal authorities seem to have taken a keen interest in their operation. Hence, the schools functioned as an important nexus between local and central authorities. Through the mediation of such institutions, reformist samurai were put in close touch not only with local power structures, which included rural samurai, religious practitioners, and village leaders, but also with potential activists from a wide range of backgrounds, some of whom would later play important roles in intradomainal struggles.

The schools became politically important in the Ansei era. Nariaki's direct involvement in bakufu politics and foreign affairs honed political consciousness in Mito to a fine edge and further exacerbated conflict between reformists, now dedicated to the slogan of "revere the emperor and expel the barbarian" (*sonnō jōi*), and anti-reformists, who increasingly received the direct support of conservative forces in the bakufu.

Having retired from bakufu politics in 1854, Nariaki was again free to devote himself to the task of domainal reform, this time through his son, Mito daimyo Yoshiatsu. The Ansei Reforms that resulted were basically an extension of the Tenpō Reforms, but with strong emphasis on the problems of mobilization and defense occasioned by the national crisis.[24] Particularly with regard to the ideological process of qualifying new subjects for action, the Ansei measures effectively finished some of what the Tenpō Reforms had only begun.

Local education formed a major focal point of the new reforms. In the Tenpō period, Nariaki seems to have adamantly opposed any sort of education to ordinary peasants. Any involvement of peasants or townsmen in the military arts, particularly, had been explicitly prohibited. In the Ansei period, in the wake of foreign crisis and intensifying conflict with conservative forces on both the domainal and national levels, major reformist efforts were expended to see that locals were allowed access to district schools and were aggressively trained in loyalist attitudes and military skills. Nine additional district schools, now often called *bunbukan* (halls for the pursuit of the liberal and military arts) were constructed in the Ansei period, and all appear to have placed major emphasis on military training. Moreover, the schools established primarily for medical training in the Tenpō period and before were now converted to the *bunbukan* style, with ample yard space devoted to drill and weapons training.

Information is not abundant regarding the relationship between the district schools and *sonnō jōi* activism by non-samurai in the 1850s and 1860s, but Seya Yoshihiko has collected evidence sufficient to indicate that the ideological momentum established as a result of Mito scholarship and the Tenpō Reforms led directly to the construction of schools for the purpose of reaching a non-samurai population. He has also demonstrated that the schools did address such a population effectively; that the curriculum placed strong emphasis on military arts and political activism; and that, on a number of occasions in the 1850s and 1860s, culminating in the Tengu insurrection of 1864, large numbers of commoners did indeed act together with samurai radicals in response to political events.

The relationship between Mito ideology and the establish-

---

24. For an account of some Ansei reforms, see Chang, *From Prejudice to Tolerance* (Tokyo: Sophia University, 1970), pp. 65–97.

ment of the *bunbukan* in the Ansei period and after is clear, not only because construction of schools appears to have been part of a unified policy of reform under the direct guidance of Nariaki, but also because the actual work of organizing, funding, and constructing many of the schools was carried out by radical activists with close connections to leading reformists, such as Tōko and Aizawa.

One such individual was Takahashi Taichirō (1813–1860), a low-ranking samurai who had studied under a disciple of Tōko and, as revealed in correspondence between them, commanded the respect of Tōko himself. He was also involved in efforts to publish Aizawa's *Shinron*. Takahashi's own radical credentials were established by his assumption of leadership in the movement to exonerate Nariaki, his arrest and demotion by conservative authorities following Nariaki's confinement, and his involvement in the Sakuradamon assassination incident. As magistrate in the northern district from 1854, Takahashi played the leading role in planning the Machida school and probably also had a hand in the establishment of two other schools in the northern district at Ōmiya and Daigo.

Another radical samurai, higher-ranking than Takahashi, was Kaneko Magojirō (1803–1861). As magistrate of the western district, Kaneko participated centrally in the land survey and other reforms. Like Takahashi, he was a leader in the movement to free Nariaki and was jailed as a result by conservatives. In 1853 he was made magistrate of the southern district and was a leading propagator of *sonnō jōi* thought. There is a record of his having on one occasion distributed copies of Aizawa's *Tekiihen*. Kaneko was instrumental in the establishment of local schools at such locations as Tamazukuri, Itako and Akiba, and in the conversion of the Keigyōkan to a *bunbukan* in 1854.[25]

Emphasis in the Ansei period on local schools as instruments for the training and mobilization of local non-samurai was linked directly to Mito philosophy as it had been formulated in the Tenpō era and before. Moreover, it is clear even from the partial information available on participants in school pro-

25. Seya, *Mito-han kyōkō*, pp. 56–59.

grams that significant elements of the rural elite and even ordinary peasants (*hirabyakushō*) were directly addressed by those institutions. A good example is provided by Takahashi's Machida school. Mobilization of the local population began even before groundbreaking ceremonies, as revealed by the list of benefactors who were honored when the school opened in 1857. Out of the 45 donors offered special thanks for money or other contributions, 20 were village leaders of various types, 3 were local physicians, 3 were rural samurai, and 4 were Shinto-oriented religious specialists. Fully 15, moreover, were ordinary peasants and carpenters.[26] The total number of donors of one kind and another seems to have been more than 1,200, revealing the degree to which even the initial construction and equipping of the schools provided occasions for local organizing by such activists as Takahashi and others.

Furthermore, attendance records for 1861 of the Machida school indicate that, of the 180 persons who came to the annual general assembly (*taikai*), 145 were classified as ordinary peasants, although 49 were of sufficient status to be allowed a surname. The rest included a mixture of rural samurai, Shinto priests, village leaders, and local physicians.[27] However, despite the high level of peasant attendance on occasions like general assemblies, the main target population of the schools seems not to have been ordinary peasants, but rather local elites. Although there were no restrictions placed on attendance by others, Shinto priests and rural samurai were more or less obliged to attend instructional sessions and gatherings on a regular basis. All were cautioned to pay primary attention to occupational and domestic duties prior to spending time on school activities.[28]

Shinto priests provide a particularly interesting example of how the Tenpō Reforms and the district schools radicalized, trained, and armed a segment of the non-samurai population. Suspicion of Buddhism and support for an accommodation between Confucianism and Shinto had been prevalent in Mito ever since the second daimyo Mitsukuni who, in the 1660s, razed 52 percent of the domain's temples and established a shrine in every village.

26. Ibid., p. 72.
27. Ibid., p. 84.
28. Ibid., p. 78.

In the Tenpō period, the Fujita-faction reformists instituted some further changes. They did away with some forty Buddhist temples that lacked resident priests and made an effort to keep Shinto temples and rites separate from Buddhist ones. They repealed the earlier system of population registration (*teraukesei*), which had forced everyone to register at the Buddhist temple, and adopted the *ujiko* system, which enforced registration at Shinto shrines. They also authorized Shinto funerals in place of the usual Buddhist ceremonies. Moreover, in 1840 the reformists under Nariaki collected a large number of bronze bells and Buddhist images from temples that were of relatively recent construction and melted them down in order to forge huge guns for coastal defense. The last measure particularly attracted the enmity of conservative forces in the domain and precipitated a successful movement to punish Nariaki.[29]

These measures had already done much to raise the status of Shinto priests, however, and predisposed many toward support for Nariaki and reformist radicalism. At the time of the first movement to exonerate Nariaki, thirty-four Shinto clergymen associated with the Kashūkan school formed an activist organization called the Green Dragon League (Seiryūgumi Kairen). Led by Miyata Tokuchika, a student of the nativist scholar Hirata Atsutane, the organization submitted at least two petitions calling for Nariaki's release and the continuation of reform.

Such radicalism was encouraged, not only by requiring priests to attend monthly sessions at the district schools, but also through patronage at the domainal level. In 1856, for example, a two-day lecture contest (*miwake*) was held for priests at the Kōdōkan. Along with prizes for lectures, the priests were provided with food, drink, and accommodations. Of the total of eighty-seven individuals who lectured, forty-nine focused on the *Analects*, twelve on the *Nihon shoki*, six on the "Age of the Gods" section of the *Nihon shoki*, six on the *Hsiao ching*, five on the *Kogoshui* (Gleanings from the archives), four on the *Engishiki* (Procedures of the Engi era), and one each on the *Kojiki*, the *Nakatomi harai* (Purification ceremonies of the Nakatomi clan), the *Kōdōkanki*, the *Shu ching*, and the *Hsiao hsueh* (Elementary learning). The strong relative emphasis on the *Nihon shoki* com-

---

29. On the religious reforms in the Tenpō period, see *Mss* II/3, pp. 285–332.

pared to the *Kojiki* seems to reflect the Mito orientation to Confucianized rather than "pure" Shinto.

Shinto representatives also had been allowed on four occasions since 1840 to take part in major military exercises and by the Ansei period and after formed a virtual paramilitary force in the service of *sonnō jōi* radicalism. Priests also participated in later actions, such as the occupation of Nagaoka station on the Mitsukaidō highway, and three were among the assassins at Sakurada-mon.[30]

The district schools also facilitated reformist efforts to organize and mobilize villagers through the central role they played in the training of peasant militia (*nōhei*). Suggested in such early texts as Aizawa's *Shinron* and initially planned in the Tenpō period, the militia system finally came into existence in September 1855. It was to consist of 1,500 peasant soldiers, with 500 from each of three groups: rural activists who had demonstrated their reformist zeal, particularly as participants in the movements to exonerate Nariaki; members of the upper stratum of peasants and townsmen who might be willing to contribute funds; and ordinary peasants and fishermen who could be assigned to coastal defense units. The preference given to "zealots" (*gimin*) who had demonstrated active support for reformist causes indicates that the militia were not only for coastal defense, but also played an important ideological role in the dissemination of *sonnō jōi* precepts and the mobilization of support. All militia were attached to rural samurai commanders, and for that purpose 53 individuals, predominantly village leaders, physicians, and other local notables, were elevated to *gōshi* status in early 1855.[31] In their directive to the militia, the domainal authorities admonished them to go immediately to their posts if a foreign ship should be sighted, while on ordinary days they were to obey village leaders, work hard at agriculture, and attend gunnery practice three times a month.

Perhaps as a result of militia participation, the majority of those who sought instruction at Machida, and presumably elsewhere, in the Ansei years and after, tended to concentrate their attention on the martial, rather than liberal, arts. Figures for

---

30. Seya, *Mito-han kyōkō*, pp. 100–21.
31. Ibid., pp. 61–66, 277–81; and Shibahara, *Meiji ishin*, p. 160.

five gatherings at the Machida school in 1861 and 1862, for example, indicate that reading sessions focusing on Chinese and Japanese classics attracted relatively few compared to those who received training in fencing and gunnery.[32]

Information is sparse concerning the literary curriculum of the schools, but a fairly common element seems to have been medical texts. Beyond that, lecturing and reading in the Japanese and Chinese Confucian classics seems to have predominated, combined with some attention to Mito texts, such as the *Kōdōkanki*. Records of a series of gatherings at the Machida school in 1861 indicate that, of the 55 participants who devoted their time to literary pursuits (compared to 180 who did only the martial arts), 16 studied the *Analects;* 12, Nariaki's book on medicine; 10, the *Ta hsueh* (Great learning); 4, the *Mencius;* 4, the *Li chi;* 2 each, the *Shih ching*, the *Kogoshūi*, the *Hsiao ching*, and the *Kōdōkanki;* and 1, the *Chung yung*.[33] Another gathering of 8 at the Kashūkan in 1862 divided their attentions as follows: 4 on the *Nihon shoki*, 2 on the *Hsiao ching*, 1 on the *Analects*, and 1 on the *Ta hsueh*. As Seya observes, it would be interesting to know if the curriculum was in any sense dictated from the domain level, but materials are insufficient to determine that.[34]

ASSASSINATION AT SAKURADA GATE

A particularly dramatic instance of joint action between radical Mito samurai and non-samurai (in this case Shinto priests) took place on March 3, 1860 with the assassination of bakufu great elder (*tairō*) Ii Naosuke outside Sakurada gate of the imperial palace. The act had originally been planned by the provincial school founders and activists Kaneko Magojirō and Takahashi Taichirō in conjunction with the Satsuma zealots Arimura Jizaemon, Arimura Yūsuke, Takasaki Itarō, Kabayama San'en, and Iwashita Sajiemon.[35] The deed as it took place, however, was perpetrated by Mito radicals with the single exception of Arimura Jizaemon from Satsuma. Original plans had called for

---

32. Seya, *Mito-han kyōkō*, pp. 86–87.
33. Ibid., pp. 87–89.
34. Ibid., pp. 225–26.
35. Jōyō Meiji Kinenkai, ed., *Mito bakumatsu fūunroku* (Mito: Toraya Shoten, reprint, 1976), p. 253.

fifty insurgents to carry out other assassinations and attacks as well, but the eighteen who actually committed themselves to action decided to limit their target to Ii.[36] Neither Takahashi nor Kaneko actually participated, because it was their assignment to assess the impact of the incident and plan further actions with their Satsuma comrades.

On March 3 the assassins were already in place when the procession of sixty-odd guards and attendants accompanied Ii from the Hikone domainal mansion in the direction of Sakurada gate. It was raining, so Ii's samurai wore raingear and had covered their sword hilts to keep them dry. When the radicals attacked, therefore, the coverings impeded the guards' defenses, and Ii was killed immediately. Four of his attendants were killed on the spot, while four others died from wounds. On the attackers' side, one was killed immediately, and four others took their own lives soon after sustaining serious injuries. Of the remaining thirteen, eight later surrendered, and five escaped. All had prepared documents resigning in advance their commissions as Mito retainers lest their deed reflect dishonorably on the Mito house.

Three of the assassins were Shinto priests; most of the rest were low-ranking Mito samurai. Their leader Seki Tetsunosuke was only a minor functionary in one of Mito's provincial headquarters and was stipended at a mere 10 *koku*. What appears from these facts to have been a willingness to flout conventional rules of subordination is in fact representative of a general turn toward egalitarian "status reversal" among Mito rebels in the post-Ansei era. As Seya observes, "The samurai [who assassinated Ii] were willing to transcend feudal status rankings and accept Seki's leadership because such rigid differentiations were irrelevant to their single-minded commitment to an objective."[37]

In their statement of purpose, the rebels criticized the treaty with the United States, the punishment of Nariaki, and so on, but expressly denied any opposition to the bakufu per se. They had acted, they said, on Heaven's behalf to punish one who had sullied the national essence. In doing so, their only objective was to "return government [*matsurigoto*] to the correct Way [*seidō*] in accord with the sacred imperial command."

36. Katsuta-shi Hensan Iinkai, eds., *Katsuta-shi shi*, p. 1030.
37. Seya and Toyosaki, *Ibaraki-ken*, p. 179.

Following the incident, a large segment of the rebel force that had occupied Nagaoka dispersed to a number of locations in the southern district of Mito domain. Often headquartering at district schools, the radicals hid from domainal authorities while collecting funds and training their troops for future actions. One of the largest concentrations centered on the Tamazukuri School and became known as the Tamazukuri force. Along with Ogawa School (the former Keiikan), which also became a radical base, the Tamazukuri facility was strategically placed between Mito castle and Edo, and yet sufficiently remote to protect rebels who were sought for their part in the Nagaoka and Sakurada-mon disturbances. In addition, the schools were clearly well-suited to the emphasis on military training, which seems to have characterized the rebel bands. Reports on the garrisons by a local official, for example, describe them as so "mad with the Japanese spirit [*Nippon damashii*]" that they trained daily.[38] About a hundred people seem to have been garrisoned at the schools for a period of nearly a year.[39]

Available sources indicate that the majority of these outlaws were "peasants," including both ordinary peasants without surnames (*hirabyakushō*) and more prominent locals, such as village leaders. It was estimated that the Tamazukuri force consisted of about sixteen samurai, two Shinto priests, two Shugendō priests, two local townsmen, and thirty-three peasants, including five with surnames.[40] The number of peasants and other locals in the movement seems to have increased with time. Virtually all four hundred or so rebels who gathered at the Minato-mura school in autumn 1863, for example, seem to have been rural in origin.[41]

38. Seya, *Mito-han kyōkō*, p. 124, quoted from *Mito-han shiryō* 2.
39. Seya, *Mito-han kyōkō*, p. 125.
40. Ibid., p. 127.
41. Ibid., pp. 136–42.

5
RITUAL AND ACTION IN THE TENGU INSURRECTION

The turn to direct political and military action by Mito partisans in the Ansei period and after and the qualification and recruitment of non-samurai as participants culminated in violent insurgency and a domain-level civil war. On March 27, 1864, the first year of the Genji era, a band of about one hundred and fifty Mito samurai, priests, and peasants climbed Mt. Tsukuba and announced their dedication to a policy of *sonnō jōi*. The action initiated an episode known variously as the "Kantō insurrection," "Genji disturbance" (*Genji no ran*), "Tsukuba war," or Tengu insurrection.

The last term is perhaps the most evocative. Tengu are mythical long-nosed mountain demons. According to Seya, the name "Tengu faction" was first applied to Mito reformists, such as Fujita Tōko and Aizawa, by conservative opponents during the Tenpō Reforms. Its intended implication was that they were low-ranking retainers who arrogantly held their noses in the air because of their rise to power on the basis of scholarship. Later, Tokugawa Nariaki is said to have actively encouraged use of the name by the Mito radicals whom he supported, on the grounds that Tengu were often thought to have superhuman powers and qualities of heroism.[1]

The leadership of the band seems to have included prominent non-samurai. In the preeminent coordinating role was Fujita Koshirō (1842–1865), son of Fujita Tōko and grandson of Fujita Yūkoku. Koshirō (or Makoto) was Tōko's fourth son, born of a concubine. He had gone to Edo with his father at the age of 12, pursued an education there, and subsequently con-

---

1. Seya and Toyosaki, *Ibaraki-ken no rekishi*, p. 181.

tinued his studies with a number of tutors in Mito. He eventually also attended the Kōdōkan. In 1863, when the Mito daimyo accompanied the shogun to Kyoto, Koshirō was able to go along.[2] There, he seems to have met the Chōshū samurai (and later Restoration leader) Kido Kōin (alias Katsura Kogorō) (1834–1877) and other *sonnō jōi* activists, and began laying the groundwork for the insurrection.

Other leaders included the rural samurai Takeuchi Hyakutarō (1830–1865), Shugendō priest Iwaya Keiichirō, and Mito municipal magistrate (*machi bugyō*) Tamaru Inanoemon (1832–1865). Takeuchi Hyakutarō (or Nobushide), also known as Takenaka Manjirō, was the son of a rich peasant who late in life had been able to purchase samurai (*gōshi*) status for 2,500 *ryō*. Hyakutarō studied under Fujita Tōko, participated in such actions as the Nagaoka occupation, and later was principal of the Ogawa school where many participants in the insurrection received their training. Iwaya Keiichirō (or Nobushige) was the son of a Shinto priest from Shishikura, which was next to the village where Takeuchi grew up. Also apparently a student of Tōko's, he had been organizer and trainer at the Itako school. He later deserted from Tengu forces during the fighting at Nakaminato. Tamaru Inanoemon (or Naonobu), a Mito samurai, played a central role in the Tenpō cadastral survey and had held a number of posts in the Mito administration. He also traveled to Kyoto with the Mito daimyo in 1863.[3]

After collecting funds from local farmers and merchants, and apparently also from Kido Kōin,[4] the insurgents soon moved by way of Nikkō to Mt. Ōhira, where a "Call to Action" (*Gekibun*—see Appendix) was issued, and the force expanded to several hundred. After some initial dissension, the force returned to Tsukuba and mushroomed into a virtual rebel army of a thousand or so troops. Morale soared when the rebels defeated soldiers from a number of domains, such as Shimoosa, Shimodate, Tsuchiura, and Yūki. Meanwhile, conservative forces from Mito under Ichikawa Sanzaemon (Hirosane) (1816–1869) oc-

---

2. For details concerning the two shogunal visits to the court, see Totman, *The Collapse of the Tokugawa Bakufu*, pp. 6–108.
3. Jōyō Meiji Kinenkai, ed., *Mito bakumatsu fūunroku*, pp. 313–26.
4. Ibid., p. 325; Yamakawa Kikue, *Oboegaki* (Tokyo: Iwanami Shoten, 1974), p. 304.

cupied Mito castle, and a bakufu army was organized against the rebels, under the leadership of Tanuma Okinori. In July the Tengu came down from the mountain, camped in the vicinity of Ogawa and Itako, and engaged the conservatives near Mito.[5]

The major struggles, however, occurred between August and October in and around the major port of Nakaminato, pitting the rebels against the combined forces of a number of domains under bakufu command. These forces appear to have numbered around five thousand, against the two thousand-odd committed by the insurgents.[6] It soon became clear that the battle was going against the Tengu, and as a result a major segment of the rebel force under Sakakibara Shinzaemon (1833–1865) entered into secret negotiations with the bakufu army. Sakakibara received assurances that he and his followers would be treated leniently if they surrendered, so in late October he took a thousand or so troops out of rebel ranks. This precipitated a realignment, as Mito elder Takeda Kōunsai, Yamakuni Hyōbu, and others, who had formerly fought alongside such moderates as Sakakibara, now refused to surrender. Instead, they chose to join Fujita Koshirō and a thousand or so compatriots in a retreat to Ōji in the northeast.

Meanwhile, bakufu troops finally entered Nakaminato and burned rebel fortifications. As it turned out, the promise of leniency was later repudiated by bakufu leaders, and in mid-November those who had surrendered were parceled out among twenty-two different domains for incarceration. Two hundred or so reportedly died in prison. Finally, in the fourth month of the following year, Sakakibara and about forty others were either executed or committed suicide.[7]

Rebel forces in Ōji, with Takeda as their newly chosen general, now decided to set out for Kyoto in an appeal to the imperial court through Nariaki's son Yoshinobu, whom the bakufu had placed in charge of defense in the region that included the

---

5. Battles at Mt. Tsukuba, Nakaminato, and elsewhere are described by Totman in *The Collapse of the Tokugawa Bakufu*, pp. 108–122. Also see E. W. Clement, "The Mito Civil War," *Transactions of the Asiatic Society of Japan* 19 (1891).
6. Totman, *The Collapse of the Tokugawa Bakufu*, p. 117.
7. Katsuta-shi Shi Hensan Iinkai, ed., *Katsuta-shi shi*, pp. 1041–47.

The Tengu Insurrection

imperial seat in Kyoto. After a long trek, which included several pitched battles against pro-bakufu armies,[8] the 823 remaining rebels surrendered in mid-December at Suruga on the Japan Sea. On February 4, 1865, Takeda and 23 others were executed, and in the next few days some 328 more met the same fate. About 280 others were banished, some to remote islands. In addition, the salted heads of Takeda, Tamaru, Fujita, and Yamakuni were placed on display in Mito for three days before being cast into the harbor.[9]

As might be expected, intense bitterness and agony accompanied this internecine warfare, which polarized not only the band of Mito retainers, but local communities and even families. Outbursts of cruel vengeance were often the result. Following the slaughter of hundreds in Suruga, for example, the close relatives of Tengu leaders met a similar fate:

> When Takeda Iga [Kōunsai]'s severed head arrived at Mito [from Suruga], his wife Toki (48), who had been imprisoned, was forced to embrace it, and then she, her daughter Toshi (11), infants Chōgan (8) and Kaneyoshi (3), and maidservant Kome (19) were all beheaded and cast off Yoshida-Sakai bridge. Hikozaemon (Takeda's eldest son), his wife Iku (Fujita Tōko's younger sister, 43), Danzaburō (15), Kaneshirō (13), and Kumatarō (10) were put to death the same day. Yamakuni Hyōbu's daughter Chi (30) and his concubine Natsu (50), Yamakuni Junichirō's wife Matsu (37), daughters Miyo (14), Seki (7), and Kuri (5), Tamaru Inanoemon's mother Iho (82), wife Natsu (58), son Seijirō (2), concubine Nami, and daughters Masu (15), Yasu (17), and Ume (10) were condemned to prison for life and most eventually died there.
>
> The executed were the family members of warriors, and they met their end in an exemplary manner. Only Takeda's youngest, Kaneyoshi, who was still a helpless suckling, clung to his mother and cried out. Even the executioner hesitated, unable to wield his sword. Seeing this, the town gendarme and witness, Shinojima, cheerfully offered to take over. The story of how he grabbed little Kaneyoshi, stuffed him between his knees, and stabbed him to

---

8. One of the battles is described by Shimazaki Tōson in his historical novel, *Yoakemae* (Before the dawn). See trans. in Edwin McClellan, *Two Japanese Novelists* (Chicago: University of Chicago Press, 1969), pp. 144–47.

9. Katsuta-shi Shi Hensan Iinkai, ed., *Katsuta-shi shi*, p. 1048.

death with a short sword invariably brought tears to the eyes of all who heard it.[10]

In the period between the end of civil warfare in Mito and the Meiji coup d'état in early 1868, domainal government rested securely in the hands of the conservatives led by Ichikawa Sanzaemon and others who had fought the Tengu. Yoshinobu, who had refused any leniency to his rebellious countrymen, became the fifteenth Tokugawa shogun in August 1866. Meanwhile, Mito retreated entirely from national politics.

However, the enmity between Tengu and the conservatives remained alive in Mito, bursting to the surface again in the months after Restoration (*ōsei fukko*) was proclaimed in December 1867. Ichikawa led Mito forces in support of the battle urged by the Aizu domain against the imperial armies, while Tengu remnants rushed to take the side of the new government. When Aizu was finally defeated in September 1868, Ichikawa and his followers returned to Mito and barricaded themselves in the Kōdōkan. After exchanging fire in October with troops led by Yamanobe Yoshitsune, Ichikawa and his men fled westward, pursued by Mito imperial loyalists. The final battle took place at Matsuyama in Chiba and ended with Ichikawa's defeat. Again, as had occurred so often in the past, the losers—as many as ninety, this time—were decapitated, and their heads sent to Mito to be gibbeted and displayed. The resourceful Ichikawa, however, eluded the Tengu again and reportedly fled to Edo where he tried to arrange passage to France. He was finally apprehended and returned to Mito for execution in February 1869.[11]

Mito's tribulations had finally ended, a full year after the overthrow of the bakufu. It is indisputable that, as the *Tōjo Nihon shi* (Japanese history as viewed from the present) records, "there were internal conflicts in virtually all the domains, especially in Chōshū, Satsuma, Tosa, Chikuzen, Kaga, and Aki"; but, surely, the account continues, "for horror and tragedy, none was the equal of Mito."[12]

10. *Mito bakumatsu fūunroku*, quoted in Hashikawa Bunsō, *Rekishi to shisō* (Tokyo: Miraisha, 1973), pp. 69–70.
11. Seya and Toyosaki, *Ibaraki-ken no rekishi*, p. 221.
12. Quoted in Hashikawa, *Rekishi to shisō*, p. 68.

MOBILIZATION AND OPPRESSION

Estimates regarding the class and occupational composition of the original Tengu force vary, but one study based on death records counted from the beginning of the fighting, places the total number of peasant (*nōmin*) casualties at 716, compared to a figure for samurai of 454. Others included 49 Shinto priests, 6 Shugendō specialists, 8 Buddhist priests, 19 doctors, and 49 rustic samurai.[13] Terms such as "peasant" are vague, of course, and Shibahara Takuji argues that the so-called peasant participants in the Tengu uprising were in fact led by the "socio-economically, militarily, and ideologically dominant stratum" of village society. He cites evidence from one group of villages that members of the local elite made up over 35 percent of the total participants.[14]

Like the district schools themselves, the Tengu force seems to have drawn its members from the upper level of the rural population and yet exploited that very population economically and militarily. As noted above in relation to Machida, even in the earliest stages of local school construction, financial and material resources, including books, had been collected in the area served by each school, rather than provided by the domain. Surely, as Seya observes, it is difficult to explain such contributions in terms of spontaneous generosity alone. A certain degree of coercion must have been involved.[15]

By the same token, it appears that Tengu forces garrisoned at the Tamazukuri and Ogawa schools supported themselves and their operation largely through extortion from rural residents. Bands of rebels would confront village leaders with demands for a "loan" in order to help "rid the nation of foreigners." If they failed to come up with an adequate amount, the intruders would destroy property and sometimes engage in violence. By the early 1860s, in fact, it appears that a general state of lawlessness and indiscriminate plunder had spread across much of northern Kantō. According to one report:

---

13. Takagi Shunsuke, "Mito-han sonnō jōi undō no sonraku shusshin giseisha," *Ibaraki-ken shi kenkyū* 13 (March 1969):54.
14. Shibahara, *Meiji ishin*, pp. 179–80.
15. Seya, *Mito-han kyōkō*, p. 72.

Beginning in early October of Bunkyū three [1863], a large force of Shinto priests, rustic samurai, and peasants gathered at the district schools in Nakaminato, Ogawa, and Itako, calling for the expulsion of foreigners [*jōi*]. They were joined off and on by a diverse collection of hangers-on from other domains. Now and then they would force their way into the homes of the rich peasants and demand contributions toward the establishment of an expulsionist army.[16]

Another, more hostile to the radicals, says,

In broad daylight with lances and swords drawn, muskets primed, they would advance upon the wealthy. They either seized or forcibly borrowed money and grain, and warned that Heaven's punishment [*tenchū*] would be meted out to those who refused . . . [for them] cutting down a peasant or townsman was no more serious than slicing off a radish shoot.[17]

In several cases in 1864, peasants were sent a message directing them to appear at an inn or private dwelling in the Itako region, south of Tamazukuri and Ogawa. When they arrived, they were threatened with violence to themselves or others if they did not come up with large sums of money, amounting in at least two cases to 200 *ryō*. After negotiation, through the intermediation of the householder or innkeeper, the amount was in all cases reduced substantially, but apparently duly paid. In one case, the name of Takeuchi Hyakutarō, one of the top Tengu leaders, was listed among the extortionists.[18] Such practices were hardly well-calculated to attract support among rural residents, and in some cases peasants reportedly helped authorities track down and arrest offenders.[19] There were also a number of violent peasant uprisings against Tengu forces before the year was out.[20]

Other documents, such as the diary of a roof-thatching con-

16. Sakai Shirōbei, *Mito kenbun jikki* (published together with Takenuma Takeshi, *Mito-han matsu shiryō*) (Tokyo: Rekishi Toshosha, 1977), p. 132.
17. *Mito-han tōsō shimatsu;* quoted in Shibahara, *Meiji ishin,* p. 183.
18. Kawamura Masaru, "Bakumatsu no Mito-han sōran to Shimoosa kuni no ichi dōkō," *Ibaraki-ken shi kenkyū* 20 (June 1971): 73–78.
19. *Mito-han shiryō* 2:53–65.
20. See Egawa Fumihiro, "Gekiha to minshū," *Ibaraki-ken shi kenkyū* 34 (March 1976), for an extended discussion of relations between the Tengu band and the peasant population.

The Tengu Insurrection

tractor in Tsukuba, tend to indicate a certain degree of initial rapport between rebels and local residents,[21] and indeed Shibahara Takuji cites the successful rebel engagement against conservative forces at Mt. Tsukuba on July 8, 1864, as their "first and last unity with the masses."[22] Clearly, however, the Tsukuba campaign as a whole was characterized by widespread extortion of money, weapons, food, and labor. Materials from Tsukuba show that a merchant suspected of trading with foreigners through the port of Yokohama was forced to contribute 30 *ryō* to avoid a raid on his life and property, and that Tengu forcibly purchased two guns, six lances, and four swords for the unfair sum of only 21 *ryō*. A general report of Tengu movements in the Tsukuba region also includes details regarding their seizure of military equipment, clothing, and funds.[23]

Neither was extortion of money the only way in which the rebels victimized local populations. A request for two years' remission of taxes submitted by villagers to domainal authorities in December 1864, after major fighting in Nakaminato, suggests the ordeals visited upon ordinary peasants by the battles that took place there:

> 1. Our village is rated at about 1,360 *koku*, and comprises about two hundred families, with a population of around 1,300. We have so few fields that in slack periods we put our energies into making straw sandals [*zōri* and *waraji*], mats, and ropes. In the vicinity of the harbor we haul for wages, sell vegetables, and perform other tasks in order to make a living. Beginning with the battle . . . in July, however, we were forced by the Tengu [rebels] to perform labor duty. . . .
>
> 2. Both large and small farmers have suffered as a result of the early droughts which have continued over the past two or three years, and again this year there was bad weather in April and May and the harvest was poor. Not only were crops ruined by floods in August, but we were subjected day and night to a labor corvée and were unable to harvest the beans. Finally, the women and old folks began to harvest in late September, but the crops were unfit even for soup paste. Nevertheless, we were commanded to provide paste [to the Tengu] and had no alternative but to do so.

21. Tsukuba-chō Shi Hensan Iinkai, ed., *Tsukuba-chō shi* (Tsukuba, 1979), pp. 1–70.
22. Shibahara, *Meiji ishin*, p. 179.
23. Ibid., pp. 152–62.

3. In August . . . the masterless samurai from other domains who fought for the Shosei [conservative side] mobilized village residents to provide a relay. As a result, we were prevented from harvesting the rice seedlings, and so were forced to live on village grain reserves. When the Tengu demanded grain, we sent a considerable amount from the same stores, but not before expending a good deal of manpower polishing it. It was the same in the case of the Shosei. We were forced to provide labor for both the rebels and the Shosei, and worked day and night with no time to eat or sleep.

4. When, in response to Tengu demands for rice on the 18th of August, we asked to be relieved of further obligation, they immediately got very angry and called the village leaders together. The Tengu said that if anyone complained, the village would be burned and its occupants beheaded. The leaders were shocked, and demanded contributions of rice from every house in the village. They were only able to collect and turn over about ten horseloads, however. It was terrible.

5. The Tengu also pressed a lot of labor into service when they occupied the Shinseikan [in Nakaminato]. Since we had no alternative, we provided the labor. Bullets flew as thick as rain, striking terror into our hearts. Only after repeated entreaties were we finally allowed to return home. The Tengu passed back and forth on both sides of the village at all hours so everyone, young and old, men and women, fled to the hills on the outskirts of the village to spend the night there. But the Tengu would ride up from nowhere to seek out workers and take them away for labor duty. There was no time for rest. While the old and young wept constantly, the women tried to work on in the fields with stray bullets flying past. The suffering they endured is indescribable.

6. Our village is next to the three shoreline villages of Minato-mura, Hiraso-mura, and Isohama-mura. When the Tengu took Minato, the residents were afraid of fire, so those who were acquainted with residents of our village, and even some total strangers, descended upon us. The times demanded mutual aid so we helped them any way we could.

7. Our village became an encampment, so many fields were left unplanted. Fields and paddies were also destroyed or dug up in the process of emplacing thirteen guns on high ground. Some dry fields were sown, but only by the method we call slash sowing, and often the women did not plow or prepare the fields in any way. Or they would sow just the seeds alone. In no case was any real crop to be expected.

8. Fires were started by the Tengu on the night of 11 September and the whole village was terror-stricken. The villagers suffered greatly, hiding their valuables and grain at Noyama. Two or three more fires were set on the night of the twentieth. The bullets were thick as rain, and the conflagration was impossible to extinguish. There was no alternative but to abandon the buildings and flee.[24]

Thus, the identity of the Tengu force was ambiguous. It was largely composed of villagers, but it neither supported nor claimed to support peasant interests. Nevertheless, the participation of rural commoners in political actions, such as those recounted above, marked a significant departure from the predominantly samurai involvement in the Tenpō Reforms. That departure was symbolized in the very appellations attached to the respective sides in the conflict. Whereas the term Tengu implied rustic upstarts, Shosei ("students") was used to designate the conservative force because of the high proportion in its ranks of young samurai who had attended the Mito Academy. In a certain sense, therefore, the conservative and rebel forces represented, respectively, the domainal academy, which had now become a bastion of conservative samurai leadership, and the provincial schools, which served as centers of learning and action for radical non-samurai.

The outlines of the process by which ideology transformed the subjectivity of commoners in Mito and qualified them to act can now be clearly seen. Even as its internal structure dictated that historical forces should be blunted and a normative system preserved, the Mito ideology in its practical dimension served to qualify and equip new historical actors who would hasten the demise of that very system. The Tenpō Reforms had sought as part of the "rectification of names" to correct landholding, taxation, retainer emoluments, and the minds of the people. But, in attempting to "rectify" social reality, the reformists succeeded also in transforming it, especially in its ideological or subjective aspect. The land survey, for example, set in motion new forms of relationship between radical samurai and commoners and expanded the possibilities for collaborative action. The district schools instilled both political awareness and fight-

24. Reproduced in Katsuta-shi Shi Hensan Iinkai, ed., pp. 1057–59.

PILGRIMAGE TO THE ORIGIN

The *Gekibun* issued from Mt. Ōhira (see Appendix) and memorials dispatched to sympathetic daimyo provide useful guides to rebel intentions. Immediately obvious in the *Gekibun* are echoes of early Mito texts, such as *Shinron*, giving evidence of continued conformity to the restorationist problematic. History as the locus of both corruption and remedial action continues to be contrasted against absolute norms, now principally the injunction to "revere the emperor and expel the barbarians." Hence, the "injurious effects of the foreign presence" and "domestic troubles and external ills" increase daily, eroding the principles of reverence and exclusionism that form the foundation of the nation.

The rebel memorial to Ikeda Mochimasa, daimyo of Okayama, recalls Aizawa's discussion of "changes in the momentum of time" in its perception of "steady deterioration, a powerful force [*ikioi*] rushing [the nation] downstream." The only remedy would be timely action designed to reestablish original norms: "Even the most lowly must hold fast to the great principle [of *sonnō jōi*] and refuse to let the moment slip." As always, action must be appropriate to circumstance but never oblivious to principle:

> Of course, if the trend of the times is not taken carefully into consideration, it will be difficult to act effectively, but, faced with the present crisis, if we look only at the trend of the times and fail to revere the great principle of *sonnō jōi*, we will succeed only in spurning the imperial will, violating the great rule of the founder, and inviting the subversion of the nation [*tenka kokka*] before our very eyes.[25]

More concretely, the insurgents seem to have been preoccupied with the need to close Japan's ports and rid the nation of foreigners. They had hoped from the outset that they could

---

25. *Mito-han shiryō* 2:579–80, 578.

The Tengu Insurrection

proceed to Yokohama as the vanguard of an expulsionist force, and, in light of stated bakufu policy at the time, this aspiration was not entirely fatuous. The bakufu had accepted an imperial demand for *jōi* that had been delivered to Edo in late 1862 by Sanjō Sanetomi (1837–1891).[26] This had initiated a period in which bakufu leaders had felt the need to pay lip service, at least, to the doctrine of *jōi*. Indeed, as Totman's account makes clear, one of the proponents of this stance of "verbal *jōi*" was Nariaki's son Yoshinobu, to whom the Tengu band would so unsuccessfully appeal during its trek toward Kyoto. Finally, however, the bakufu announced clearly in spring 1864 that Yokohama would be closed to foreign intercourse. At last the Tengu leaders could plausibly claim to be obeying not only the imperial will, but the order of the bakufu as well.[27]

However, the Tengu band was never able to march on Yokohama. Instead, after gathering at Mt. Tsukuba on March 27, the rebels left almost immediately for Utsunomiya, near Mt. Nikkō, where they arrived on April 5. On the sixth, Tengu leaders met with sympathetic Utsunomiya samurai and expressed their desire to camp at Nikkō. On the eighth, however, they were told that Utsunomiya commissioner Okura Masayoshi would allow no more than ten people to enter the sacred area, and then only for a single visit. After initial resistance, the Tengu complied, sending a small group of leaders to pay their respects at the tomb of Ieyasu. On the eleventh, they repaired to Kanuma in Shimotsuke, and from there to Mt. Ōhira.[28]

In her recent interpretation of those years, Yamakawa Kikue suggests that the Tengu leaders saw Nikkō primarily in military terms as a haven that, because of its sacredness, would be immune to attack by bakufu troops.[29] That may indeed have been an important factor. At the same time, however, it almost certainly had symbolic meaning as a point of origin, where the aura of an age prior to historical decay and foreign desecration was still tangible.

The close relationship in the popular mind between Nikkō

---

26. Totman, *The Collapse of the Tokugawa Bakufu*, p. 39.
27. Ibid., p. 109.
28. Ibaraki-ken Shi Hensan Iinkai, ed., *Ibaraki-ken bakumatsushi nenpyō* (Mito Ibaraki-ken, 1973), pp. 153–56.
29. *Oboegaki*, p. 304.

and the sacred origins of the polity was the result of a series of stratagems employed in the mid-seventeenth century by the shogunal adviser and Tendai priest Tenkai. Working in conjunction with the third shogun Tokugawa Iemitsu (1603–1651), Tenkai had Ieyasu's remains laid to rest in Nikkō and later transformed the burial site into an ornate mausoleum at an expense to the bakufu of 500,000 *ryō*. Tenkai further contributed to Nikkō's sacred aura by deifying Ieyasu: through a reconstruction of the Shinto-Buddhist Sannō tradition, Tenkai presented Ieyasu as the reincarnation of the Sun Goddess and avatar of the "universal god of all gods, who precedes creation, yin and yang, and is superior to all Buddhas."[30] As a result, Nikkō was turned into a ritual center that rivaled and, in some ways, actually superseded the Ise complex, which enshrined the ancestress of the imperial line. In 1645 the court began to send imperial messengers to Nikkō every year, further reinforcing the impression that Nikkō and Edo were the new national centers of ritual and authority. Although initially only daimyo were invited to Nikkō, by the second half of the Tokugawa period, access was allowed to commoners, who visited at the rate of about 30,000 per year.[31]

A suggestion of the aura that surrounded Nikkō is captured in a poem reportedly written by Tengu leader Satō Sajiemon as the band negotiated with officials at Utsunomiya:

> The barbarians have invaded Eastern seas.
> Yet the soul of the founder is with us
> Even as we shed tears of gratitude
> In melancholy worship from afar—Mt. Nikkō.[32]

Also significant for an interpretation of the meaning of Tengu orientations to Nikkō is Eliade's observation that a "symbolism of the center" is often closely related to the archaic mystique of origins, and the most common representation of centrality is a sacred mountain. A pilgrimage to the center symbolizes the transition "from chaos to cosmos" and thus is difficult but supremely meaningful: "attaining the center is equivalent to a

---

30. Ooms, *Tokugawa Ideology*, p. 177.
31. Ibid., pp. 183, 60.
32. Jōyō Meiji Kinenkai, ed., *Mito bakumatsu fūunroku*, p. 335.

The Tengu Insurrection

consecration, an initiation; yesterday's profane and illusory experience gives place to ... a life that is real, enduring, and effective."[33]

Such insights are extremely suggestive regarding the symbolic functions of the trek to Nikkō. In the Tenpō period and before, language and institutions had been manipulated as efficient means toward the eventual representation of a natural, unmediated polity. Now, this separation of means from ends is rejected, and action is required to represent directly the possibility of a natural order. In terms used originally by Ferdinand Toennies, there was a transition from arbitrary will, in which means are merely expedient and perhaps even antithetical to ends, to essential will, in which means and ends are an "organic whole."[34]

It is surely possible, therefore, to detect in the Tengu gesture toward Nikkō—as well as in the initial choice of the prominent Mt. Tsukuba and the later trek toward the imperial seat—a strong, symbolic orientation to the "center" similar to that described by Eliade. In the political and religious context of late Tokugawa Japan, the visit to Nikkō could well be interpreted as an attempt to signify—to represent not in texts or institutions, but rather in a dramatic gesture—the relevance of original principles in a time of crisis.

It is unnecessary, of course, to deny the importance of what Quentin Skinner would call other "motives" behind the act.[35] For example, Yoshinobu recorded retrospectively his view that, despite their rhetoric about revering the emperor and expelling the barbarian, Tengu leaders were actually concerned only with the power struggle going on in Mito between radical and conservative factions.[36] Undoubtedly, the Tengu mobilization responded to a number of political, economic, and social considerations, among which were factional conflicts. Such motives do not, however, affect the proposition that the Tengu leaders intended in making the gesture toward Nikkō (if not by it) to associate their movement with the aura of original purity and

33. Eliade, *The Myth*, pp. 12–17, 18.
34. Werner J. Cahnman and Rudolph Heberle, eds., *Ferdinand Toennies on Sociology* (Chicago: University of Chicago Press, 1971), p. 66.
35. Quentin Skinner, "Motives, Intentions and the Interpretation of Texts," p. 400.
36. Osatake Takeki, *Meiji ishin* 2 (Tokyo, 1943):551.

wisdom surrounding Tokugawa Ieyasu and to suggest a regeneration of the spirit of his administration in order to nullify the degenerative forces of change.

Moreover, intentionality itself is seldom simple or unambiguous. Certainly, the strategic significance of Nikkō and all other mountains is undeniable, and virtually all the maneuvers of the Tengu force reveal a strong element of military instrumentality. Yet that is not necessarily the only factor involved. As von Wright has observed, the explanation of collective behavior requires a "second order of understanding," according to which data about individuals is "colligated" under a general concept. For example:

> I see crowds of people in the street moving in the same direction, shouting things in unison, some waving flags, etc. What *is* it that is going on? I have already understood the "elements" of what I see intentionalistically. The people are "themselves" moving and not being swept by a wind or torrent. They are shouting—and this is to say more than that sounds emanate from their throats. But the "whole" which I observe is not yet clear to me. Is this a demonstration? Or is it perhaps a folk festival or a religious procession that I am witnessing?[37]

By the same token, one might ask for purposes of the present interpretative exercise whether the march to Nikkō was primarily a military maneuver or a symbolic gesture in the form of a pilgrimage. For Yamakawa Kikue, as indicated above, it was unequivocally the former, with the sacred aura of Nikkō serving only to insure the Tengu forces against bakufu attack. In the context of the Mito ideology as a whole, however, it is also likely that the action had certain characteristics of a pilgrimage. A movement through space to the "center" symbolized also a leap back through time to the beginning and thus dramatized the critical and regenerative possibilities of a restoration.

The work of Victor Turner on ritual and pilgrimage also contains useful clues to the message contained in Tengu attacks. For Turner, "pilgrimages are liminal phenomena,"[38] suffused

---

37. Georg Henrik von Wright, *Explanation and Understanding* (Ithaca: Cornell University Press, 1971), p. 132.
38. *Dramas, Fields, and Metaphors*, p. 166.

with elements of communitas, which is one of two basic "models for human interrelatedness." The first model, "is of society as a structured, differentiated, and often hierarchical system of politico-legal-economic positions with many types of evaluation, separating men in terms of 'more' or 'less.'" The second, which he calls communitas, "emerges recognizably in the liminal period" and connotes "society as an unstructured or rudimentarily undifferentiated *comitatus*, community, or even communion of equal individuals, who submit together to the general authority of the ritual elders."[39] Of course, liminality as Turner uses the term is rooted in the *rites de passage* of primitive societies, and the ritual process remains the prototype for communitas. As rituals, therefore, pilgrimages "seem to be regarded by self-conscious pilgrims both as occasions on which communitas is experienced and as journeys toward a sacred source of communitas, which is also seen as a source of healing and renewal."[40]

In the case of the Tengu pilgrimages, however, more is involved than an experience for the pilgrims themselves. Rather than merely self-renewing celebrations, the Tengu actions must be understood as gestures that designated certain referents and communicated a certain content concerning them. The pilgrimage model serves to highlight important aspects of the active "statement" contained in the Tengu gestures. A willingness to defy existing laws and conventions, for example, is obviously consistent with a view of pilgrimage as antistructural communitas. The rebel memorial to Itakura Katsukiyo, daimyo of Bitchū Matsuyama, for example, stated:

> We sincerely apologize if we should happen to break the law. Nevertheless, even though under present circumstances we may violate a few petty ordinances, justice demands that we obey the great principle of the founder [*sonnō jōi*]. If we do not soothe the imperial heart, how else are we to repay our indebtedness for three thousand years of benevolence?[41]

39. *The Ritual Process*, p. 82. I employ Turner's conceptualization of communitas despite its static bias. In his view, communitas functions primarily to regenerate structure (ibid., pp. 169–70). I argue that, in the case of Mito, this was not necessarily true, and perhaps this indicates that the model should not be used here. On the other hand, Turner's static analysis seems to fit well with the anti-historical aims of the Mito rebels.
40. Turner, *Dramas, Fields, and Metaphors*, p. 203.
41. *Mito-han shiryō* 2:579–80.

Whereas in the Tenpō period institutions were seen as necessary vehicles for administration in accord with the Way, the urgency of the new situation demanded that stable structures be set aside in service to the higher duty of actualizing the principle of *sonnō jōi*. As the *Gekibun* asserts, "A deadly disease is not to be treated with common everyday remedies. If extraordinary measures are not adopted, there will be no extraordinary effects."[42]

The general applicability of the pilgrimage model to the Tengu trek is further substantiated by the correlation pointed out by Turner between liminality and status elevation or reversal.[43] As noted above, the Tengu band consisted largely of nonsamurai from rural areas who had been initiated into the Mito ideology through the district schools. Even the leaders were of relatively low status, and their own frequent mention of that fact indicates that it was considered meaningful by the Tengu themselves. The memorial to Ikeda Mochimasa, for example, begins, "We are aware that for small men such as we commoners and hermits to exceed the limits of their station and presume to discourse on policy for the realm is no small infraction."[44] The attempt to cultivate an aura of purity and ingenuousness is unmistakable.

Elements of liminality and communitas only suggested by the Nikkō pilgrimage, however, emerge with greater clarity in the later Tengu decision to march westward in an appeal to the court through the good offices of Tokugawa Yoshinobu.[45] The immediate political objective was to gain official sanction to serve as part of an imperial force to repel the barbarians. In their earlier memorial to Nariaki's ninth son, Ikeda Mochimasa, for example, they had entreated, "If through your good offices you could intercede on our behalf in order to secure imperial sanction for our force as the vanguard of expulsionism, we should express appreciation with our very lives."[46] Ikeda complied, dispatching memorials of his own to both court and

    42. Ibid., p. 576.
    43. Turner, *The Ritual Process*, p. 85.
    44. *Mito-han shiryō* 2:579–80.
    45. See Osatake, *Meiji ishin* 2:558; and Jōyō Meiji Kinenkai, ed., *Mito bakumatsu fūunroku*, p. 548.
    46. *Mito-han shiryō* 2:581–82.

The Tengu Insurrection

bakufu. In the latter, he referred to the Tengu as the *Yashū ikki* (uprising in Shimotsuke), and, though he agreed that the rebellion should be put down, he suggested that, in the event the bakufu were to adhere to a policy of expelling the foreigner, the Mito rebels should be put in the forefront of an expulsionist force.[47] However, in the case of Yoshinobu, who was now Supreme Commander of Imperial Defense, the rebels misjudged. Not only was he not disposed to provide aid, but he played a major role in their defeat.[48]

The Tengu appeal to the court brings us full circle, back to the function of the Great Thanksgiving Ceremony as a representation of the origin. As a movement through space to the center, which, like most pilgrimage sites, was the place where "some manifestation of divine or supernatural power had occurred,"[49] the trek toward Kyoto exemplified the spatial counterpart of the backward leap through time in the thanksgiving ceremony. Indeed, Turner's model highlights the profoundly "antistructural" as well as antihistorical mood of the thanksgiving ritual itself. As noted above, that ceremony dramatizes the symbolic consanguinity of all Japanese as descendants of the gods and is closely correlated with a notion of ritualistic government that transcends all historically determined, institutional structures. The common focal point of both rituals—thanksgiving ceremony and pilgrimage—is the imperial presence, itself the major tangible manifestation of the timeless, unchanging national essence.

Frustrated in their attempts during the Tenpō era to represent natural forms by shaping institutions, Mito radicals turned to dramatic, often violent, gestures as a means of calling attention to the accessibility of origins and the possibility of renewal. Nikkō, as the sacred resting place of the founder of the Tokugawa polity, provided them with a vivid representation of the need to reform institutions, on the domainal level and for the nation as a whole. In the final analysis, however, institutions, like history, were only relative and conditional, inadequate to a strategy of unmediated actualization. Hence, even when both

---

47. Jōyō Meiji Kinenkai, ed., *Mito bakumatsu fūunroku*, p. 345.
48. See Osatake, *Meiji ishin* 2:561–80.
49. Turner, *Dramas, Fields, and Metaphors*, p. 189.

domain and bakufu resisted the restorationist reform of administrative structures, the imperial symbol continued to offer the possibility of a rejuvenating "escape" from history that might provide the basis for a new start.

NEW POLITICAL SPACE

Related to the turn to a strategy focused directly on Ieyasu as the founder of the bakuhan system and on the emperor as the symbol of timelessness and antistructural communitas was an abandonment of the domain as a political field. Implicit, at least, in rebel actions was the production of a new political space cutting across the barriers to horizontal movement that were characteristic of Tokugawa rule. As Maruyama Masao has pointed out, the Tokugawa system as a whole relied on a hierarchical structure in which "the values of the total social system are diffused and embedded in each closed social sphere." Control is indirect in such a system, and therefore "any problem ... must be solved at the place [*ba*] in which it occurs." Every effort must be made to "prevent the horizontal extension of incidents."[50]

Obviously, the maneuvering by Tengu from domain to domain and particularly the march all the way to Suruga on the Japan Sea were in open violation of laws and conventions regulating horizontal movement. In conjunction with the slogan of "revere the emperor and expel the barbarian," which dramatizes the danger facing not just a particular domain, but the nation as a whole, such movements demonstrated the possibility of a nationwide political arena unfettered by "feudal" barriers.[51] Moreover, by acting through the domain, they symbolically transformed it from the representational medium it had been in the Tenpō period into an active, potentially autonomous subject. At least through its self-designated representatives, the domain (*han*) could now act in, and even for, the whole. In other words, in place of the Tenpō strategy by which normative principles were to be represented only through the

---

50. *Studies*, p. 244.
51. On the development of a broader political space in the era leading to the Meiji Restoration, see H. D. Harootunian, *Toward Restoration*, p. 37 and passim.

The Tengu Insurrection

mediation of the domain as microcosm, the Tengu radicals were now able to act directly in and on the nation as a whole, implying in the process how that nation might be transformed into something new.

It is certainly true, as Osatake and others have pointed out, that texts related to the Tengu rebellion do not openly employ anti-bakufu rhetoric.[52] Ieyasu, as the founder of the Tokugawa house and symbolic originator of the principle of "revere the emperor and expel the barbarian," was lionized, but even the existing bakufu administration was generally the object of only muted criticism. As in the *Gekibun,* Tengu actions were commonly presented as "supplementing the bakufu's judgment" or "assisting the shogun." Nowhere was there even a suggestion that the ultimate objective might be to replace the bakuhan system with anything else.

However, Tengu actions were clearly a challenge not only to conservative forces in the domain, but to the bakufu itself. Despite the absence of anti-bakufu pronouncements, the authorities in Edo did not misunderstand for a moment the threat to the established order posed by the rebellion. They began almost immediately to mobilize forces to put it down. The Tengu hoisted the flag of rebellion on Mt. Tsukuba on March 27, and by April 7 the bakufu had issued the first of many exhortations to domains in the area to prepare for the rebels and, if necessary, to "pacify" them militarily.[53] Hence, despite the moderate Tengu rhetoric, there could have been no doubt in the mind of any rebel that, for all practical purposes, the bakufu was the enemy.

52. Osatake, *Meiji ishin* 2:544.
53. Ibaraki-ken Shi Hensan Iinkai, ed., *Ibaraki-ken bakumatsushi nenpyō,* pp. 153–54.

CODA: MITO IDEOLOGY AS TEXT

Despite the debilitating impact of their rebellion on the bakufu, the political actors formed in Mito did not themselves overthrow the old regime or establish the Meiji state. Instead, their activism was fated to dissipate in internecine battles and to play itself out in what is best understood as a dress rehearsal for revolution.[1] In order to comprehend more fully the relationship between the occurrences in Mito and the comprehensive revolutionary event that was completed several years later, it is again necessary to turn away from a chronological mode of historical reasoning back to the analogy of the text. That is, rather than "causing" the Meiji Restoration, or "influencing" those who did, Mito simply offered its texts to be read and its meaningful actions to be reenacted by others, thereby giving them new importance beyond their original contextual relevance.[2]

The late Mito writings, particularly Aizawa's *Shinron,* were widely disseminated among radicals. As noted in the introduction, Maki Izumi, Yoshida Shōin, Kusaka Genzui, and Umeda Unpin all read Mito works and all visited Mito at least once between the mid-1840s and early 1860s. Of course, their readings exploited the full plurivocity of such texts as *Shinron* and *Kōdōkanki jutsugi* and construed them in new ways. Tōyama Shigeki argues that the *shishi* "read in" to Mito texts implications that were far more radical than anything intended by the authors:

> The number of *shishi* from across Japan who read works by Fujita and Aizawa and then proceeded to engage in anti-bakufu actions is by no means small. Yet this is not to be explained with reference to

---

1. The metaphor is Harootunian's, although he applies it to different events (*Toward Restoration*, chap. 5).
2. The distinction between the situational "relevance" of events and their omnitemporal "importance," which allows them to be reenacted and thus reinterpreted in later social contexts, is developed by Ricoeur ("The Model of the Text," pp. 543–44).

qualities inherent in Mitogaku itself, but rather with respect to its readers and the circumstances that surrounded them. Mitogaku sought, from the perspective of the top [of the bakufu power structure], to stimulate feelings of responsibility and self-reflection on the part of *bushi* [samurai] at the bottom. That was its original content; yet the *shishi* read it as criticism of bakufu policies and as anti-bakufu tracts. They read in [*yomikae*] the implication that the shogun and the daimyo were not meeting their responsibilities (to promote *sonnō* and *jōi*) and thus construed it as an assignment of responsibility from the bottom upwards [directed at the bakufu].[3]

Moreover, radicals in the 1850s and 1860s almost certainly "read" not only writings, but meaningful acts as well. Yoshida Shōin, for example, seems to have been deeply impressed by the active involvement of peasants in such actions as the January 1852 exoneration movement. One scholar even attempts to show that Shōin's experience in Mito demonstrates a direct intellectual link between late Mitogaku and the organization of the Kiheitai units in Chōshū.[4]

Clearly, Mito texts of both the printed and the kinetic varieties lent themselves to appropriation in other historical contexts, despite their manifestly antihistorical content. Indeed, the antihistorical, representational thrust of the Mito project may have been responsible in part for the widespread reading its texts received. That is, Mito activists had sought to *inscribe* the Way of Heaven on the face of the earth, not only in the lines that delineated parcels of land during the cadastral survey, but in ritualistic patterns of human interaction and even in the habits of the human mind. Mito ideology was above all a "writing"—a purposeful fixing of meaning that would resist the forces of time. Having been so assiduously preserved in "marks," it is not surprising that the Mito text(s) should have attracted readers and interpreters. Of course, the intent in writing had been to close off discourse by providing a solution to flux and ambiguity; the result was precisely the opposite, because, as Ricoeur observes, writing is open: "addressed to an unknown reader and potentially to anyone who knows how to read."[5]

3. *Meiji ishin to gendai* (Tokyo: Iwanami Shinsho, 1968), p. 114.
4. Yoshida Toshizumi, "Kōki Mitogaku to Kiheitai shotai," pp. 92–102.
5. *Interpretation Theory*, p. 31.

Appendix: *Gekibun* (Call to Action)

Sonnō jōi [Revere the emperor, expel the barbarians] is, of course, the great principle of the divine land [of Japan]. Since the glorious creation of the divine land, an unbroken line of emperors has inherited the sun in heaven and ruled the four seas, their bountiful authority giving them preeminence over the countries of the world. Even in later ages, there were many who displayed a heroism peculiar to Japan, such as Hōjō Tokimune who annihilated the Mongols and Hideyoshi who sent an expedition to Korea. Their obedience to the radiant teachings inherited from Amaterasu Ōmikami is profoundly moving. Tokugawa Ieyasu, particularly, exercised the utmost care and solicitude in establishing the foundation for several hundred years of peace, premising it on the great duty of *sonnō jōi*. It is valiant in the extreme that among the great principles of the Tokugawa house none was put above *sonnō jōi*.

Now the injurious effects of the foreign presence become more excessive day by day. Stability in the popular mind has been snatched away before our very eyes, and charlatans have taken advantage of the times to parlay pseudo-Confucianist nonsense. Domestic troubles and external ills increase daily, until it appears doubtful that the imperial will can be accomplished or the great teachings of the founder [Ieyasu] upheld. In fact, the divine land has never suffered greater ignominy and danger. How can those who are born in the divine land and bathe in its blessings stand by for even a moment in silent idleness? Fortunately, we ourselves were born in the divine land and, while our actions may be inadequate to the present crisis, we have made up our minds to die in order to save the nation [*kokka*] and repay the wealth of blessings we have received. Accordingly, we have deliberated, being aware that a fatal disease is not to be treated with common everyday remedies. If extraordinary measures are not adopted, there will be no extraordinary effects. How is it possible to soothe the sacred imperial heart above and, below, to supplement the decisive judgment of the bakufu by cleansing away past insults?

Unable to quiet our indignation, we have agreed to meet likeminded comrades at Nikkō, carrying a palanquin enshrining the soul of Tokugawa Nariaki. We are sworn to serve the legacy of Ieyasu, rectify the sins of those who have misled us, stave off the insults of the barbarians and spies, and repay our debts to court and bakufu. Alas, in these trying times is there none willing to make effective retribution? Is there no one who will refuse to curry favor with the foreigner and decline submission to his rule? Is it not unbecoming a son of the divine land, when he has recognized the need for effective action and deeply resents the machinations of the foreign barbarian, to vacillate and temporize ignobly, praying for a divine wind? We beg those consumed with loyalty in other domains to act quickly and join us in a cooperative effort. Serving the court above and assisting the shogun below, we intend to spread the authority of the divine land over the nations of the world. As the spirit of Ieyasu in heaven is our witness, this is our humble petition. (*Mito-han shiryō* 2:576–77)

Bibliography

JAPANESE-LANGUAGE WORKS

Aizawa Seishisai. *Shinron* [A new thesis], *Tekiihen* [On the way to proceed]. Ed. by Tsukamoto Katsuyoshi. Tokyo: Iwanami Bunko, 1931.

Bitō Masahide, ed. *Ogyū Sorai*. Nihon no meicho 16. Tokyo: Chūō Kōronsha, 1974.

Chihōshi Kenkyū Kyōgikai, eds. *Ibaraki-ken no shisō bunka no rekishiteki kiban* [The historical basis for the thought and culture of Ibaraki prefecture]. Tokyo: Yūzankaku, 1978.

Egawa Fumihiro. "Gekiha to minshū—Genji gannen Tsukuba kyohei o chūshin to shite" [The rebels and the people, with particular attention to the Tsukuba mobilization]. *Ibaraki-ken shi kenkyū* [Studies in Ibaraki prefectural history] 34 (March 1976): 70–83.

Haga Tōru, Matsumoto Sannosuke, and Minamoto Ryōen, eds. *Edo no shisōka tachi* [Intellectuals of the Edo period]. Tokyo: Kenkyūsha, 1979.

Hashikawa Bunsō. *Rekishi to shisō* [History and thought]. Tokyo: Miraisha, 1973.

———. ed. *Fujita Tōko*. Nihon no meicho 29. Tokyo: Chūō Kōronsha, 1974.

Hayashiya Tatsusaburō, ed. *Bakumatsu bunka no kenkyū* [Studies in late Tokugawa culture]. Tokyo: Iwanami Shoten, 1978.

Ibaraki-ken Shi Hensan Iinkai, ed. *Ibaraki-ken bakumatsushi nenpyō* [A chronology of events in Ibaraki prefecture in late Tokugawa]. Mito: Ibaraki-ken, 1973.

Imai Usaburō, Seya Yoshihiko, and Bitō Masahide, eds. *Mitogaku* [Mito scholarship]. Nihon shisō taikei 53. Tokyo: Iwanami Shoten, 1973.

Inui Hiromi. "Mito-han tōsō no ichi kōsatsu: Tenpō kenchi no bunseki o tsūjite" [An interpretation of the Mito conflict, based on analysis of the Tenpō cadastral survey]. *Rekishigaku kenkyū* [Historical research] 232 (Aug. 1959): 11–22.

Inui Hiromi and Inoue Katsuo. "Chōshū-han to Mito-han" [The house of Chōshū and the house of Mito]. In *Iwanami kōza Nihon rekishi* [The Iwanami essays on Japanese history] 12, pp. 262–323. Tokyo: Iwanami Shoten, 1976.

Jōyō Meiji Kinenkai, ed. *Mito bakumatsu fūunroku* [An account of events in late Tokugawa Mito]. Mito: Toraya Shoten, 1976. Reprint.

Katsuta-shi Shi Hensan Iinkai, ed. *Katsuta-shi shi: chūseihen, kinseihen* [History of Katsuta city: medieval and early modern]. Katsuta: Katsuta Shiyakusho, 1978.

Kawamura Masaru. "Bakumatsu no Mito-han sōran to Shimoosa kuni no ichi dōkō" [The upheaval in late Tokugawa Mito and trends in Shimoosa]. *Ibaraki-ken shi kenkyū* [Studies in Ibaraki prefectural history] 20 (June 1971): 73–78.

Maruyama Masao, ed. *Rekishi shisō shū* [An anthology of the philosophy of history]. Nihon no shisō 6. Tokyo: Chikuma Shobō, 1972.

Matsumoto Sannosuke. *Tennōsei kokka no seiji shisō* [Political thought under the emperor system]. Tokyo: Miraisha, 1969.

Mito-han shiryō [Documents of Mito house]. 4 vols. Tokyo: Yoshikawa Kōbunkan, 1915.

Mito-shi Shi Hensan Iinkai, ed. *Mito-shi shi* [History of Mito city]. 4 vols. Mito: Mito Shiyakusho, 1971–76. Cited as *Mss*.

Nakamura Akira. "Mitogaku no kokka-ron" [The Mito scholars' view of the state]. *Ibaraki-ken shi kenkyū* [Studies in Ibaraki prefectural history] 34 (March 1976): 1–18.

Nakamura Kōya, ed. *Seikatsu to shisō* [Life and thought]. Tokyo: Shōgakkan, 1944.

Noguchi Takehiko. *Edo no rekishika: Rekishi to iu na no doku* [Historians of the Edo period: The poison called "history"]. Tokyo: Chikuma Shobō, 1979.

Osatake Takeki. *Meiji ishin* [The Meiji Restoration]. 2 vols. Tokyo: Hakuyōsha, 1943.

Rai Tsutomu, ed. *Soraigakuha* [The Ogyū Sorai school]. Nihon shisō taikei 37. Tokyo: Iwanami Shoten, 1972.

Sakai Shirōbei and Takenuma Takeshi. *Mito kenbun jikki* [First-person accounts of events in Mito], *Mito-han matsu shiryō* [Documents on the end of Mito house]. Tokyo: Rekishi Toshosha, 1977.

Seya Yoshihiko. *Mito-han kyōkō no shiteki kenkyū* [Historical study of the Mito district schools]. Tokyo: Yamakawa Shuppansha, 1976.

Seya Yoshihiko and Toyosaki Takashi. *Ibaraki-ken no rekishi* [History of Ibaraki prefecture]. Tokyo: Yamakawa Shuppansha, 1973.

Shibahara Takuji. *Meiji ishin no kenryoku kiban* [The power base of the Meiji Restoration]. Tokyo: Ochanomizu Shobō, 1965.

Suifu-mura Shi Hensan Iinkai, ed. *Suifu-mura shi* [History of Suifu village]. Suifu: Ron Shobō, 1977.

Suzuki Fusako. "Mito-han Tenpō kaikaku no ichi kōsatsu" [An interpretation of the Tenpō Reforms in Mito]. *Ochanomizu shigaku* [Ochanomizu historical studies] 15 (1972).

Tahara Tsuguo. "'Jinsei' no shisō to 'oie' no shisō" [The ideology of "benevolence" and the ideology of the "house"]. *Shisō* [Thought], no. 633 (March 1977):65–81.
Takagi Shunsuke. "Mito-han sonnō jōi undō no sonraku shusshin giseisha" [Rural-origin victims of the Mito movement to "revere the emperor and expel the barbarian"]. *Ibaraki-ken shi kenkyū* [Studies in Ibaraki prefectural history] 13 (March 1969):53–78.
Takasu Yoshijirō, ed. *Fujita Tōko zenshū* [Complete works of Fujita Tōko]. 6 vols. Tokyo: Shōkasha, 1935.
———, ed. *Mitogaku taikei* [Anthology of Mito scholarship]. 8 vols. Tokyo: Mitogaku Taikei Kankōkai, 1941.
Tōyama Shigeki. *Meiji ishin* [The Meiji Restoration]. Tokyo: Iwanami Zensho, 1951.
———. *Meiji ishin to gendai* [The Meiji Restoration and recent history]. Tokyo: Iwanami Shinsho, 1968.
Tsukuba-chō Shi Hensan Iinkai, ed. *Tsukuba-chō shi: Shiryōshū, dainihen.* [History of Tsukuba: Documents 2]. Tsukuba: Tsukuba-chō Yakuba, 1979.
Tsuyuguchi Takuya. "Bakumatsu ni okeru kokkateki rinen no sōshutsu" [The construction of a national ideal in the late Tokugawa period]. *Bunka shigaku* [Cultural history] 31 (Dec. 1975):44–58.
Yamakawa Kikue. *Oboegaki: Bakumatsu no Mito-han* [A reminiscence of Mito in the late Tokugawa period]. Tokyo: Iwanami Shoten, 1974.
Yoshida Toshizumi. "Kōki Mitogaku to Kiheitai shotai—Kōki Mitogaku no saihyōka o motomete" [Late Mitogaku and the special militia—Toward a reevaluation of the impact of late Mito scholarship]. *Ibaraki-ken shi kanpō* [Ibaraki prefectural history gazette] 2 (Feb. 1975):89–102.

ENGLISH-LANGUAGE WORKS

Althusser, Louis. *Lenin and Philosophy and Other Essays.* Trans. by Ben Brewster. London: New Left Books, 1971.
———. *For Marx.* Trans. by Ben Brewster. London: New Left Books, 1977.
Althusser, Louis, and Etienne Balibar. *Reading Capital.* Trans. by Ben Brewster. London: New Left Books; 2nd ed., 1977.
Backus, Robert L. "The Kansei Prohibition of Heterodoxy and its Effects on Education." *Harvard Journal of Asiatic Studies* 39, no. 1 (1979):55–106.
———. "The Motivation of Confucian Orthodoxy in Tokugawa Japan." *Harvard Journal of Asiatic Studies* 39, no. 2 (1979):275–338.

Beasley, W. G. *Select Documents on Japanese Foreign Policy, 1853–1868.* London: Oxford University Press, 1955.

———. *The Meiji Restoration.* Stanford: Stanford University Press, 1972.

Cahnman, Werner J., and Rudolph Herberle, eds. *Ferdinand Toennies on Sociology: Pure, Applied, and Empirical.* Chicago: University of Chicago Press, 1971.

Chan, Wing-tsit, ed. *A Source Book in Chinese Philosophy.* Princeton, N.J.: Princeton University Press, 1969.

Chang, Richard T. *From Prejudice to Tolerance: A Study of the Japanese Image of the West.* Tokyo: Sophia University, 1970.

Clement, E. W. "The Mito Civil War." *Transactions of the Asiatic Society of Japan* 19 (1891): 393–418.

Coward, Rosalind, and John Ellis. *Language and Materialism: Developments in Semiology and the Theory of the Subject.* London: Routledge and Kegan Paul, 1977.

Craig, Albert M. *Chōshū in the Meiji Restoration.* Cambridge: Harvard University Press, 1961.

Craig, Albert M. and Donald H. Shively, eds. *Personality in Japanese History.* Berkeley and Los Angeles: University of California Press, 1970.

Davis, Winston. "Pilgrimage and World Renewal: A Study of Religion and Social Values in Tokugawa Japan, Part I." *History of Religions* 23, no. 2 (Nov. 1983): 97–116.

———. "Pilgrimage and World Renewal: A Study of Religion and Social Values in Tokugawa Japan, Part II." *History of Religions* 23, no. 3 (Feb. 1984): 197–221.

de Bary, Wm. Theodore, and Irene Bloom, eds. *Principle and Practicality: Essays in Neo-Confucianism and Practical Learning.* New York: Columbia University Press, 1979.

Eliade, Mircea. *The Myth of the Eternal Return or, Cosmos and History.* Princeton, N.J.: Princeton University Press, 1971.

Ellwood, Robert S. *The Feast of Kingship: Accession Ceremonies in Ancient Japan.* Tokyo: Sophia University, 1973.

Fingarette, Herbert. *Confucius: The Secular as Sacred.* New York: Harper Torchbooks, 1972.

Foucault, Michel. *The Order of Things: An Archaeology of the Human Sciences.* New York: Vintage, 1973.

———. *The Archaeology of Knowledge and the Discourse on Language.* Trans. by A. M. Sheridan Smith and Rupert Sawyer. New York: Harper and Row, 1976.

Hall, John W., and Marius B. Jansen, eds. *Studies in the Institutional History of Early Modern Japan.* Princeton, N.J.: Princeton University Press, 1968.

Harootunian, H. D. *Toward Restoration*. Berkeley and Los Angeles: University of California Press, 1970.
Holtom, D. C. *The Japanese Enthronement Ceremonies*. Tokyo: The Kyo Bun Kwan, 1928.
Huber, Thomas M. *The Revolutionary Origins of Modern Japan*. Stanford: Stanford University Press, 1981.
Jameson, Frederic. *The Political Unconscious: Narrative as a Socially Symbolic Act*. Ithaca: Cornell University Press, 1981.
Kumazawa Banzan. "*Dai Gaku Wakumon:* A Discussion of Public Questions in the Light of the Great Learning." Trans. by Galen M. Fisher. *Transactions of the Asiatic Society of Japan* 16, ser. 2 (1938).
Lau, D. C., trans. *Mencius*. London: Penguin Books, 1970.
Legge, James, trans. *The I Ching*. New York: Dover, 1963. 2d ed.
McClellan, Edwin. *Two Japanese Novelists: Sōseki and Tōson*. Chicago: University of Chicago Press, 1969.
McEwan, J. R. *The Political Writings of Ogyū Sorai*. London: Cambridge University Press, 1969.
Maruyama, Masao. *Studies in the Intellectual History of Tokugawa Japan*. Trans. by Mikiso Hane. Tokyo: University of Tokyo Press, 1974.
Najita, Tetsuo, and J. Victor Koschmann, eds. *Conflict in Modern Japanese History: The Neglected Tradition*. Princeton, N.J.: Princeton University Press, 1982.
Najita, Tetsuo, and Irwin Scheiner, eds. *Japanese Thought in the Tokugawa Period: Methods and Metaphors*. Chicago: University of Chicago Press, 1978.
Nakai, Kate Wildman. "The Naturalization of Confucianism in Tokugawa Japan: The Problem of Sinocentrism." *Harvard Journal of Asiatic Studies* 40, no. 1 (1980): 157–99.
Nosco, Peter, ed. *Confucianism and Tokugawa Culture*. Princeton, N.J.: Princeton University Press, 1984.
Ogyū Sorai. *Distinguishing the Way [Bendō]*. Trans. with intro. and notes by Olof G. Lidin. Tokyo: Sophia University, 1970.
Ooms, Herman. *Charismatic Bureaucrat: A Political Biography of Matsudaira Sadanobu, 1758–1829*. Chicago: University of Chicago Press, 1975.
———. *Tokugawa Ideology: Early Constructs, 1570–1680*. Princeton, N.J.: Princeton University Press, 1985.
Passin, Herbert. *Society and Education in Japan*. Tokyo: Kodansha, 1982.
Pocock, J. G. A. *Politics, Language and Time: Essays on Political Thought and History*. New York: Atheneum, 1973.
Ricoeur, Paul. "The Model of the Text: Meaningful Action Considered as a Text." *Social Research* 38, no. 3 (Autumn 1971): 529–62.
———. *Interpretation Theory: Discourse and the Surplus of Meaning*. Fort

Worth: Texas Christian University Press, 1976.

Scheiner, Irwin. "The Mindful Peasant: Sketches for a Study of Rebellion." *Journal of Asian Studies* 32, no. 4 (1972–73): 579–91.

Skinner, Quentin. "Meaning and Understanding in the History of Ideas." *History and Theory* 8, no. 1 (1969): 3–53.

———. "Motives, Intentions, and the Interpretation of Texts." *The New Literary History* 3, no. 2 (1972): 393–408.

Smith, Thomas C. *The Agrarian Origins of Modern Japan.* Stanford: Stanford University Press, 1959.

Therborn, Göran. *The Ideology of Power and the Power of Ideology.* London: Verso Editions and NLB, 1980.

Totman, Conrad. *The Collapse of the Tokugawa Bakufu, 1862–1868.* Honolulu: University Press of Hawaii, 1980.

———. "Tenpō Reforms." *The Encyclopedia of Japan* 8. Tokyo: Kodansha, 1983.

Tsunoda, Ryusaku, Wm. Theodore de Bary, and Donald Keene, eds. *Sources of Japanese Tradition.* 2 vols. New York: Columbia University Press, 1958.

Turner, Victor. *The Ritual Process.* London: Penguin Press, 1969.

———. *Dramas, Fields, and Metaphors: Symbolic Action in Human Society.* Ithaca: Cornell University Press, 1974.

von Wright, Georg Henrik. *Explanation and Understanding.* Ithaca: Cornell University Press, 1971.

Wakabayashi, Bob Tadashi, "Aizawa Seishisai's Shinron and Western Learning, 1781–1828." Ph.D. dissertation, Princeton University, 1982.

Waley, Arthur, trans. *The Analects of Confucius.* New York: Vintage, 1938.

Webb, Herschel. "What is the *Dai Nihon Shi*?" *Journal of Asian Studies* 19, no. 2 (Feb. 1960): 135–49.

INDEX

Abe Masahiro, 139, 141
Aizawa Seishisai, 3, 8, 19, 42–43, 51, 56–81, 103, 131, 145, 152, 173; on education, 121–122; on history, 57–64, 162; on instrumental action, 77–80, 100; and Kōdōkan, 114–115, 118; as moderate, 142; on obedience to bakufu, 128; on ritual and *kokutai*, 64–77; on social problems, 30–32
Aizu, 156
Aki, 156
Akiba, 145
Alternate attendance (*sankin kōtai*), 14, 15, 109
Althusser, Louis, 6, 26, 52, 130
Amaterasu Ōmikami, 62, 65–73, 77, 80, 116, 126, 164, 175
Analects (Confucius), 44, 64, 115, 121, 147, 149
Ancestor worship, 61–62, 66, 70–75, 80, 128
Ancient studies (*kogaku*), 10, 54
Ansei period, 114, 124, 131, 134, 142–145, 148; purge in, 142; reforms in, 143–144
Aoyama Nobumitsu, 118
Aoyama Nobuyuki, 115, 118
Arai Hakuseki, 45–47
Arimura Jizaemon, 149
Arimura Yūsuke, 149
Artisans, 33, 90, 137
Asaka Tanpaku, 40, 42
Asami Keisai, 50
Ashikaga Yoshimitsu, 59

Bakufu, 79, 97, 118, 139, 143, 149–150, 169, 170, 176; accommodation with court, 142; censure of Tokugawa Nariaki by, 138, 140–142; criticism of, 174; exclusionist position of, 56–57, 60, 163; ideology of, 126–127; judgment of, 175; Kamakura and Muromachi, 59; movements against, 3, 20–21; overthrow of, 1–4, 156; reforms of, 15–16, 104; relation of, to emperor and daimyo, 47–48, 127; as religious focus, 8, 164; suppression of Tengu insurrection by, 154–156, 166, 171, 173–175
Bakuhan system, 4, 14, 126–27, 170, 171
Benevolent government (*jinsei*), 26, 45, 58, 75, 76, 86–87, 92–93, 99, 123, 126, 167
Bitō Masahide, 36, 43
Bogo imperial rescript, 142
Buddhism, 7, 12, 50, 61, 62, 140, 157; enmity toward, in Mito, 31, 32, 146–147
bunbukan. See Halls for the pursuit of liberal and military arts
Bunka era, 136
Bunroku cadastral survey, 95
Bunsei era, 133, 136
bushi. See Samurai
Bushi dochaku no gi (Fujita Tōko), 107–109, 111

Cadastral survey (*kenchi*), 82–101, 106, 109, 111, 113, 114, 122, 132–139, 143, 145, 153, 161, 174; in Keichō period, 95
Cash equivalent (*kuramae*, or *mononari*) stipend system, 104–107, 111, 132
Center, symbolism of, 156, 164–166, 169
Centralized rule (*gunken*), 59, 107
Changes in the momentum of time (*jisei no hen*), 58, 60, 63, 77
China, 42, 47, 59, 62, 90, 107, 116–117
Chinese civilization, 12, 14, 51, 108; assumptions of, 42; classics of, 39, 124, 149; histories, 34–35, 41, 46, 60; nomenclature, 45; tradition, 9, 43, 52, 58, 66; values, 65
Chōshū, 1, 20–23, 153, 156, 174
Chou dynasty, 107–108, 121, 123
Chou-li, 121
Christianity, 32n, 61–62, 67n
Chuang-tzu, 53
Chu Hsi, 7, 8, 35, 37, 50, 53
Ch'un-ch'iu, 45, 121

183

Chung yung, 75, 80, 115, 149
Cities, 12, 30–31, 90, 102, 107, 109–110
Civil war, Mito (Tengu insurrection), 1, 4, 16, 43, 144, 152–171
Coastal defense, 103, 109–110, 148. *See also* Military
Commerce, 23, 81, 83, 90, 102, 137; treaty of, with U.S., 141, 150. *See also* Economic affairs; Market
Commoners, 5, 10, 12, 33, 42, 129, 130–153, 164; anti-feudal energy of, 22; education of, 122–125, 142–149, 161, 168; in historiography, 61; love of profit of, 31; in *Mencius*, 87; in military forces, 21–22, 113–114, 134, 143; purchase of samurai status by, 100, 133; samurai hegemony over, 21, 22, 26; subjectivity of, 16, 21–23, 27, 131, 134–139, 161. *See also* Artisans; Merchants; Peasants
Communitas, 167, 170
Confucianism, 4, 11, 12, 14, 20, 33, 39, 43–52, 61–63, 65, 87, 116, 146, 149, 175
Confucius, 4, 15, 44–46, 48, 61–64, 116, 117, 119
Confucius Hall (Kōshirō), 117, 119
Corvée, 91, 104, 113

Daigaku wakumon (Kumazawa Banzan), 14
Daijōkan. *See* Grand Council of State
Daijōsai. *See* Great Thanksgiving Festival
Dai-Nihon shi, 2, 9, 13, 34–43, 57, 60
Dazai Shundai, 83
Decentralized rule (*hōken*), 58, 103–104, 107, 108, 121
Demonstrative action, 13, 34, 55, 80, 129, 166
Depopulation, 31, 83, 85, 86, 135
Discourse, 5–6, 10, 13, 17, 27, 49, 52, 54, 77, 80, 83, 99, 103, 129, 131
dochaku. *See* Grounding the samurai
Doctors. *See* Physicians
Dutch Studies (Rangaku), 63
Dynastic overthrow (*ekisei kakumei*), 37, 44

Economic affairs, 15, 23, 77, 81–84, 97–98, 102, 107, 123. *See also* Taxation; Market

Edo, 85, 93, 109–111, 115, 118, 139–143, 149–151, 156, 171
Education, 4, 73, 74, 114–125, 143–149. *See also* Mito academy; Schools
ekisei kakumei. *See* Dynastic overthrow
Ekishūkan, 123, 125
Eliade, Mircea, 70, 71, 77, 130
Emperors, 41, 47, 62, 63, 78, 127, 128, 141; legitimacy of, 36, 45; name of, 48; unbroken line of, 4, 35–38, 40, 44–46, 58, 65–67, 75, 76, 115, 116, 128, 175
Engishiki, 147
England, 56, 57
Eternal return, 4, 64
Europeans, 65
Evils of heresy (*jasetsu no gai*), 58, 61, 64, 77
Exoneration movement, 138–142, 145, 147, 148, 174
Expulsion (*jōi*), 158, 163, 168, 169

Famine, 31, 93, 118, 133, 135
Fief system (*jikata chigyō*), 104–114
Filial piety, 26, 53, 54, 59, 62, 64–68, 71–72, 75, 76, 117, 119, 122
Financial difficulties, 29, 30, 38, 82, 103, 105, 118, 133, 139
Five Relationships, 50, 53
Flexibility, 77, 79
Foreigners, 20–21, 80, 115, 162; doctrines of, 114; as enemies, 32, 56, 63, 164, 175–176; ships of, 21, 56–57, 141, 148; trade with, 24, 159
Foucault, Michel, 5
France, 156
Freedom and Popular Rights Movement, 18
Fuchū, 140
Fujikō, 13, 32
Fujita faction, 81–84, 114, 147
Fujita Koshirō, 152–155
Fujita Teisei, 118
Fujita Tōko, 4, 26, 42, 66, 82, 83, 145, 152, 153, 155; on administration, 123, 131; on cadastral survey, 92–94, 134; on *dochaku*, 105–113; on education, 122; on failure of samurai class, 33; on Kōdōkan, 114–118; mythical narrative of, 48–53, 67; opposition of, to sale of samurai status, 133; punishment of, 140; restorationism of, 100

Index

Fujita Yūkoku, 2, 26, 56, 152; on bakufu, 127; on domainal decline, 29; opposition of, to sale of samurai status, 133; on rectification of names, 38, 43–49, 51, 52, 91; on rural reform, 82–92, 95, 99–100, 106, 134; and Shōkōkan, 40, 43, 57, 81
Fujiwara, regency of, 47, 59
Fujiwara Seika, 7, 8
Fuju-fuse sect, 32

Gakkō gohimon, 115
Gekibun, 153, 168, 171, 175–176
Genroku era, 29, 86, 89, 91, 104
gimin. See Zealots
gōnō. See Peasants, rich
gōshi. See Rustic samurai
Grand Council of State (Daijōkan), 62
Great Thanksgiving Festival (Daijōsai), 67–71, 74, 75, 169
Grounding the samurai (*dochaku*), 15, 80, 84, 85, 101–114, 122, 134
gunken. See Centralized rule

Halls for the pursuit of liberal and military arts (*bunbukan*), 144, 145
Hamada village, 42
Hamamatsu, 79
Harootunian, H. D., 41
Harris, Townsend, 142
Hayashi Gahō, 45, 46
Hayashi Razan, 35, 37
Heian period, 47
Hikone, 141, 150
Hiraso village, 160
Hirata Atsutane, 12, 147
Historiography, in Mito, 2, 29, 34–48, 57
History, 22, 42, 89; abolition of, 70, 169; contradiction between nature and, 55; degenerative concept of, 16, 19, 26, 57–64, 70, 71, 78, 80, 89, 116, 123, 163, 166; escape from, 170; relativist concept of, 54; terror of, 130
Hitachi, 116
Hitotsubashi Keiki. See Tokugawa Yoshinobu
Hōei period, 29
Hōjō Tokimune, 175
hōken. See Decentralized rule
Hotta Masayoshi, 141
"House," ideology of, 125–127

Hsiao ching, 118, 125, 147, 149
Hsiao hsueh, 147

I ching, 74
Ichikawa Sanzaemon (Hirosane), 153–156
"Ideological drift," 76
Ideological hegemony, 22, 139
Ideology, 6–7, 139; of Confucianized Shinto, 16; definition of, 6–7, 130–131; function of, 22, 26; of Mito, 17, 27, 144, 161, 166, 168, 174; of natural order, 18; of *sonnō jōi*, 21–23, 148; in Tokugawa period, 7, 13, 77, 126–131
Ii Naosuke, 1, 141–143, 149, 150
Ikeda Mochimasa, 162, 168
ikioi. See Momentum
Ikokusen uchiharai-rei. See Order to repel foreign ships
Imperial court, 41, 59, 128. See also Emperors, unbroken line of
Imperial presence, 169
Imperial regalia, 58, 66, 69, 77
Imperial will, 150, 162, 163, 167, 175–176
Infanticide, 31, 83
Instrumentalism, 4, 10, 11, 14, 27, 34, 53–55, 88, 100, 103, 129, 166
Intentionality, 5, 6, 88, 129, 166
Inui Hiromi, 127, 136–137
Invention (*sakui*), 17–19, 80
Ise Jingū, 164
Isohama village, 160
Itako, 135, 136, 138, 145; district school in, 153–154, 158
Itakura Katsukiyo, 167
Iwashita Sajiemon, 149
Iwaya Keiichirō, 153

Jameson, Frederic, 9
jasetsu no gai. See Evils of heresy
Jesus, 63
Java, 63
jikata chigyō. See Fief system
Jingikan. See Office of Deities
Jingū, Empress, 36
Jinmu, Emperor, 58, 61
jinsei. See Benevolent government
jisei. See Momentum of time
jisei no hen. See Changes in the momentum of time
Jiyōkan, 123
Jōge fuyū no gi (Fujita Tōko), 105

Kabayama San'en, 149
Kaga, 146
Kaiho Seiryō, 11, 12, 54
Kamakura period, 59
Kan'ei Reform, 85, 93, 95–97, 104–105
Kaneko Magojirō, 145, 149, 150
Kannō wakumon (Fujita Yūkoku), 85, 95
Kansei Reforms, 8, 15, 81
Kanuma village, 163
Kashima Jingū, 116, 119
Kashūkan, 123, 124, 147
Katsura Kogorō. *See* Kido Kōin
Keichō cadastral survey, 95
Keigyōkan, 123, 145
Keiikan, 123, 151, 158
Keiō era, 119
kenchi. See Cadastral survey
Kido Kōin (Katsura Kogorō), 153
Kiheitai. *See* Special militia
Kii, 2, 97, 109, 127, 140
Kimon school, 8, 39, 49, 51
Kōdōkan. *See* Mito academy
Kōdōkan gakusoku (Aizawa Seishisai, Aoyama Nobuyuki), 119
Kōdōkanki (Fujita Tōko), 114–119, 121, 122, 147, 149
Kōdōkanki jutsugi (Fujita Tōko), 33, 48, 66, 173
kogaku. See Ancient studies
Kōgeikan. *See* Kashūkan
Kogoshui, 147, 149
Kojiki, 39, 147, 148
Kōken, Empress, 62
Kokushi-hen (Tokugawa Nariaki), 125
kokutai. See National essence
Kōmei, Emperor, 141
Komiyama Fūken, 40; on *dochaku*, 113–114; establishment of Nobukata Gakkō by, 123; on infanticide, 83; opposition to Kōdōkan, 118; pragmatism of, 84; on rural reform, 99–100, 137
Konkōkyō, 13
Korea, 50, 175
Kōshi-rō, *See* Confucius Hall
Kumazawa Banzan, 14, 15, 103
Kurozumikyō, 13
Kusaka Genzui, 3, 173
Kyōhō era, 31, 104
Kyōhō Reforms, 15, 81, 104
kyōkō. See Schools, district
Kyoto, 30, 36, 71, 82, 153–155, 163, 169

Language, 5, 34, 53, 129; as aspect of natural order, 43; of Confucianism, 12; Confucius on, 44; corrosive power of, 16, 101; as means to natural polity, 165; Mito ideology as, 80; signifying power of, 48. *See also* Names and statuses; Rectification of names; Writing
Lao-tzu, 53
Laws, 12, 53, 80, 87–92, 95, 122
Laxman, Captain Adam, 56
Li chi, 121, 149
Lotus Sutra, 32
Luxury, 31, 82, 89, 90
Loyalty, 10, 176; and filial piety, 26, 53, 54, 59, 62, 64–68, 72, 75, 76, 117, 119
Luzon, 63

Machida district school, 145, 146, 148, 149
Maki Izumi, 3, 173
Makino Tadayuki, 140
Market, 23, 24, 30, 102, 130
Maruyama Masao, 17–20, 23, 39, 128, 170
Matsudaira Sadanobu, 15
Matsudaira Yorimasa, 140
Matsudaira Yorinori, 140
Matsudaira Yoritane, 140
Matsuyama, 156, 167
Measurement of land, 94–96
Medical training, 123–125, 144
meibun. See Names and statuses
Meiji Restoration, 1, 3, 17–20, 22, 23, 25, 173
Meiji state, 19, 173
Men of high purpose (*shishi*), 3, 173, 174
Mencius, 86–88, 121, 149
Merchants, 11, 12, 16, 21–23, 30, 31, 33, 78, 81, 82, 89, 90, 102, 131, 159
Military, 10, 19, 47, 64, 66, 77–80, 97, 103, 109, 114, 120, 126, 149, 166; duties, 106, 112, 134; exercises (Oitorigari), 119, 148; morale, 76; production, 141; training, 16, 25, 144, 151; unity with letters (*bun*), 84, 117; weakness, 57
militia (*nōhei*), 114, 141, 148
Minamoto Yoritomo, 59
Minato village, 123, 160
minshin. See Popular will
Mito academy (Kōdōkan), 84, 85, 108, 114–121, 139, 147, 153, 156, 161

Index

Mitogaku, 3, 17, 19, 20, 23, 36, 40, 174
Mito historiographical institute (Shōkō-kan), 29, 34–36, 38–40, 42, 56n, 57, 81, 118
Mitsukaidō, 142, 148
Miyata Tokuchika, 147
Mizuno Tadakuni, 15, 140
Mobilization, 25, 68, 77, 113, 134, 141, 144–146, 148, 157, 165
Modernity, 17
Momentum (*ikioi*), 60, 162
Momentum of time (*jisei*), 106, 121, 137
Mongols, 175
mononari. See Cash-equivalent system
Moriyama, 140
Motoori Norinaga, 12, 39, 49, 53, 54
Mountain ascetics (*yamabushi*), 118, 121
Muromachi period, 59, 126
Myth, 9, 26, 39, 49–52, 58, 65, 68, 70, 76, 81, 84, 130

Nagaoka, occupation of, 143, 148, 151, 153
Nagayama village, 135, 138
Najita, Tetsuo, 23
Nakaminato village, 154, 159, 160; district school in, 158
Nakatomi harai, 147
Nakayama, Bizen-no-kami, 111, 139
Names and statuses (*meibun*), 20, 38, 43, 46, 47, 53, 76, 83, 86, 127
Nation, Japanese, 1, 2, 9, 21, 27, 57, 60, 63, 64, 76, 129, 136, 139
National essence (*kokutai*), 1, 16, 64–77, 115, 125, 150; domain as representation of, 125, 129; and national destiny, 76; relation of, to imperial line and ritual, 75–76, 169; relation to loyalty and filial piety, military arts, and popular welfare, 64; relation of, to origins, 65, 67, 72, 127; survival of, 60, 63, 103; and the universal way, 65, 72
Nativism, 12, 37, 39, 73, 124
Natural order, 14, 16, 26, 123, 127, 165; and artifice, 48–57; confidence in, 103; economic basis of, 83; logic of, in Ogyū Sorai, 19; reconstitution through practical action, 101; relation to history, 54; relation to names, 43, 44; society as, 17; and the Way, 51
Naturalism, 12, 53, 54, 100
Nemuro, 56

Neo-Confucianism, 7, 8, 11, 14, 17, 35, 36, 39, 53, 84
Nihon shoki, 9, 118, 147, 149
Nikkō, 1, 153, 163–71, 175
Nobukata district school, 123
Noguchi Takehiko, 37, 41
nōhei. See Militia
Noyama village, 161

Oda Nobunaga, 7
Office of Deities (Jingikan), 62
Ogawa village, 123, 154, 157; district school in, 158
Ogyū Sorai, 10, 11, 14, 15, 17–19, 30, 37, 39, 40, 53, 54, 80, 83, 87, 88, 103, 122, 131
Ōhira, Mt., 153, 162, 163
Ōji village, 154
Ōjin, Emperor, 36, 161
Okayama, 162
Okura Masayoshi, 163
Ōkubo village, 123
Ōmiya, 145
Ōnuma village, 110
Ooms, Herman, 7, 9, 10
Order to repel foreign ships (*Ikokusen uchiharai-rei*), 56, 60
Origins, 49, 163, 169; archetype of, 127; gratitude to, 61; imperial, 71; of Japan, 46, 65, 67, 72, 75, 125; of the Way, 115, 116
Osaka, 93
Osatake Takeki, 171
Ōshio Heihachirō, 93
Ōta village, 123
Ōtomo, Prince, 36
Owari, 2, 97, 109, 127, 140
Ōzu village, 93

Peasants, 11, 21–25, 31, 33, 86–88, 94–99, 111–113, 123, 124, 130–139, 142–144, 146, 151, 157–162, 174; movements of, 13; rebellion by, 29, 92–93; rich (*gōnō*), 21–23, 25, 90n, 98, 121, 131–139, 153, 158
Perry, Commodore Matthew, 141
Physicians, 146, 148, 173
Pilgrimage, 1, 27, 162–170
Po I, 34
Politics, unity with scholarship, 4, 5, 29, 40, 75, 117, 122. *See also* Religion and politics
Po-lu-tung shi-yüan chieh-shih (Chu Hsi), 50

Popular will (*minshin*), 32, 33, 58, 67, 117, 163, 175
Population, 31, 91
Practicality, 3, 12, 14, 15, 27, 29, 53, 77, 79, 83, 84, 100, 101, 117, 119, 122
Profit, 11, 31, 33, 54, 78, 84, 106

qualification, 7, 23, 26, 27, 129, 131, 139, 143, 152, 161

Rai Mikisaburō, 140
Rai Sanyō, 60, 140
Rangaku. *See* Dutch Studies
Rebellion, 10, 38, 58, 67, 79, 100
Rectification, 16, 29–55, 81, 122, 138; of institutions, 84; of landholding, 83, 101; of names, 4, 38, 43–48, 52, 83, 84, 161; of names and status distinctions, 26, 37, 67, 80; of relationships, 121, of social order, 4
Relativism, 13, 14, 26, 59, 87, 130, 169
Religion and politics, 8, 68–71, 74–77
Religious reform, 133, 147
Restorationism, 15, 23, 34, 49, 51, 52, 87, 89, 100, 101, 103, 107, 108, 125, 128, 135, 162, 166, 170
Revenue, domainal, 97–98
"Revere the emperor and expel the barbarian" (*sonnō jōi*), 1, 3, 20, 21, 41, 128, 141, 144–145, 148, 152, 162, 167–171, 174, 175
Reverence (*kei*), 10, 26, 27, 47, 66, 69, 72, 73, 76, 77, 162
Reward and punishment, 75, 122–123
Ricoeur, Paul, 5, 174
Ritual, 5, 27, 43, 48, 62; and abolition of time, 70; Confucius on, 44; Daijōsai as, 68–77, 169; as element of the Way, 53; and eternal return, 64–77; focus on Ieyasu's tomb, 8, 164; in *I ching*, 74; and "magical" government, 80; pilgrimage as, 169; as source of order, 26; tension with instrumentality, 4, 55
Russia, 56, 57

Sakakibara Shinzaemon, 154
sakui. See Invention
Sakuradamon assassination incident, 145, 148–151
samurai (*bushi*), 5, 12, 14, 15, 20–23, 27, 29–34, 80, 81, 87, 101–114, 174; economic predicament of, 32; failure of, 33; income of, 29, 99, 104–107; as intellectuals, 29; relation of, to the land, 78; rustic (*gōshi*), 21, 90, 94, 118, 121, 132–133, 140, 143, 146, 148, 153, 157, 158; weakening of, 102
Sanjō Sanetomi, 163
sankin kōtai. See Alternate attendance
Satō Issai, 115
Satō Sajiemon, 164
Satsuma, 1, 20, 149–150, 156
Schools, district (*kyōkō*), 16, 26, 85, 109, 114, 121–125, 143–149, 151, 157, 161, 168
Seidan (Ogyū Sorai), 15
Seimeiron (Fujita Yūkoku), 43–48
Seki Tetsunosuke, 150
Seya Yoshihiko, 82, 144, 152, 157
Shamanism, 61
Shibahara Takuji, 101, 133, 134, 157, 159
Shih chi (Ssu-ma Ch'ien), 34
Shih ching, 122, 149
Shimodate, 153
Shimoosa, 153
Shimotsuke, 163, 169
Shinron (Aizawa Seishisai), 3, 16, 30, 56–80, 100, 114, 128, 145, 158, 162, 173
Shinto, 7–9, 54, 61, 64–66, 84, 116, 118, 146–151, 153, 157, 158; Confucianized, 16, 39, 49, 50, 64, 65, 76; Ise, 8; Mito favor toward, 32n; priests and radicalism, 146–148; Suika, 8; Yoshida, 8; Yuiitsu, 140
shishi. See Men of high purpose
Shishikura village, 153
Shoguns, name of, 45–46
Shōkōkan. *See* Mito historiographical institute
Shōmu, Empress, 62
Shōtoku Taishi, 62
Shu ching, 147
Shugendō, 118, 151, 153
Sinocentrism, 39
Skinner, Quentin, 5, 165
Smith, Thomas C., 23
Soga no Umako, 62
sonnō jōi. See "Revere the emperor and expel the barbarian"
Special militia (Kiheitai), 21, 174
Spontaneity, 10, 14, 26, 33, 49, 51, 53, 69, 70, 73, 75, 76, 80, 83, 84, 122
Ssu-ma Ch'ien, 34, 35
Status reversal, 150, 168
Structuralism, 5. 19

Index

Subjects, 6; of action, 131; of history, 7; mobilization of, 22n; of the prince, 7; production of, 26
Subjection, 7, 22, 23, 26, 27, 76, 131, 143
Subjectivity, 10, 22, 135, 161, 170; of commoners, 16, 21–23, 27; 134–139, 161; production of, 26; restorationist, 135; transformation of, 6, 17, 27
Suda Gennosuke, 98, 136
Suda Mojūrō, 138
Sugiyama Chūryō, 118
Sujin, Emperor, 58, 61
Sukegawa village, 110
Sumptuary laws, 16, 81, 93, 94, 137
Surnames, sale of, 25
Suruga, 155, 170
Suzuki Shōsan, 7

Ta hsueh, 149
Tachihara Suiken, 36, 39–43, 81–84, 99
Tahara Tsuguo, 126
Taiheisaku (Ogyū Sorai), 15
Taika Reforms, 59
Takahashi Taichirō, 146, 149, 150
Takamatsu village, 140
Takasaki Itarō, 149
Takeda Kōunsai, 140, 154, 155
Takemi-katsuchi-no-kami, 116, 119
Takeuchi Hyakutarō, 158
Tamaru Inanoemon, 153, 155
Tamazukuri village, 145, 151, 157
Tanuma Okinori, 154
Taoism, 53, 100
Taxation, 78, 81, 85–88, 91, 96, 98, 104–107, 111–113, 135
Technological development, 24–25
Tekiihen (Aizawa Seishisai), 54, 128, 145
Tenchi, Emperor, 59
Tendai Buddhism, 8, 164
Tengu insurrection. *See* Civil war, Mito
Tenkai, 8, 164
Tenmei era, 31, 133, 135
Tenmu, Emperor, 36
Tenpō era, 124, 125, 144, 145, 148
Tenpō Reforms, 1, 15, 16, 52, 81–140, 144, 146, 152, 161
Tenrikyō, 13
Therborn, Göran, 6, 26
Thought and action, 4–7, 19, 34, 38, 54, 114
Toda Tadahisa, 118

Toennies, Ferdinand, 165
Tōjō Nihonshi, 156
Tokiwayama Tōshōgū, 140
Tokugawa Harumori, 40, 133, Tokugawa Harutoshi, 41
Tokugawa Iemitsu, 164
Tokugawa Iesada, 141
Tokugawa Ieyasu, 7, 15, 47, 59, 89; as founder of bakuhan system, 78–80, 102, 103, 116, 170, 171, 175; legacy of, 176; as restorationist, 128; as Shinto-Buddhist avatar, 8; tombs of, 1, 8, 164
Tokugawa Mitsukuni, 2, 3, 9, 34–38, 40, 41, 57, 86, 89, 107, 116, 117, 132, 146
Tokugawa Nariaki, 1, 20, 29, 42, 43, 141, 152, 154, 163, 168; and Ansei Reforms, 143–144; bakufu censure of, 138, 141–142, 150; enshrining of, 175–176; frugality of, 82; movement to exonerate, 138–139, 140, 145, 147, 148; role in bakufu politics of, 139, 143; and Tenpō Reforms, 85, 86, 92, 93, 99, 109–112, 114–120, 124–129, 132–137
Tokugawa Narinobu, 56
Tokugawa Tsunaeda, 34, 41, 132
Tokugawa Yorifusa, 86, 89, 116, 117, 132
Tokugawa Yoshiatsu, 111, 143
Tokugawa Yoshimune, 15
Tokugawa Yoshinobu (Hitotsubashi Keiki), 141, 154, 163, 165, 168, 169
Tokugawa Yoshitomi (Iemochi), 142
Tokushi yoron (Arai Hakuseki), 47
Tomobe village, 110
Tosa, 23, 132, 156
Tōyama Shigeki, 20–23, 101, 173
Toyota Tenkō, 3
Toyotomi Hideyoshi, 7, 59, 78, 102, 103, 175
Tsuchiura, 153
Tsukuba, Mt., 152, 153, 159, 163, 165, 171
Turner, Victor, 5, 166–169

Uete Michinari, 61
Ugai Yoshizaemon, 142
Umeda Unpin, 3, 173
Universality, 11, 36, 37, 55, 62, 65, 66, 72, 125, 127
Ushibori village, 135, 138
Utsunomiya, 163

von Wright, Georg Henrik, 166

Webb, Herschel, 36
Well-field system, 86–88
Wen, King, 47
Western nations, 2, 9, 56, 67n
World renewal (*yonaoshi*), 13, 134
Writing, 51–52, 84–85, 101, 174

yamabushi. *See* Mountain ascetics
Yamaguchi Tokumasa, 118
Yamakawa Kikue, 163, 166

Yamakuni Hyōbu, 154, 155
Yamanobe Yoshitsune, 110–111, 140, 156
Yamazaki Ansai, 8–10, 14, 16, 26, 27, 39, 50, 51, 53, 76
Yokohama, 159, 163
yonaoshi. *See* World renewal
Yoshida Shōin, 3, 173, 174
Yoshinari Mataemon, 138–140
Yoshino, southern court at, 36
Yūki village, 153

Zealots (*gimin*), 140, 149

Designer: Betty Gee
Compositor: G&S Typesetters
Text: 11/13 Baskerville
Display: Baskerville

www.ingramcontent.com/pod-product-compliance
Lightning Source LLC
Chambersburg PA
CBHW021708230426
43668CB00008B/761